Marking Time in the Golden State

In recent decades, the nature of criminal punishment has undergone profound change in the United States. This case study of women serving time in California in the 1960s and 1990s examines two key points in this recent history. The authors begin with a look at imprisonment at the California Institution for Women in the early 1960s, when the rehabilitative model dominated official discourse. To this they compare women's experiences in the 1990s, at both the California Institution for Women and the Valley State Prison for Women, when the recent "get tough" era was near its peak. Drawing on archival data, interviews, and surveys, their analysis considers the relationships among official philosophies and practices of imprisonment, women's responses to the prison regime, and relations between women prisoners. The experiences of women prisoners reflected the transformations Americans have witnessed in punishment over recent decades, but they also mirrored the deprivations and restrictions of imprisonment that seem to transcend time and place.

Candace Kruttschnitt is Professor of Sociology at the University of Minnesota. She was visiting Fellow at the University of Cambridge in 2004 and Visiting Professor at the University of Helsinki in the Department of Social Policy. She has published widely in journals, including *Law & Society, Crime & Delinquency, Journal of Research in Crime & Delinquency, Journal of Criminal Law & Criminology, Criminology, Violence & Victims, Criminal Behavior and Mental Health, Aggression and Violent Behavior,* and *Women and Criminal Justice.*

Rosemary Gartner is Professor of Criminology and Sociology at the Centre of Criminology, University of Toronto. She has taught at the University of Iowa and the University of Minnesota and is currently Chair of the Crime, Law, Deviance Section of the American Sociological Association and Executive Counselor of the American Society of Criminology. She has coauthored *Murdering Holiness: The Trials of Franz Creffield and George Mitchell* (2003) and *Violence and Crime in Cross-National Perspective* (1984).

Cambridge Studies in Criminology

Edited by

Alfred Blumstein, *H. John Heinz School of Public Policy and Management, Carnegie Mellon University*
David Farrington, *Institute of Criminology, University of Cambridge*

Other books in the series:

Marking Time in the Golden State

Women's Imprisonment in California

Candace Kruttschnitt
University of Minnesota

Rosemary Gartner
University of Toronto

PUBLISHED BY THE PRESS SYNDICATE OF THE UNIVERSITY OF CAMBRIDGE
The Pitt Building, Trumpington Street, Cambridge, United Kingdom

CAMBRIDGE UNIVERSITY PRESS
The Edinburgh Building, Cambridge CB2 2RU, UK
40 West 20th Street, New York, NY 10011-4211, USA
477 Williamstown Road, Port Melbourne, VIC 3207, Australia
Ruiz de Alarcón 13, 28014 Madrid, Spain
Dock House, The Waterfront, Cape Town 8001, South Africa

http://www.cambridge.org

First published 2005

Printed in the United States of America

Typeface ITC New Baskerville 10/12 pt.   *System* LaTeX 2_ε [TB]

A catalog record for this book is available from the British Library.

Library of Congress Cataloging in Publication Data
Kruttschnitt, Candace.
    Marking time in the Golden State : women's imprisonment in California /
Candace Kruttschnitt and Rosemary Gartner.
        p.   cm. – (Cambridge studies in criminology)
    Includes bibliographical references and index.
    ISBN 0-521-82558-X – ISBN 0-521-53265-5 (pbk.)
    1. Women prisoners – California.   2. Female offenders – California.
3. Criminal justice, Administration of – California.   I. Gartner,
Rosemary, 1952–   II. Title.   III. Series.
    HV9305.C2K78   2005
    365′.43′09794 – dc22   2004046569

ISBN 0 521 82558 x hardback
ISBN 0 521 53265 5 paperback

Contents

Figures and Tables

Figures

Tables

Acknowledgments

Without the generosity of David Ward and Gene Kassebaum, this book would not have been written. We are particularly grateful to David Ward for providing us the research materials from their study of the California Institution for Women (CIW) in the early 1960s; for his willingness to share his memories of CIW, its administration, and its prisoners; for his advice over the course of this project; and for his comments on drafts of the book manuscript.

We have benefited from the helpfulness and expertise of many other individuals and institutions over the nearly ten years since we began this project. We must first acknowledge the California Department of Corrections (CDC) and John Berecochea, Chief of the CDC's Research Branch; Warden Susan E. Poole at CIW, and Warden Lew Kuykendall at Valley State Prison for Women (VSPW) for granting us permission to conduct research at CIW and VSPW. Wardens Poole and Kuykendall also gave generously of their time by allowing us to interview them at length. Our research was facilitated by a number of administrators and staff at the prisons, including Ross Dykes, Chief Deputy Warden, John Lee, Associate Warden Operations, and Corrine Abspoel at CIW; and Bill Stebbins, Public Information Officer at VSPW. Judith Angell, at the Research Branch of the CDC, assisted us in a number of ways, in particular by compiling CDC data on women in prison in California. We are grateful to staff at CIW and VSPW who volunteered to be interviewed, especially Lt. Bob Sebald at CIW, who provided us with invaluable information about CIW during the 1970s and 1980s.

We are fortunate to have had the help of several excellent research assistants. At the University of Minnesota, Amy Miller and, in particular, Kristin Carbone-Lopez contributed to the analysis of the survey and interview data from CIW and VSPW in the 1990s. At the University of California, Santa Cruz, Julie Beck collected extensive historical and contemporary data on imprisonment in California. At the University of Toronto, Elizabeth Griffiths compiled census data for women in California. At the University of California, Riverside, Doreen Anderson-Facile provided invaluable assistance in managing the logistics of the survey administration at CIW. Most of our interviews were transcribed at the University of Minnesota by Dena Sanford.

Our work has been improved by the generous assistance, advice, and encouragement of colleagues at various universities. At the University of Minnesota, Ross Macmillan guided us patiently and carefully through the analysis reported in Chapter 6; and Jeylan Mortimer made a number of useful comments on early drafts of our survey. At the University of Toronto, Mariana Valverde and Kelly Hannah-Moffat read and commented on early drafts of some of the material in Chapters 2, 4, and 5. At the University of California at Riverside, Robert Nash Parker provided us with assistance through the Presley Center for Crime and Justice Studies. Barbara Owen, at California State University at Fresno, smoothed our introduction to California's newer prisons for women in Chowchilla. Alison Liebling, Cambridge University, offered very useful and detailed comments on a draft of the entire manuscript. We also thank David Farrington and Al Blumstein, editors of the Cambridge Studies in Criminology series, for encouraging us to submit this manuscript to them and for helping it through to publication.

We have benefited from comments from colleagues who attended presentations about our research at the Department of Sociology, University of Iowa; the Department of Sociology, University of California at Davis; the Faculty of Law, University of Victoria; the Department of Sociology, Pennsylvania State University; the Department of Sociology, University of Minnesota; the Department of Sociology and the Centre of Criminology, University of Toronto; and the Institute of Criminology, Cambridge University. We are grateful to both the Department of Sociology at the University of Minnesota and the Centre of Criminology at the University of Toronto for their collegial and supportive environments.

Financial assistance for this research was provided by the National Science Foundation (grant #SBR-9617285); the Graduate School of the University of Minnesota; the Life Course Center, University of Minnesota; and the School of Graduate Studies, University of Toronto.

We owe a particularly deep debt to the seventy women serving time at the California Institution for Women or Valley State Prison for Women who agreed to be interviewed and to the thousands of women at the two prisons who completed our survey. Without their cooperation, their openness, and their insights, we could not have attempted this research, let alone completed it. The officers and representatives of the Women's Advisory Council at both prisons were not only enormously supportive and encouraging, they also gave of their time by commenting on early drafts of the survey, by publicizing the survey to their housing units, and by meeting with us at different points over the course of our research to discuss findings and interpretations.

Finally, and most importantly, we owe the most to those who have remained closest to us throughout this process. CK thanks Tom, Erica, and Lindsay for the tremendous support, love, and encouragement they offered at every phase of this project, even when she couldn't be with them. RG thanks her parents, Jeanette and David, and, in particular, Jim Phillips, for their love, faith, and encouragement. They have contributed to this book in ways that cannot be captured in words.

Marking Time in the Golden State

Introduction

THIS BOOK DESCRIBES a study of women's imprisonment in California in the early 1960s and the late 1990s, bridging a period that many scholars argue encompasses some of the most significant changes in penal policy during the last century. Although punishment in general and prisons as a central site of state punishment have long been subjects of both popular fascination and debate in democractic societies, this has been particularly true of the last few decades (see e.g., Beckett 1997; Garland 2001; Pratt 2002). In the United States, this period witnessed the fading of the rehabilitative ideal and the attendant view of the deviant as a product of poor socialization; the politicalization of crime – or what Simon (1997) calls "governing through crime" – and the widening of the criminal justice net to include not only a correctional apparatus anchored in community settings but also increasingly severe custodial sanctions (Bottoms 1983; Cohen 1985). While debate continues as to the precise nature and causes of these transformations in state control, and the most effective way of capturing or understanding these developments (Garland 2003), there is a consensus among scholars that the landscape of criminal punishment was very different at the end of the twentieth century than it had been only four decades earlier.

These changes, both in policy and in practice, have had profound consequences for female offenders. Historically, long-standing assumptions about criminal women and normative femininity have tended to shape both judicial responses to women's law breaking as well as the restrictions imposed on them in carceral settings. As a consequence, women's imprisonment, until recently, was characterized by numerical stability and continuities in forms and ideologies that seemed to transcend political fads and fashions. However, in the last quarter of the twentieth century, women were swept into jails and prisons in record numbers. Between 1965 and 1995 the female imprisonment rate in the United States increased sixfold and at the start of the twenty-first century more than 166,000 women were held in U.S. prisons and jails (Kruttschnitt and Gartner 2003). While in absolute numbers the imprisonment binge had a larger impact on males than on females, the rate of growth has been more dramatic for women and it has had a more profound effect on the composition of populations of state prisons for women than prisons for men.[1] As a result of the war on drugs, over the past fifteen years the proportion of women imprisoned for drug offenses almost tripled, while the proportion imprisoned for violent offenses decreased. By contrast, the proportion of men incarcerated for violent crimes has remained relatively constant since 1986 (Kruttschnitt and Gartner 2003: table 3).

These dramatic shifts in both the numbers of incarcerated women and the types of offenses for which they were imprisoned have been accompanied by efforts to alter perceptions of female offenders and the models for their imprisonment. The media and some scholars have placed an exaggerated emphasis on the danger posed by female offenders, constructing their specific incarnation – from the violent outlaw to the pregnant crack addict or teenaged gang-banger – to fit the latest moral panics (Faith 1993). These commentators, however, generally ignore the actual women convicted of crimes – often homeless, impoverished, and addicted – who are more in need of social assistance than social condemnation. Such depictions are also inconsistent with how prison administrators have seen their charges even as new structures of control, different organizational objectives, and carceral spaces for women developed. The maternalistic philosophy that guided women's institutions for most of the past century has been systematically dismantled in favor of ostensibly less gender-stereotypic regimes. The domestic orientation, reinforced through cottage-style architecture and therapeutic management, has been gradually replaced in many jurisdictions by industrial-style modular institutions, gender equity in programming, and regimes that view women offenders as agents responsible for their own rehabilitation (Hannah-Moffat 1995, 2001; Shaw 1992a; Carlen 2002).

As we will show these shifts in imprisonment were particularly evident in California, a state that is known for setting all manner of trends, including those affecting crime and punishment. The sheer scale of the criminal justice system in California, the largest in the free world, means that any innovation in punishment not only has a large net effect in California (Zimring, Hawkins, and Kamin 2001: 17) but also that it often sets precedents for change in other states. Not surprisingly, then, it was California that led the nation in the rehabilitation movement after World War II; it was California that subsequently led the nation in the prisoners' rights movement, racial

---

[1] Of course, the relative growth in women and men's imprisonment rates are affected by their initial base rates. Because women's initial base rates are substantially smaller than men's, changes in their rates produce larger proportional increases.

antagonism and violence in prisons, and, subsequently, in a host of reforms (Irwin 1980: xxiii–xxiv), including those that have now been characterized as central components of the "penal harm movement." These so called reforms include the passage of the nation's most draconian "Three Strikes Law" and the notorious growth in California's prison population over the last two decades (see Zimring et al. 2001).

Our research addresses this later movement, but it begins before it emerged. We start when the first large-scale descriptive studies of women in prison were conducted at the height of the rehabilitative era: David Ward and Gene Kassebaum's study of the California Institution for Women (1965) and Rose Giallombardo's study of the federal facility at Alderson, West Virginia (1966). Research on the male prison world was flourishing during this period, as scholars vigorously debated the merits of different theoretical perspectives – functionalist, situational functionalist, and importation – designed to explain prisoners' adaptations to institutional life. The work of Ward and Kassebaum and of Giallombardo not only grew out of this "golden age of prison sociology" (Simon 2000) but also made a significant contribution to it, as the experiences and coping mechanisms of female prisoners, up until that time, were virtually unknown. Today these large-scale studies of imprisonment have all but disappeared from American sociology, although there are selected exceptions (Owen 1998).

The absence of research on prison communities, once viewed by sociologists as a central piece of "institutional analyses" (Jacobs 1977: 1–2), is surprising given both the unprecedented growth in the correctional population (Simon 2000) and the growing scholarly attention devoted to the "new culture of crime control" (Garland 2001), or what scholars have variously termed a postmodern trend in penology, the "new penology," or the "new punitiveness" (Smart 1990; Feeley and Simon 1992; Reiner 1992; Pratt 2000). Addressing macrolevel changes in penal ideologies and practices, this new scholarship seeks to understand the causes and contradictions in the apparent reconfiguration of crime control during the latter part of the twentieth century. For example, from some scholars we learn that public opinion and values, influenced by a moral panic, have crystallized in a political culture of intolerance of offenders and acceptance of imprisonment as a first-order response to crime (Jacobs and Helms 1996; Caplow and Simon 1999). Others focus on the prison as an institution, arguing that we have seen the emergence of the bureaucratic prison over the last quarter of the twentieth century. Prison authority has been centralized in various departments of corrections that emphasize classification of prisoners and staff training while deemphasizing other methods of informal social control (Adler and Longhurst 1994; Irwin and Austin 1994). Still others cast a wider net, conceptualizing changes in penal policy and the treatment of offenders as a "new penology" evident in the discourse of risk and probability, identification and management, and classification and control techniques that measure and assess risk (Feeley and Simon 1992).

Debate also rages over whether we are in fact witnessing a postmodern penal movement, especially among those scholars who study and direct our attention to the front lines of corrections (Haney 1996; Lynch 1998). In this debate, the emphasis has switched to the pragmatics of program implementation and the ways in which this new discourse has been realized, if at all (Garland 1997; Hannah-Moffat 1999; Riveland 1999). Penal sanctions are viewed as uneven and diverse, combining at once elements of discipline (e.g., in boot camps), rehabilitation (in prison industry/enterprise), and incapacitation (warehousing prisoners) (O'Malley 1992, 1999). The application of criminal justice sanctions reflecting this movement is also acknowledged to vary by actors' abilities to absorb new technologies and ideologies surrounding punishment (see e.g., Harris and Jesliow 2000).

We do not focus on this debate or the merits of various conceptualizations of the current changes in criminological discourse and the American penal system, although we see our research contributing to these.[2] Instead, in this study we direct our attention to what we see as an important omission – the question of whether and how shifts in penality have affected the daily lives of prisoners, specifically female prisoners. This is where we begin.

The Study Unfolds

The questions of primary concern to us are: (1) what can women's experiences in prison tell us about the practices of punishment over time and in different institutional contexts and (2) during the era of hyperincarceration, how do women do time and what are the relative contributions of their backgrounds and prison experiences in shaping their responses to prison life?

We examine women's prison experiences in three different contexts to determine whether and how shifts in penality have translated into changes in the experiences of those subject to criminal punishment. These contexts are the California Institution for Women (CIW) in the 1960s, CIW in the 1990s, and Valley State Prison for Women (VSPW) in the 1990s. Our first context is circumscribed by Ward and Kassebaum's research at CIW in the 1960s. We were given access to the data they collected on the female prisoners at CIW in the early 1960s – transcripts of interviews, aggregate survey data, and various prison and Department of Corrections' publications. This provided us with a unique opportunity to conduct a temporal study of women's imprisonment, one that would replicate and build on Ward and Kassebaum's work. As such,

---

[2] For excellent discussion of how we might best characterize and understand contemporary penal developments, see Garland (2003) and Simon and Feeley (2003).

the interviews we conducted at CIW in the late 1990s relied on the same four orienting themes they employed, and our survey included some of the same questions they asked of the female prisoners they studied forty years ago. This methodology allows us to compare women's carceral experiences at two critical times in the recent history of women's imprisonment: the height of the rehabilitative regime and the height of the neoliberal regime. If it is true that we are witnessing a new penal era, then we should see variations over time in the expectations of prisoners, how they are treated, and explicit and implicit messages about who they are. We would also expect these differences to be reflected in how prisoners relate to other prisoners, to the staff, and to the prison regime.

VSPW is the newest and largest prison for women in California; it epitomizes the central elements of the new penology in its preoccupation with danger, security, and efficient management of prisoners. Because it provides a contrast to CIW, the oldest prison for women in California and the prison that perhaps retains the strongest ties to its rehabilitative heritage, a comparison of these two institutions allows us to be more explicit about the ways in which macrolevel shifts in penal policy and ideology shape women's responses to prison within this new punitive era. We know, for example, that policies and ideologies are often subverted, ignored, or manipulated by agents charged with applying them (Haney 1996; Lynch 1998). Demands of running a prison mean that certain organizational requirements take precedence and can be conditioned by traditions and habits. Further, organizational characteristics and processes can change more slowly than policies and discourses as the habits of organizational actors often militate against change. All of these factors suggest that the effects of changes in punishment and penal policy may be conditioned by specific institutional contexts. We draw attention to this possibility in our examination of women's experiences at CIW and VSPW in the 1990s. As Medlicott (2001: 210) suggests in her study of suicidal male prisoners, if we want to describe the experiences of individuals, we "must recognize both structure and experience, for the life of an individual cannot be adequately understood without references to the institutions within which his biography is enacted."

But in drawing attention to institutional context, we also acknowledge that the prison is a unique institution, being relatively impermeable to the comings and goings of social life on the outside.[3] While activities in the

---

[3] This conceptualization of the prison draws from Goffman's (1961) depiction of prisons as total institutions. We are aware that this perspective has been criticized (Irwin 1970, 1980; Jacobs 1977, 1983), and that prisons have been significantly influenced by various religious and political social movements, and that today televisions and other forms of mass media play a significant role in providing alternative social worlds for prisoners (Jewkes 2002). Yet none of these influences erase the monotony of the temporal and spatial structures of prison life (see Medlicott 2001).

free world are dispersed among different individuals and across public and private spaces, prisons confine virtually all interaction – work, socialization, rest – within their walls to a limited set of actors. In the classic era of prison sociology, this realization led to an important theoretical perspective on prisoner behavior, one that posited that regardless of the particulars of an institution or an individual's biography, prisoner's behaviors could be predicted and explained as a result of living in such a constrained and emotionally deprived environment (Sykes 1958). From this perspective, time and institutional context should matter little. Women's lived prison experiences and their responses to imprisonment should transcend both time and place as the prison's "overwhelming power to punish" (Carlen 1994: 137), which is so integral to its logic and function, overrides the particularities of different penal philosophies and regimes.

Overview

In this book we present the findings of our temporal and cross-institutional study, findings that speak directly to these different perspectives on prisoners' responses to their carceral lives. Chapter 2 sets the stage for our research by describing the social and political environment for women in California over the period of our investigation: 1960–1998. We consider the broader political and legislative shifts that shaped this period (e.g., the demise of rehabilitation and the move to determinant sentencing) as well as the specific factors that bear on women's imprisonment: demographic trends pertaining to women's education, family formation, employment and poverty, and arrest and imprisonment rates, and the perceptions of the female offender. As Garland (2001) has shown, criminal justice policies are intimately tied to perceptions and everyday realities of crime as well as social and economic life. We try to portray how these factors shape women's imprisonment in California.

In Chapter 3, we enter the prisoners' world. We provide a description of how we carried out our research, moving from our initial acquisition of Ward and Kassebaum's data to conducting interviews at CIW and VSPW. We discuss how these interviews helped to shape the content of our prisoner survey and both the successes and problems we encountered in administering the surveys in two vastly different prison environments.

Chapters 4 through 6 provide the central analyses and findings of the study. Chapter 4 focuses only on CIW, contrasting the experiences of imprisonment for women and their reactions to imprisonment in 1963 and 1998. Here we rely heavily on the interviews Ward and Kassebaum conducted and our interviews with prisoners to explore how women responded to other prisoners, the staff, and the prison regime itself in these two time periods. In Chapter 5, we introduce the third context by including VSPW in our analysis. We consider the same questions we examined in the previous chapter – how women respond to other prisoners, the staff, and the prison regime – to determine how institutional and temporal variations influence women's prison experiences. The interviews are also supplemented with selected responses to survey items that were included in both Ward and Kassebaum's and our survey. These data allow us to gauge the extent to which prisoners living in these varying contexts shared similar constructions of, and reactions to, prison life. In the final analytic chapter (Chapter 6), we return to a concern central to the golden age of prison sociology and focus on the question of how women do time. While our analysis draws heavily from this earlier period of research, it is also informed and shaped by the more recent scholarship on women's imprisonment and prison adjustment. This work draws attention to how some aspects of women's backgrounds and experiences take on a particular salience in the prison context, ultimately producing different styles of adaptation, resistance, and coping. Here we rely primarily on a quantitative analysis of our survey data enriched by the prisoners' depictions of how they manage their prison time.

In the concluding chapter, we consider both the practical and theoretical implications of this research. Remarkably few studies of women's experiences in prison have been conducted during the past two decades, despite the expansion of women's imprisonment and, as we noted, despite the thriving and sophisticated scholarly literature on penality. As a result, relatively little is known about the social order of women's prison lives in the 1990s. Is the heightened punitiveness of this era having adverse effects on women prisoners, the vast majority of whom will eventually be released back into the community, and do their adaptations hinge on the specific regime to which they are subject? While this study directly addresses these omissions in the research on female penality, we believe that it goes further. Both our research design and our larger goals reflect a call issued more than twenty years ago by Jacobs (1983: 32) for more longitudinal and comparative studies of prisons: "these types of macrosociological research . . . may add much to our basic knowledge of the dynamics of total societies. Imprisonment is the keystone of coercive control in modern society. Knowing how the prison and its segments articulate with the larger society will increase our understanding of society's distribution of power, stratification, and system of legal rights and obligations." While we concur, we would add that it will do so only if it systematically addresses the imprisonment of women as well as of men.

Women, Crime, and Punishment in California

THE POST–WORLD WAR II period was a time of reform and innovation in the California criminal justice system. Optimism about the system's ability to remold offenders through novel rehabilitative programs and therapeutic regimens was widespread, encouraged by the state's booming economy and its self-image as "America's laboratory for social change" (Cross 1968: 110). Through the 1960s and into the 1970s that optimism was sustained even in the face of rising crime rates, social unrest, and an economic slowdown. But by the late 1970s, California had embarked on a series of legislative initiatives that marked the beginning of an "era of hyper-incarceration" (Simon 2000) in the state. These initiatives gained momentum over the next fifteen years as public faith in the government's ability to deal with social problems declined, the disparity between rich and poor expanded, and the state's population grew increasingly more diverse ethnically and racially.

In this chapter we consider how these political, economic, and social changes shaped women's crimes and criminal punishment in California. We describe how female criminals, traditionally seen as less culpable and more redeemable than their male counterparts, were caught up in the state's expanding crime control complex. To do this, we first provide an overview of trends both in criminal justice policies and in public attitudes toward crime and criminals in California during the last four decades of the twentieth century; and we consider the larger demographic, economic, and social context within which these trends occurred. We then turn our attention to women in California, tracing changes in their demographic characteristics and economic prospects, with particular attention to the types of women at greatest risk of coming into conflict with the law. We also document women's involvement in crime in California between 1960 and 1998. The chapter concludes with a discussion of the major trends in and issues surrounding women's imprisonment in California during these four decades.

Crime, Criminal Justice, and Politics in California, 1960 to 1998

California's reputation as a trendsetter for the nation was well-established by the mid-twentieth century and developments in its criminal justice policies over the next forty years both sustained and reflected that reputation. In the 1950s and 1960s, California was the state that, in the words of Jonathan Simon, "went the furthest in attempting to build a scientifically informed and rehabilitative penal system," but by the mid-1970s it became "among the first to repudiate that vision" (Simon 1993: 13). The reasons for that repudiation are complex and still debated, but popular writers and scholarly analysts agree with Abramsky (2002: xvi) that political rhetoric – reinforced by the media's fascination with crime and popular concerns over a decline in morality – was transformed from "a language of inclusion and hope to one of cynicism and fear." This discourse helped to construct a set of justifications for and technologies of punishment that sent increasing numbers of convicted felons to prison. As a consequence, California's prison growth during the 1980s and 1990s put it "in a class by itself," according to Zimring and Hawkins (1994: 83), not just nationally but internationally.

For politicians and criminal justice officials working in the booming California of the early 1960s, growth of this magnitude, at least with regard to imprisonment, was completely unanticipated. Instead, most state officials had their sites set on how to best manage the apparently unending expansion of California's postwar economy and the enormous growth in its population. When David Ward and Gene Kassebaum began their two-year study at the California Institution for Women (CIW) in 1961, the state's population, at more than sixteen million, was poised to exceed that of New York. Immigration from within and outside the United States was diversifying the racial and ethnic composition of the state's population and, together with the postwar baby boom, had helped lower the state's median age to just thirty years. Job opportunities for the state's younger and more heterogeneous workforce were plentiful. As a result of massive federal spending on defense, which fueled the state's aerospace and electronics industries, the state's economy was thriving. The gap between the state's richest and poorest citizens continued the decline that began with the start of World War II, and by 1960 the family poverty rate in California was substantially lower than that for the nation as a whole.

In the election of 1958, the Democratic Party had taken charge of the state's executive office for only the second time since the turn of the century.

Governor Edmund G. Brown did not, however, propose a radical new direction for state government. Instead, he committed himself to a bipartisan and neoprogressive approach that Governor Earl Warren, a Republican, had established during his ten-year term (1943–1953).[1] Almost fifteen years had passed since Warren had ordered a reorganization of the state's penal system and created the California Department of Corrections (CDC) to centralize and rationalize the management and operations of the state's prisons. Under the new system, headed by Warren's handpicked director, Richard A. McGee, a series of programs emphasizing rehabilitation through individualized treatment was launched. Prisoners were given greater freedoms in exchange for their participation in a comprehensive therapeutic apparatus that featured behavior-modification techniques and group counseling conducted by psychiatrists and trained counselors as well as by chaplains, librarians, educators, correctional officers, and prisoners themselves. McGee, who remained director of the CDC until 1961, was convinced – as were other officials who embraced what Garland terms "penal-welfare principles" – that his rehabilitative goals could be accomplished through such programs both in and outside of prisons and without lengthening the amount of time prisoners served.[2] As Garland observes (2001: 35), such principles "tended to work against the use of imprisonment, since the prison was widely regarded as counter-productive from the point of view of reform and individual correction."

McGee and other state correctional officials were not alone in their efforts to build on the state's well-established reputation as a trendsetter in the areas of criminal justice and law. Reform and innovation were also on the agendas of the state's judiciary and law enforcement agencies. In the early 1960s, California was one of the first states to launch a major reform of its penal code, an effort that would continue into the 1970s, although with consequences not initially envisioned by its initiators.[3] The California Youth Authority (CYA), which had been established in 1953 with the express

[1] For a discussion of the influence of progressivism in California in the 1940s and 1950s, see Putnam (1994).

[2] Brian Traugher (1991: 137), a member of the 1990 Blue Ribbon Commission on Inmate Population Management, illustrated McGee's concerns about relying too much on imprisonment with a memo McGee wrote to Governor Brown in March 1964. In the memo, McGee – who in 1961 had been appointed the first director of the state's Youth and Adult Correctional Agency – "excoriated the Adult Authority for failing to sufficiently reduce median time served, but praised the Women's Board of Terms and Parole for having dropped the median time served for women felons in California from twenty-two months to thirteen months. The memo concluded, 'The Women's Board has saved you, Governor, $10 million, 500 women and one institution.'"

[3] Among those consequences was the lengthening of prison terms and an increase in prison populations that followed on the passage of the Uniform Determinate Sentencing Act in 1976. For more about efforts to reform the California penal code, see Berk, Brackman, and Lesser (1977), and Gordon (1981).

purpose of moving from retribution to the treatment and training of young offenders, also underwent major revisions in 1961. Under the CYA's new procedures young people charged with crimes would be provided legal counsel in felony cases as well as greater opportunities for pretrial diversion. The nature and direction of these reforms were not ultimately determined, however, by the reformist ideals of criminal justice lobbyists in ways consistent with a professional-elite model of legislation. Instead, the negotiations and compromises among legislators, lobbyists for various interest groups, and criminal justice officials, which were necessary for the successful passage of these reforms, planted within the reforms the potential for outcomes quite at odds with those imagined by correctional officials such as McGee.

The idealistic belief in the malleability of humans that inspired many people working in California's correctional system in the 1960s was only one of several complex forces driving these various efforts at reform and experimentation. Another was growing trepidation over signs of social disintegration that began emerging in the mid-1960s. Despite the array of experimental correctional programs the state had developed, by the mid-1960s California had established itself as a national leader in its rate of serious crime. In 1965, the California Crime Index (CCI) rate had reached 1,873 per 100,000 population, 30% higher than the rate had been in 1960 (see Figure 2-1).[4] Most of that increase was driven by a rise in the property crime portion of the CCI. But serious violent crimes – homicide, rape, robbery, and aggravated assault – were also up by more than 10%. Moreover, California's economic growth had slowed, and with cuts in federal defense spending the state was about to begin a two-year long recession. Although overall economic inequality was still on the decline, by the mid-1960s the gap between the incomes of African Americans and whites was increasing, and the unemployment rate for blacks was double that for whites.[5] In recognition of these warning signs, Cross (1968: 110) began her chapter on California as "America's Laboratory for Social Change," with a cautionary note: "California in the sixties is the pacemaker in the struggle against poverty, crime, addiction . . . In many ways, she leads out of necessity. For while becoming America's richest and fastest-growing state, she has developed ominous social blight."[6]

---

[4] The California Crime Index (CCI) combines six categories of crimes known to the police: homicide, forcible rape, robbery, aggravated assault, burglary, and motor vehicle theft. To create the CCI violent crime rate the first four of these are combined; to create the CCI property crime rate the last two are combined.

[5] For an analysis of the economic fortunes of African Americans in California in the 1950s and 1960s, see Gibbs and Bankhead (2001).

[6] Cross went on to describe some of the experimental programs carried out in California's prisons in the early 1960s, including one which trained convicts on their release from prison to be community development workers and members of state legislators' research staffs. Another, known by the acronym ICE (Increased Correctional Effectiveness), provided "group

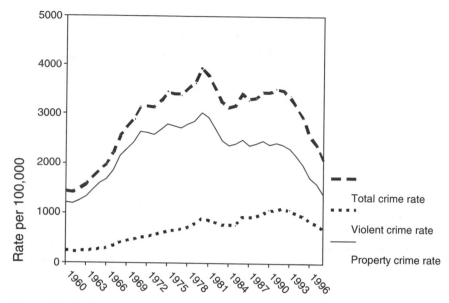

Figure 2-1. California Crime Rates, 1960–1998
Source: California Bureau of Criminal Statistics. (Various years) Crime and Delinquency in California. Sacramento: California Department of Justice.

Concerns about crime, as much criminological research has shown, often do not correlate strongly with trends in crime rates. It is perhaps not surprising, then, that in the last half of the 1960s when crime was increasing Californians appeared relatively uninterested in it. Public opinion polls rarely listed crime among the choices of "problems facing the state" that were offered to respondents. But if crime per se was not a high profile issue, disrespect for the law and other signs of social disorder were. In 1967 a conservative political upswing brought Ronald Reagan into the governor's office. Much of his support among voters was generated by his agenda for cutting taxes and reducing government spending on social services and welfare. But another important element of his appeal was his uncompromising stance on student protest and civil unrest. His 1966 gubernatorial campaign marked one of the first appearances of law and order rhetoric in a state election, setting a model that would increasingly characterize subsequent campaigns.[7]

living that was more helpful and more civilized than the usual incarceration – a five-day work week in pleasanter surroundings, backed up with intensive group therapy and regular community and family meetings" (Cross 1968: 115–116).

[7] For an overview of Reagan's use of law and order as a campaign issue in 1966, see Dallek (2000) and Kotkin and Grabowicz (1982).

Politicians, according to Scheingold (1984: 54–55), do not induce the public to be intolerant of social disorder so much as exploit what are pre-existing conservative and punitive tendencies residing in American culture. Whether this was true of Reagan in his 1966 campaign is uncertain, but the rebellions in Watts in 1965 and a year later in San Francisco's Hunter's Point, had raised the fears of many middle-class white Californians, making them receptive to politicians, such as Reagan, who stressed the need for greater respect for the law. Even so, Reagan's economic agenda and his belief in reducing the size of government trumped any inclinations he might have had toward expanding the state's correctional apparatus in response to civil unrest. As Austin, Irwin, and Kubrin (2003: 462) point out, upon assuming office, Reagan "instructed the parole board to reduce the prison popula-tion." Because of the leeway allowed by the state's indeterminate sentencing system, within two years the prison population had dropped from 28,000 to less than 18,000. What is significant about Reagan's directive is not, however, its seeming incongruity with his law and order politics. Rather, it is notewor-thy because it marked the beginning of a trend toward greater involvement by the state's politicians in setting agendas for the criminal justice and cor-rectional systems, a trend that would soon have very different results for the size of the prison population.

By the late 1960s, elected officials from both the Republican and Demo-cratic Parties were aware of a growing consensus among experts that the criminal justice system was not only ineffective at rehabilitating offenders but had created disparities in their treatment that needed to be rectified. The death knell on California's progressive penology and its professional-elite model of criminal justice legislation, according to Berk and his col-leagues (1977), had begun to strike. Moreover, the naive, oppressive, and inequitable aspects of the criminal justice system's commitment to individ-ualized treatment were becoming apparent both to prisoners and prison staff, many of whom recognized that "[t]he treatment-era California prison had introduced reforms it could not fulfill and probably never intended to" (Cummins 1994: 15).[8] Among these reforms was an expansion in the civil rights of prisoners, which opened the door to what would become a flood of prisoner litigation in the 1970s. Ironically, then, official commitment to

---

[8] Cummins provides a comprehensive overview of imprisonment and a detailed analysis of the prison movement in California from 1950 to 1980. He argues that prisoners, individually and collectively, used the rhetoric of rehabilitation to manipulate the courts and public opinion as well as prison officials, to achieve a variety of goals not envisioned by the originators of the state's rehabilitative regime. Further, according to Minton (1971: 319) prisoners in California were highly skeptical about the effectiveness and purposes of treatment programs: in a 1966 survey of seventy parolees, 57% said treatment programs were not effective, 55% believed the California Department of Corrections (CDC) saw these programs as a means to increase their budgets, and 28% believed the programs were designed primarily to control prisoners (see also Hallinan 2001).

rehabilitation had provided one of the means by which prisoners would end up challenging key elements of the rehabilitative regime, such as indeterminate sentencing.[9] Along with the growth in prisoner litigation and civil rights, the late 1960s also saw an increase in prison violence and prison gang activity in men's prisons, a harbinger of what was to come.

As a result of the law and order rhetoric of state and federal politicians, extensive media coverage of a series of high profile killings,[10] prison uprisings,[11] and the illegal activities of radical political groups, by the early 1970s crime and disorder had moved to the top of the public's list of problems facing the state. Popular sensibilities about crime and criminals also toughened and by the mid-1970s three-quarters of the state's populace supported capital punishment, up from only 50% in 1960. But despite the strength of these sentiments, state officials had not only been unwilling to increase spending to build more prisons but had made efforts to reduce the state's prison population. In 1972, during yet another economic recession, the state's criminal justice planning agency, the California Council on Criminal Justice (CCCJ), developed a plan to close two state prisons by the end of 1976. A year later, the CCCJ again recommended reducing prison populations as well as improving rehabilitative programs, psychiatric and health care services, and public volunteer programs in prisons (California Council on Criminal Justice 1972, 1973). And as late as the mid-1970s, state legislators again expanded prisoners' civil rights by enacting the Inmate Bill of Rights. Thus, support on the part of many state officials for alternatives to incarceration, for rehabilitation as a purpose of punishment, and for civil rights for prisoners coexisted with increasingly punitive popular sentiments, at least through the first half of the 1970s.

For many scholars of punishment, the mid-1970s signaled a shift to a distinctly different period of penal policy and public understanding of crime and its solutions in the United States. As Simon and Feeley (2003: 84) describe it, "the Great Society period of the 1960s and the early 1970s, which embraced a modified version of Progressive penology," was quickly superceded by "a new period that began in the mid-1970s and that David

---

[9] The 1968 Convict Bill of Rights, for example, amended Section 2600 of the penal code and rationalized parole practices with the aim of releasing prisoners on their minimum parole eligibility. Among other things, this bill also granted prisoners greater scope for confidential correspondence and for receiving various types of printed matter through the mail.

[10] The series of murders committed by people associated with Charles Manson in 1969 were among the first and most notorious of these. Three of the women involved in these killings – Susan Atkins, Patricia Krenwinkle, and Leslie Van Houten – were convicted of first-degree murder, sentenced to death, and sent to CIW in 1971. Their sentences were subsequently commuted to life imprisonment. All three of them continue to serve their time at CIW.

[11] Between 1970 and 1974, 116 prisoners and 11 correctional officers – all of them male – died in a series of gang wars, rebellions, and escape attempts in California's prisons (May 1995: 16).

Garland has termed 'the culture of control.'" This subsequent "culture of control," according to Garland (2001: 1), was "almost exactly the contrary of that which was anticipated as recently as 1970," when what he calls "penal welfarism" still characterized the field of crime control. In California, the event that perhaps most clearly epitomizes this abrupt transition is the passage of the Uniform Determinate Sentencing Act (UDSA) in 1976.

Indeterminate sentences were a hallmark of penal welfarism because they granted correctional officials and professional specialists enormous discretionary power in the name of rehabilitation and individualized treatment. It was this discretionary power of experts, exercised largely without public oversight, that state legislators, prison rights activists, and prisoners themselves objected to – especially faced with growing evidence that the experts did not know "what works." For people with a variety of interests and very different political leanings, the UDSA appeared to offer a solution to this problem, in part, because it offered "a set of practices that was not closely linked to ideologies or normative traditions" (Zimring et al. 2001: 212). When the UDSA was passed it was widely hailed as the necessary first step in doing away with sentencing disparities and other perceived injustices of the indeterminate system.[12] Of enormous symbolic importance, the act opened with the statement that "The Legislature finds and declares that the purpose of imprisonment for crime is punishment." Rehabilitation was thus formally and explicitly rejected as an objective of imprisonment in California when the act went into effect in 1977.

The introduction of determinate sentencing marked the beginning of a major transformation in both the discourse around and the practice of criminal punishment in California. By establishing both mandatory minimum sentence enhancement legislation and maximum sentences for certain crimes, the UDSA very quickly lead to longer sentences, larger prison populations, and decreased use of probation and parole.[13] By the beginning of the 1980s imprisonment had become a first-order response to crime

[12] Determinate sentencing systems in California and elsewhere shifted the formal authority to influence sentences from correctional officials to prosecutors and other courtroom actors. However, some analysts such as Jonathan Simon (1991: 77–78), have argued that "the functional power to distribute punishment ... moved back toward corrections and parole ... [which] has a tremendous amount of discretion over those coming out on parole."

[13] As early as 1981, Biles reviewed the results of five evaluations of the impact of California's Uniform Determinate Sentencing Act and found these were largely consistent in showing a decrease in sentencing disparity, but an increase in both sentence length and in prison populations. However, some evaluations of the impact of the act have found evidence that it did not increase the proportion of defendants sent to prison or the rate of guilty pleas (see e.g., Casper, Brereton, and Neal 1982).

Among the act's immediate consequences for prisoners was its allowance of good-time credits for working. However, the act also provided for the loss of those credits for misconduct, and the amount of time lost for misconduct was increased by the state legislature throughout the 1980s.

in California. With the system no longer defined by any rehabilitative ideals, operational goals related to detaining and managing large numbers of convicted offenders – one of the hallmarks of Feeley and Simon's (1992) "new penology" – had assumed priority.[14] And these numbers were reaching record levels as crime rates continued their sharp upward trajectory. As measured by the California Crime Index, the rates of both violent and property crimes peaked in 1980 (see Figure 2-1), as did arrest rates for virtually every type of crime (California Bureau of Criminal Statistics 1980).

A major contributor to the growing crime rate was a parallel increase in income inequality. The gap between California's economically disadvantaged and prosperous citizens had grown throughout the 1970s and then picked up its pace in the 1980s. As the state's stock of affordable housing – particularly in urban areas – diminished, and as welfare and entitlement programs contracted, the state's homeless population rose. Especially hard hit were families headed by women. In the lowest paid sectors of the service economy, where women workers predominated, the minimum wage (in real dollars) shrank. The state's family poverty rate rose throughout the 1980s, as poverty became even more concentrated in California's inner cities. But living outside of cities did not protect the economically marginalized; rural poverty rates were also on the rise.[15]

In times of economic uncertainty, public attitudes toward crime often become harsher and popular sentiment in California in the 1980s was no exception. In 1982, voters overwhelmingly approved Proposition 8, known as the "Victims' Bill of Rights"[16] and in 1986, they failed to reconfirm the state's chief justice, Rose Bird, and two other supreme court justices because of what was seen as the court's soft-on-crime stance.[17] Each of these was a step toward greater popular involvement in criminal justice policymaking, a trend which extended well beyond California. As Pratt describes (2002: 163), in his analysis of criminal punishment in English-speaking countries, "there was a growing sense of public dissatisfaction with the way in which the axis of penal power was then operating... [T]he mood of the public changed from indifference to anxiety." Such anxiety was widespread and free-floating in California in the 1980s. Even though the state's crime rate dropped each year between 1980 and 1985, by the mid-1980s close to 90% of Californians

---

[14] This managerial orientation, which emphasizes aggregate control and system efficiency, has been described as one of the defining features of late twentieth-century penality, which "measure[s] its success against its own production processes" (Feeley and Simon, 1992: 456).

[15] For an analysis of growing rural poverty in California, see Taylor, Martin, and Fix (1997). For detailed information on homelessness in California, see Housing California (2000), California Department of Housing and Community Development (2000), and Quigley, Raphael, and Smolensky (2001).

[16] The Victims' Bill of Rights gave victims and their next of kin the rights to speak during criminal proceedings about the consequences of their victimization and to receive restitution.

[17] Rose Bird was the first Supreme Court Justice in the state's history to fail to be reconfirmed.

felt that crime was on the increase in their city or town, more than 80% supported the death penalty, and 50% favored cutting other government services in order to build more prisons.

In response to this anxiety, voters displayed an increased willingness to reach into their wallets. In 1981, they passed the first of a series of prison bond issues launching a building boom that would continue into the 1990s. Between 1984 and 1988, eight new state prisons came on line, two of them – Avenal State Prison and Mule Creek Prison – the first of several built at the request of local communities. These were joined in 1989 by Pelican Bay State Prison, the state's fourth maxi-max prison and the first with a high-tech Secure Housing Unit (SHU) which could hold more than 1,000 prisoners.[18] Built for 2,080 prisoners and costing more than a quarter of a billion dollars, Pelican Bay was officially opened in June 1990 by Governor George Deukmejian. Lest anyone doubt how state leaders balanced the competing justifications for imprisonment, Deukmejian declared that Pelican Bay "symbolizes our philosophy that the best way to reduce crime is to put convicted criminals behind bars" (Austin and Irwin 2001: 127). As the state's prison population approached 100,000, Deukmejian approved a budget for operating the nine new and twelve older state prisons that was 360% larger than it had been in 1982.

The prison building boom of the 1980s did little, however, to relieve public concerns about crime. Just as they had in the early 1970s, in the early 1990s the public ranked crime first among all the problems facing the state. Moreover, citizen distrust of the government's ability to deal with crime was also reaching new levels (Baldassare 2000) and culminated in a series of punitively oriented citizen initiatives. An upturn in the state's crime rate from the late 1980s through the early 1990s – and some particularly shocking killings – helped to fuel these grass roots efforts. But there was more than fear of crime or concern about the ineffectiveness of the criminal justice system behind this public punitiveness. As Tyler and Boeckmann (1997) have demonstrated in their study of Californians' attitudes toward the three-strikes law, support for punitive responses to crime may be tied more closely to a belief that moral and social cohesion is diminishing. In explaining why California was unusually susceptible to the tough-on-crime movements of the 1990s, Zimring and his colleagues (2001) also point out that what changed was not public attitudes about crime, but attitudes about what the government should do in response to crime. In other words, citizens became more likely to act on the punitive sentiments that they had held for many years. Criminals were an easy target for these sentiments, as Gaubatz (1995: 165) found in her interviews with residents of Oakland, California in 1987: "To a significant degree, they have placed criminal offenders beyond the

---

[18] See Austin and Irwin (2001: 127–128) for a more detailed discussion of Pelican Bay.

pale. They are not imputing to them good intentions; they are not looking upon them as really just like us. Forgiveness and the avoidance of vengeance may be important standards for the commerce of everyday life...but the treatment of criminals is not a part of everyday life."

California's politicians were masters at feeding off of and reinforcing the public's anxieties in the 1980s and 1990s, perhaps out of what they saw as necessity. Deukmejian, governor from 1983 to 1991, had worked hard – as a state assemblyman, senator, and attorney general – to build a reputation as a crime fighter, by ushering in hundreds of bills creating new crimes and increasing sentences for existing crimes through the state legislature. But for many, Pete Wilson exemplified the political exploitation of public opinion about crime, winning two terms as governor "largely because he portrayed himself as the toughest, meanest crime buster around" (Abramsky 2002: 6). As mayor of San Diego in the 1970s and early 1980s, Wilson had appointed a crime control commission that recommended redirecting expenditures on prisons toward community corrections. But as a U.S. senator he sponsored the Comprehensive Crime Control Act of 1984, that increased the number of prisoners in federal custody by 32%. If Wilson was the poster boy for Californians hungry for harsher justice, he was not alone in trying to appear tough on crime. To do otherwise was to court electoral disaster in many political analysts' minds. And so, in the gubernatorial election of 1990, Wilson's opponent, Dianne Feinstein – who had opposed capital punishment and favored rehabilitative responses to drug offenders in the 1960s and 1970s – announced her support for the execution of murderers and proposed a one-half cent sales tax to raise money for more police officers. Despite Feinstein's efforts, Wilson won the election with 49% of the vote to Feinstein's 46%.

Wilson assumed office in 1991, when tens of thousands of blue-collar jobs in the state's defense industry and natural resource-based sectors were drying up. Both the state's unemployment rate and its family poverty rate were about to surpass those for the nation as a whole. The booming high tech sector and financial markets made for healthy gains among the state's economically well-off, but contributed to the continued growth in income inequality in the state (California Department of Finance 1999; California Employment Development Department 2000; Office of Economic Research 2000; U.S. Bureau of the Census 1999). Wilson very soon faced a major budget crisis: at an impasse with the Democratically controlled state legislature, he was forced to operate without a budget for a record sixty-one days, and by the summer of 1993 the state faced an $11 billion shortfall on a total budget of $52 billion. With an election year looming, Wilson turned to the strategy that had helped him in previous campaigns: making crime the focal issue and selling his abilities to deal with it. He enthusiastically threw his support behind Proposition 184 – the "Three Strikes" initiative – promising, if elected, to fight off any efforts to weaken it. Ahead in the polls until a few months before the election, his Democratic opponent, Kathleen Brown, tried to counterpunch with her own tough-on-crime rhetoric. But the California Correctional Peace Officers Association (CCPOA) threw its support and over $500,000 behind Wilson's campaign, and Wilson emerged victorious.[19]

Wilson's November 1994 election coincided with the passage of Proposition 184, popularly known as the Three Strikes Law. The success of Three Strikes was, according to Zimring and his colleagues (2001), a product of the same process of limiting the discretion of judges and parole boards that lead to the Uniform Determinate Sentencing Act and other legislation that assigned mandatory minimum sentences to various crimes.[20] But unlike the UDSA, which was not designed to increase levels of criminal punishment,[21] Three Strikes was "deliberately confrontational and destabilizing in intention... It was drafted with the explicit ambition of creating large and abrupt changes in punishment practice across a broad category of offenses" (Zimring et al. 2001: 23) – for example, by doubling sentences for a second conviction on a violent or serious felony and mandating life in prison for a third felony. With its passage came even more pressure on politicians and policymakers to develop legislation demonstrating their commitment to punitive responses to crime. At the same time, after 1994 other bills were introduced in the state legislature that sought to develop alternatives to imprisonment for some types of offenders and treatment rather than imprisonment as a response to some drug offenses. If California was "peculiar in its vulnerability to extreme versions of punitive law reform," it also remained an innovator in its efforts to develop a range of responses to crime (Zimring et al. 2001: 177).

For some years, state-sponsored commissions had been proposing a slow down in the growth of prison populations. In 1990, for example, the Blue Ribbon Commission on Inmate Population Management recommended reducing prison overcrowding and expanding alternatives to imprisonment for nonviolent and first-time offenders.[22] Nevertheless, in the same year a $450 million prison bond issue – the fifth in a decade – was passed by

---

[19] This contribution was the largest independent campaign contribution in California's history. By the early 1990s, the California Correctional Peace Officers Association (CCPOA) was collecting about $8 million annually in dues and spending about one-quarter of this on campaign endorsements (see Schiraldi 1994).

[20] Among other bills passed in the wake of Proposition 184 was Assembly Bill 2716, that required violent offenders to serve at least 85% of their sentences in prison.

[21] According to the (UDSA), the basis for calculating determinate sentences was the average time served under the previous indeterminate system: this was "a deliberate method of keeping criminal punishment nearly equal to previous levels" (Zimring et al. 2001: 23).

[22] For an analysis of the views of criminal justice officials on the recommendations and impact of the Blue Ribbon Commission, see Davies (1996).

voters, helping to fund eleven more prisons, which opened between 1991 and 1997.[23] Staffing the correctional bureaucracy and its institutions added to these costs. By the middle of the 1990s, the California Department of Corrections – with approximately 40,000 employees – was the largest department of state government and its annual budget had reached $3.4 billion. According to its own projections, the CDC concluded that by 2006 seventeen more prisons would be needed to accommodate an anticipated 74,000 additional prisoners, which would bring the total prison population to 240,000.

Between 1995 and 1998 – the period in which we carried out our research at the California Institution for Women and Valley State Prison for Women (VSPW) – the number of voices expressing concerns about both an overreliance on imprisonment and the inadequacy of prison training and treatment programs continued to grow. The state legislature passed a bill in 1995 that encouraged putting rehabilitation as a purpose of imprisonment back on the CDC's agenda, at least for some offenders. The bill, Penal Code 1170(2), charged the department with developing rehabilitative programs for nonviolent, first-time felons. In 1998 the state's Little Hoover Commission (LHC) released a report that again recommended reducing overcrowding in prisons and jails, developing intermediate sanctions for nonviolent drug and property offenders, and expanding drug treatment and cognitive skills programs in prisons. However, similar to other state-sponsored commissions, the 1998 LHC did not challenge the goals expressed in the sentencing legislation of the 1980s and early 1990s and did not back away from the CDC's plan for building more prisons. In the report, the commission noted that its recommendations were "intended to support Three Strikes and other sentencing enhancements enacted in recent years by ensuring there always is room in state prisons for the worst of the worst." The commission also called for competitive procedures that would allow private and public agencies to submit proposals for new prison construction (Little Hoover Commission 1998: v). In other words, the Little Hoover and other commissions were not urging California to turn away from imprisonment as the first-order response to many types of crimes and criminals, but instead encouraging the development of alternative ways to deal with some types of crimes and criminals. This bifurcated approach (Bottoms 1977) is another important element of late-modern penality, whereby offenders are divided "into groups, the first normal, run-of-the mill, rational, routine, and relatively harmless; and the second abnormal, serious, dispositionally pathological, and dangerous" (Morgan 2002: 1115). California's Little Hoover

---

[23] Although they passed the 1991 bond issue to finance more prison building, the state's citizens had clearly become less enamored with the costs of the imprisonment boom. A 1991 poll found that 75% of respondents wanted the state to find less expensive ways of punishing offenders, according to Austin and Irwin (2001: 47).

Commission, then, still envisioned a growing prison population made up of serious offenders, as the three-strikes law and other sentence enhancement legislation mandated.

Similar to previous Little Hoover Commission studies (1994a, 1994b, 1995) and many other investigations into crime and imprisonment in California, the 1998 LHC report did not single out women's imprisonment for detailed analysis or comment, even though the imprisonment rates for women had doubled between 1989 and 1998 and women made up a disproportionate number of the types of offenders thought best suited for rehabilitative programs.[24] In his comments at a conference devoted to the final report of the 1990 Blue Ribbon Commission on Inmate Population Management, Zimring (1991: 12–13) suggested why this was so: "In the case of women, we do know that female imprisonment is not responsible for a large share of the California fluctuations because females in prison... are just not an important part of the population... [W]hen you have got as much of a change as we do in a system, which is 95% male... you are not going to be looking hard at the females in the system." The approximately 10,000 women in the state's prisons thus remained at most an afterthought to analysts of California's imprisonment binge.

We, however, are going to be looking hard at the females in the system and at the prisons that incarcerated them, because we think women are not just an important part of the prison population but may also have been differentially affected by some of the changes in penality and penal policy we have discussed in this section. But first we turn to an overview of women in California in the late twentieth century and summarize some of the social, economic, and political trends relevant to their lives, their involvement in crime, and the popular and official reactions to their criminality.

Women, Crime, and Criminal Justice in California, 1960 to 1998

In 1960 the approximately eight million women in California, similar to women throughout the United States, were only beginning to shake off the burden of the "feminine mystique" that had defined their place in a family-centered, consumer-oriented household during the 1950s.[25] For

---

24 The Blue Ribbon Commission did not completely ignore women in prison. In its report, it commented on the fact that the state women's prisons were overcrowded and noted the resource disadvantages female prisoners faced relative to male prisoners.

25 According to Waren (1987) women's place in the traditional family structure of California in the 1950s affected both their experience of psychiatric problems and the ways in which these problems were labeled. Warren argues that the decade of the 1950s was a transition period for Californian women, a period that isolated them in their households with problematic consequences for their mental health. She also describes the transformation of the mental health system in California in the 1970s and 1980s, which saw most state hospitals closed and others emptied of many of their long-term inmates.

most women, marriage and motherhood marked their transition to adult-
hood. Two-thirds of women over the age of fifteen were married and living
with a spouse in 1960, and half of them had at least one child (see Table 2-1).
The postwar emphasis on women as homemakers meant that fewer Californian women had graduated from college in the 1950s than in the 1920s,
and by 1960 only one-fifth had attended college at all. For many poor and
working-class women, higher education was completely out of reach; instead, economic survival required that they combine unpaid work in the
home with paid employment. Just over one-third of women in California
worked outside of the home in 1960, most of them concentrated in low paying jobs, and they earned, on average, 62% of men's earnings.[26] The state's
female population was also young (almost a third were less than fifteen
years old) and predominately white in 1960. The official census figures that
are reported in Table 2-1 underestimate California's ethnic diversity in 1960,
however, because they do not include a separate category for Hispanics (and
would not until the 1980 census).

Throughout the 1960s and 1970s California's political arena remained
largely closed to women, except in an unofficial capacity. In 1960 no women
held state elective office; as late as 1975, the state ranked forty-eight in the
percentage of state offices held by women. Nonetheless, throughout the
1960s political activism among many middle-class and professional women
grew from a hobby to a vocation. The emerging feminist movement of the
late 1960s saw women's groups in California successfully lobbying for liber-
alization of the state's divorce and abortion laws.[27] In 1967, Ronald Reagan
refused to veto legislation that gave California the most progressive abortion law in the country, and in 1971 California again lead the nation, this
time with the introduction of no-fault divorce. However, despite these and
other ostensible advances for women's rights, when the California Advisory
Commission on the Status of Women released its first major report in 1971
the news for women was mixed.[28] The number of female-headed households on welfare had nearly doubled in just two years and there were spaces
in day care facilities for only 125,000 of the more than one million children of working mothers. Although the number of women in California's

---

[26] By 1970 women in California were earning only 60% of what men earned.

[27] Nevertheless, public opinion about women's rights and the women's movement was decid-
edly mixed in California. According to a poll conducted by the Fields Institute in 1970 only
35% of the state's population supported the movement, while 38% opposed it, and 27%
were neutral.

[28] Subsequent research has shown that for women the consequences of more liberal divorce
laws are complex and often negative (see e.g., Weitzman 1985). In the late 1980s, Zillah
Eisenstein argued that "[a]lthough California divorce law moves to the point of treating
women as like men – as independent individuals – it does so within the context of a marriage
and labor market system that treats women as unequal – in wages, in job opportunity, and
so on" (1988: 80).

Table 2-1. *Selected Characteristics of the Female Population in California, 1960 and 1990*

	1960	1990
Age distribution		
% 0–14	30%	22%
% 15–24	13%	14%
% 25–34	13%	18%
% 35–44	15%	16%
% 45–59	16%	14%
% >59	13%	16%
Racial/ethnic distribution		
% White	92%	69%
% African American	6%	7%
% Hispanic	n.a.	12%
% American Indian	<1%	1%
% Chinese	<1%	1%
% Japanese	1%	1%
% Other	<1%	8%
Marital status (females >14)		
Never married	14%	25%
Married, spouse present	65%	49%
Married, spouse absent	2%	2%
Separated	2%	3%
Divorced	5%	11%
Widowed	12%	10%
Number of Children (females >14)		
No children	50%	58%
One child	19%	19%
Heads of household		
All women (>14)	17%	28%
White women	16%	30%
African American women	23%	48%
Hispanic women	n.a.	11%
Labor force status (females >14)		
% employed	34%	54%
% unemployed	2%	4%
% not in labor force	64%	42%
Education (females >20)		
% high school graduate (only)	35%	31%
% with some college	21%	53%
Total female population	7,879,306	14,910,663

Sources: U.S. Bureau of the Census 1963; U.S. Bureau of the Census 1993.

workforce had increased by more than 50% between 1960 and 1970 most remained in low paying jobs. Almost half of women workers were single, divorced, separated, or widowed, and 20% of them earned less than $3,000 annually (compared to 8% of men). The expectations of economically disadvantaged young women suggested little reason for optimism that their life chances would be any better. A survey of teenaged girls from low income families conducted in the early 1970s found that 40% of them were unsure if they would finish high school and none of them planned to continue their education if they did graduate (California Advisory Commission on the Status of Women 1971).

Over the next two decades, growing economic inequality in the state would have particularly pronounced effects on women's lives, especially the lives of minority and immigrant women. The face of poverty in California became more feminized and racialized throughout the 1970s and 1980s. This trend would continue through the 1990s due in part to growing rates of divorce, nonmarital childbearing, and teen pregnancy (East and Felice 1996; Waller 2001). However, for economically advantaged women, opportunities to participate in public life expanded as more of them moved into higher education, politics, and the professions. For less economically advantaged women, however, the decline of well paying blue-collar jobs forced more and more of them into the service sector that paid substantially lower wages. At the same time, more of these women were heading households and raising children on wages that were declining in real dollars. Both legal and illegal immigration to California also became more feminized, as women from countries experiencing political violence and economic decline moved into minimum wage agricultural and domestic jobs, and into the underground economy.[29]

Between 1960 and 1990, the state's female population almost doubled, reaching just under fifteen million, and became distinctly more diverse racially and ethnically (see Table 2-1). Together, Hispanic and African American women constituted close to one-fifth of the state's female population, while non-Hispanic white women accounted for less than 70%. Women in California in 1990 were also much less tied to the traditional nuclear family structure than they had been thirty years earlier. Only half of them were married and living with spouses, and the proportion that either had never married or were divorced had almost doubled since 1960, rising to 36%.

---

[29] For analyses of the immigration of women to California and immigrant women's lives in the California labor market, see Hart (1997), Kohpahl (1998) and Mathews (2003). For a discussion of how economic restructuring lead to a rise in nativism in California, with particular consequences for poor women of all races, see Zavella (1997). And, for an analysis of the increased risk of poverty for Latinas and African Americans in Los Angeles as a result of child-care constraints and commuting penalties, see Johnson, Bienenstock, Farrell, and Glanville (2000) and Stoll (2000).

Although women were much less likely to be married in 1990, they were only somewhat less likely to have children than they were in 1960. As these figures on marital and parental status suggest, the proportion of women who were heads of households in 1990 was much greater than it had been in 1960.[30] Partly as a consequence of the increasing economic demands on them, women had moved into California's labor force in growing numbers over these three decades. They remained concentrated, however, in low paying occupations – more than a third were employed in clerical jobs in 1990 – and on average still earned less than 70% of what males earned.

Thus, despite important strides in the participation of women in the labor force and in higher education, women in California in the 1990s made up a larger proportion of the state's economically disadvantaged population than they had in the previous three decades. Their poverty rates were growing faster than men's, as were their rates of homelessness. In the early 1990s, families accounted for 40% of the estimated 350,000 homeless population, and 80% of these families were headed by women. Although the representation of women in the state legislature had grown,[31] this did not stop the dismantling and restructuring of the state's welfare system in the 1990s, a move that pushed more single women and their children below the poverty line. As Reingold (2000: 243) observes in her study of gender and legislative behavior in California and Arizona, "[w]hile the women of these state legislatures did seem better connected to their female constituents and more willing to take the lead on some women's issues, they were no different from their male counterparts in several other respects." One of these other respects appears to have been a failure to provide the means to prevent a growing rate of poverty among women, especially those raising children on their own.

By 1997, almost one in four families in California was receiving Temporary Aid to Needy Families (TANF), which had replaced Aid to Families with Dependent Children (AFDC) with President Clinton's administration's restructuring of welfare. One of the features of the federal welfare reform package was the introduction of a lifetime exclusion for parents who were convicted drug felons. This restriction disproportionately affected women, especially minority women, according to some (Adams, Onek, and Riker 1998; Gibbs and Bankhead 2001), both because single mothers greatly outnumbered single fathers on welfare roles and because drug arrests constituted such a large proportion of total female arrests (see Table 2-2). But this provision had considerable popular support nationwide and in

---

[30] This total figure obscures substantial differences across racial and ethnic groups. For example, in 1990 nearly half of all African American women were household heads, compared to only 11% of Hispanic women.

[31] Sixteen percent of California state legislators were women in 1990.

Table 2-2. *Female Felony Arrests by Type of Crime, 1960s and 1990s*

	1960–1964	1994–1998
Total female arrests	10,200	95,400
Total female arrest rate	202	675
% of all female arrests	100%	100%
% of total arrests (m + f)	10%	18%
Female arrests for homicide	165	245
Homicide arrest rate	3.3	2.2
% of all female arrests	1.6%	.3%
% of all homicide arrests	14%	11%
Female arrests for robbery	585	2,500
Robbery arrest rate	12	23
% of all female arrests	6%	3%
% of all robbery arrests	6%	10%
Female arrests for ag. assault	1,500	18,800
Aggravated assault rate	30	170
% of all female arrests	15%	19%
% of all ag. assault arrests	12%	15%
Female arrests for burglary	1,550	11,800
Burglary arrest rate	31	107
% of all female arrests	15%	12%
% of all burglary arrests	6%	19%
Female arrests for gr. theft	1,200	12,800
Grand theft arrest rate	24	115
% of all female arrests	12%	14%
% of all grand theft arrests	16%	23%
Female arrests for forgery	1,900	5,300
Forgery arrest rate	38	48
% of all female arrests	19%	5%
% of all forgery arrests	19%	37%
Females arrested for narcotics	1,700	28,600
Narcotics arrest rate	34	260
% of all female arrests	16%	30%
% of all narcotics arrests	15%	20%

Notes: Figures are five-year averages. Rates are calculated on the basis of the female population aged 18–69.
Sources: California Bureau of Criminal Statistics (1960–1964; 1994–1998) Crime and Delinquency in California. Sacramento: California Department of Justice.

California where the public's attitudes toward women on welfare and teen mothers had hardened considerably in the 1990s. The state's politicians were more than willing to exploit these sentiments and they did so through a tried-and-true method – by linking poor, single mothers to crime. In a 1995 campaign speech, Governor Pete Wilson received applause for his claim that "the fourteen-year-old unwed mother all too often produces the fourteen-year-old predator" (Dietrich 1998: 3). By tapping into popular anxieties that connected dangerousness with family breakdown and moral decline, Wilson placed poor, single mothers at the center of those anxieties.[32]

Wilson's comments are an example of what Gomez (1997) has termed a broader mother blaming trend in the United States in the late twentieth century, a trend that was strongly racialized. In California, it was expressed in the "discovery" of prenatal drug exposure as a social problem in the mid-1980s. Sustained by a barrage of media coverage portraying an explosion in births of drug-addicted babies, a number of state legislators and prosecutors devoted enormous effort to attempting to criminalize drug using women. Between 1985 and 1992, the state's two largest newspapers (*Los Angeles Times* and *San Jose Mercury News*) published 148 stories on the topic, most of them featuring crack cocaine users as the source of the so-called epidemic. Crack cocaine was said to make women promiscuous and destroy their maternal instincts, with the consequence that they gave birth to drug-addicted babies they had no attachment to or interest in caring for. As Gomez (1997) points out, women of color were overrepresented as the subjects of these cautionary tales, in effect racializing the image of the unfit mother. In response to the moral panic generated by these stories, state legislators introduced fifty-seven bills aimed at criminalizing or regulating pregnant drug using women between 1986 and 1996. Remarkably, despite the legislature's willingness to increase criminal penalties more generally, none of the bills criminalizing prenatal drug use was passed. Instead, at the urging of the medical profession and many women's rights groups, state legislators chose to support a series of therapeutic responses to the problem, following in a long tradition of medicalizing rather than criminalizing problem women. But also consistent with this tradition, women were targeted for intervention primarily because of their sexual and reproductive activities not because of what drug addiction cost them.[33]

---

[32] It is this sort of anxiety that Tyler and Boeckmann (1997) have identified as an important source of Californians' punitive attitudes toward lawbreakers. More generally focusing on women's contribution to crime through their roles as reproducers of a criminal class has a long historical tradition.

[33] In the early 1990s, the media and some politicians helped generate a minor moral panic around another type of problem female: teenaged girls involved in gangs. Academic research on gangs in California did not challenge the claim that girls – especially African American and Hispanic girls – were joining gangs in growing numbers but did question media claims about the extent to which these girls participated in serious violence. Nevertheless, media hyperbole characterizing female gang members as particularly wild or cold-blooded found support in some academic work. For example, Vigil (2002: 24) resurrected the stereotype of females as even more deviant than males when they cross normative boundaries in his depiction of Latina gang members in Los Angeles: "It is not unusual for some females to take on the persona of a crazy person, as for instance the Chicanas who embrace the

Summary

At the time we began our research at CIW in 1995, the women of California were different in many respects from their counterparts of the early 1960s, when Ward and Kassebaum had conducted their research. They were more ethnically and racially diverse, they participated at higher rates in the labor force, and their choices about their family lives were less constrained. But with more than half of all marriages ending in divorce and many women choosing not to marry, a woman's chances of being the sole earner for her family had almost doubled, as had the likelihood that she and her family would live in poverty. The transformation of the household economy had created a cadre of job seeking women, but their opportunities for work remained overwhelmingly concentrated in female-dominated occupations that paid less than other jobs. The changes in women's lives in California were largely beneficial for economically advantaged and educated women; but these changes can not be said to have improved the prospects for economically marginalized women. Some women – in particular, single mothers, women on welfare, and women of color – faced not just fewer opportunities for economic independence but also more callous and coldhearted public attitudes, particularly if they turned to drugs or alcohol. These women also faced greater risks of coming into conflict with the law and, as a consequence of a constellation of popular concerns over increasing crime, declining morality, and society's growing diversity (Tyler and Boeckmann 1997), greater risks of being sent to prison, as we will see.

Women and Crime in California, 1960 to 1998

Given women's growing prominence within California's economically, socially, and politically disenfranchised population, it is not surprising that their involvement in crime also grew over time, at least according to arrest statistics (see Figure 2-2). The rate at which women were arrested for violent crimes[34] rose slowly but steadily from the 1960s until 1980, dipped briefly, and then turned sharply upward from the mid-1980s onward. Thus, despite the decline in the rate of violent crimes known to the police in the 1990s (see Figure 2-1), arrests of females for violent crimes did not drop during this period. This suggests that women may have faced a greater likelihood of arrest for their violent offending in the 1990s than they had in earlier

---

nickname Loca and live up to it. Male gang members generally walk more gingerly around such homegirls – there is crazy, then there is crazier!"

[34] The violent crime rate includes arrests for homicide, forcible rape, robbery, assault, and kidnapping. Arrests for assault account for, on average, between 80% and 90% of women's arrests for violent crimes.

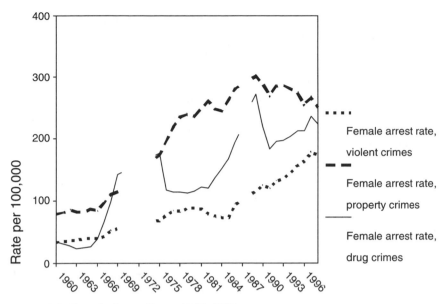

Figure 2-2. Female Arrest Rates, 1960–1998
Source: California Bureau of Criminal Statistics. (Various years) Crime and Delinquency in California. Sacramento: California Department of Justice.

decades. The rate at which women were arrested for property crimes also rose from the early 1960s to the mid-1980s. In contrast to their arrest rate for violent crimes, however, women's arrest rates for property crimes turned downward thereafter.[35] The rate at which women were arrested for drug crimes was considerably more volatile over time, which reflects changes in enforcement patterns at least as much as changes in patterns of women's drug use. Similar to arrest rates for violent and property crimes, the female arrest rate for drug crimes was stable through the mid-1960s. But between 1966 and 1969 it increased fourfold, briefly surpassing the property crime arrest rate. After leveling off in the 1970s and through the early 1980s, the rate at which women were arrested for drug crimes shot upward again, a consequence of the war on drugs. Between 1982 and 1988, their arrest rate for drugs doubled before reaching its peak in 1989.[36] It dropped sharply in the early 1990s but began inching upward again in 1992.

---

[35] The property crime rate includes arrests for burglary, theft, motor vehicle theft, forgery, and arson.

[36] Possession of small amounts (one ounce or less) of marijuana became a misdemeanor rather than a felony in California in 1976. This explains the lower rate of drug arrests in the late 1970s compared to the late 1960s and early 1970s.

As women's arrest rates rose over this period, their contribution to the total arrest rate also grew (see Table 2-2). In other words, the population of arrested felons in California became less male dominated over time, with females accounting for a larger proportion of arrests for robbery, aggravated assault, burglary, grand theft, forgery, and drug crimes in the 1990s than they had in the 1960s.[37] Homicide was the exception to this trend. Not only did women's arrest rate for homicide drop (from an average rate of 3.3 per 100,000 adult females in the early 1960s to an average rate of 2.2 in the mid-1990s), their contribution to total arrests for homicide also declined, from 14% to 11%. The upturn in homicide in California in the last third of the twentieth century therefore was essentially a male phenomenon, and homicide became a more male-dominated crime over time.

The crimes for which women were arrested changed somewhat between the 1960s and the 1990s. A smaller proportion of female arrestees were charged with homicide, robbery, and especially forgery and related crimes. But a much larger proportion of female arrestees were charged with drug crimes. In the early 1960s, only 16% of all female arrests were for drug crimes. By the mid-1990s, drug arrests accounted for 30% of all arrests of women. Women in California were therefore coming into conflict with the law more often in the 1990s, not primarily because of greater involvement in serious, violent crimes but because of the war on drugs.[38] This conclusion is supported by other research that has examined data from California and other states, including work by Marc Mauer and his colleagues (1999), that suggest that the war on drugs had a disproportionately negative impact on women, especially African American and Hispanic women.[39]

---

[37] Some of the increase in female arrests for less serious crimes should be attributed to a growing willingness of criminal justice officials to arrest women and girls over time. Official recognition of differential treatment of male and female suspects is acknowledged in various publications, including *Crime and Delinquency in California* in which it was noted that female offenders in rural areas may have faced lower risks of arrests compared to both male offenders and female offenders in urban areas: "At least part of the reason for this is the lack of adequate or separate facilities for female prisoners in the smaller counties. The police attempt to use other logical alternatives to formal arrest and detention if it is at all possible" (California Department of Justice 1969: 75).

[38] In a comparison of the likelihood of arrest for California birth cohorts of 1956 and 1959, Tillman (1990) found an increase in the percentage of females who had incurred at least one arrest from 11.6% to 13%. He attributes this increase to the war on drugs in California. We were not able to obtain annual data on female arrests disaggregated by offense and race. Nevertheless, other sources indicate that this war on drugs disproportionately affected African American women in California. For example, the California Judicial Council Advisory Committee, in its discussion of the treatment of minority defendants in California courts, highlighted the disproportionate number of women of color imprisoned for drug offenses (see California Judicial Council Advisory Committee 1997).

[39] Barbara Bloom and her colleagues (1994), Barbara Owen (1999), and Stephanie Bush-Baskette (1999, 2000) have made similar claims about how the war on drugs affected women in California and in the United States as a whole.

Similar arguments have been made about the consequences for women of other policy and legislative changes that extended the scope and harshness of California's criminal justice system. For example, the growth of mandatory minimum sentences in California since the 1980s has increased the likelihood of imprisonment largely for less serious crimes, such as burglary and drug crimes. As Table 2-2 indicates, women accounted for a larger proportion of persons arrested for these offenses (compared to serious, violent offenses), suggesting that they may have been disproportionately affected by mandatory minimum sentences.[40]

In addition, some have argued that Three Strikes laws and other laws that conflate dangerousness with persistence may also have affected women disproportionately.[41] For example, Barbara Hudson (2002: 45), in her analysis of gender issues in penal policy, has suggested that "[i]f sentencing is concerned with previous record and with risk of re-offending, then the number of women prisoners can be expected to rise ... as dangerousness and seriousness become even less significant as the thresholds for imprisonment." In an analysis of California's Three Strikes law, however, Zimring and his colleagues (2001: 55–61) found evidence that it had a disproportionate effect on African Americans but not on women.[42] Nevertheless, the question remains: did such apparently gender-neutral policies have far from gender-neutral consequences? What is not in question, however, is that women in conflict with the law in California were at growing risk of going to prison over the last third of the twentieth century.

An Overview of Women's Imprisonment in California, 1960 through 1998

Growth in Women's Imprisonment

If female criminals were not the intended targets of the punitive turn in California's criminal justice system, increasing numbers of them, nonetheless, were caught up in the wider net cast by the state's correctional apparatus. Despite the rise in female arrest rates through the 1960s and 1970s, imprisonment rates for women dropped from 17 per 100,000 adult females

---

[40] Changes in responses to and women's involvement in burglary illustrate this point. In 1981 the California state legislature passed the Beverly Bill, and as a consequence offenders convicted of residential burglary were denied the possibility of probation, even on a first conviction (Davies 1996). Burglary, as Table 2-2 shows, is the index crime for which women's relative contribution grew the most between the early 1960s and the mid-1990s.

[41] Mona Danner (1998) discusses other ways in which Three Strikes laws have had gender-specific effects on women.

[42] They conclude their analysis by noting that "although the California statute is one of the most extreme of its kind, the offenders it singles out for special treatment are probably far closer to typical felons than the targeted population of other Three Strikes laws" (Zimring et al. 2001: 60).

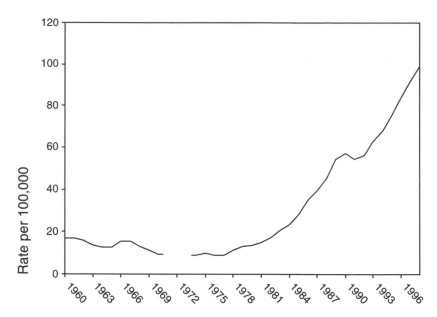

Figure 2-3. Female Imprisonment Rates, 1960–1998
Source: California Department of Corrections. (Various years) Characteristics of Population in California State Prisons by Institution. Sacramento: California Department of Corrections.

in 1960 to between 9 and 10 by the late 1970s (Figure 2-3). But beginning in 1983 what had been a slight increase in women's imprisonment quickly turned into major escalation. Female imprisonment rates doubled from the mid-1980s to 1990, and nearly doubled again by the end of the 1990s. In absolute numbers, this growth was unprecedented in the history of women's imprisonment. The state's female prison population increased more than tenfold between the early 1970s, when approximately 600 felons and 300 nonfelons[43] were imprisoned at CIW, and the late 1990s, when almost 11,000 women were imprisoned at the state's four prisons for women.

To deal with the ever larger numbers of female prisoners, in the early 1980s CIW began double bunking its cells, converted its auditorium to a dormitory, and put up bunks in hallways and storage rooms. But by the mid-1980s, with a population approaching 2,000, CIW was bursting at the seams. The same was true for men's prisons throughout the state. Concerns about

---

[43] Nonfelons incarcerated at CIW in the 1960s and 1970s included "mentally disordered sex offenders, county diagnostic cases, Mental Hygiene, Youth Authority wards, federal prisoners, and California Rehabilitation Center narcotics addicts received under W&I Code Section 3000 et seq." (California Department of Corrections 1970).

overcrowding and expectations about further growth in the prison population lead to the introduction of five prison bond issues between 1981 and
1990. Voters passed each of them, making an additional $3 billion available
for prison construction. Among the prisons built from these funds was the
Northern California Women's Facility (NCWF) in Stockton, which had a design capacity of 400. However, within months of opening in 1987, NCWF's
population exceeded 600 and it could not meet the demand for cell space.
In response, a wing of the state prison for men at Avenal was converted to
incarcerate women and building plans for two more women's prisons were
approved. One of these, the Central California Women's Facility (CCWF)
opened in 1990 and its population also quickly surpassed its design capacity
of 2,500. Its twin sister, Valley State Prison for Women – built according to
the same design and directly across the road from CCWF – opened in 1995;
it too filled to capacity within months. In spite of the addition of these three
prisons, by 1998 CIW's population remained around 1,800, over twice what
it had been built to accommodate. The same was true of the other three
women's prisons: at the end of 1998 NCWF's population was 765, CCWF's
population had reached 3,600, and VSPW, with a population of over 3,700,
had taken the title of "largest women's prison in the world" away from its
sister prison, CCWF.[44]

Public (Non)Interest in Women's Prisons

Despite this enormous growth in the female prison population, for a variety
of reasons female prisoners and women's prisons in California rarely gar-
nered the same attention that their male counterparts received. Certainly –
as suggested by Zimring's comment noted earlier – the fact that women
accounted for only about 5% of the total prisoner population is one of the
reasons, as is the fact that there was only one prison for women in California
until 1987. In addition, women's prisons have historically been relegated to
the background in discussions of punishment, and, in Carlen's words, have
been routinely talked about as "something other than they are" (2002: 4).
Thus was CIW, in the words of someone who had worked there in the 1970s,
"isolated... pretty much a world unto itself, not really part of the system"[45]
Until the late 1970s, staff at CIW were regulated by a separate set of rules

---

[44] Until the Central California Women's Facility (CCWF) was opened, CIW had been the
largest women's prison in the world. These prison population totals include felons and
nonfelons and are taken from the California Department of Corrections annual report
entitled "Characteristics of Population in California State Prisons by Institution." The total
female prison population in 1998 also included approximately 800 women at the California
Rehabilitation Center (CRC), a medium security facility for male and female felons and civil
narcotics addicts, and approximately 350 women at various prison camps throughout the
state.

[45] From a telephone interview conducted in March 2000.

and procedures from those that applied at the state men's prisons and their training manual was written by CIW's superintendent and staff, not by the CDC. The rules and regulations applied to prisoners at CIW were also distinct in important ways. For example, there was no inmate classification system at CIW until the mid-1970s and until 1992 state law mandated that the prison be run by a woman.

Most, but not all, of the public activism and official attention around prison reform in the late 1960s and 1970s that we described earlier were directed at men's prisons and male prisoners, just as the most conspicuous political organizing, collective protests, and violence were carried out by male prisoners. But as the women's movement gained strength in California, it encouraged efforts to ameliorate conditions in women's prisons and to address abuses of particular relevance to female prisoners.[46] In 1976 and 1977, the California Assembly Select Committee on Corrections held public hearings on women's imprisonment that lead to a number of recommendations for improving the academic, vocational, and health care programs at CIW. However, in a pattern reminiscent of women's prison reform efforts in other times and places, these hearings were followed not by any substantial changes in the conditions of life for women at CIW but by further hearings and additional reports documenting the same litany of problems. Partly in response to these problems, throughout the 1980s the California Department of Corrections moved to bring CIW into compliance with the rules and regulations under which the state men's prisons operated. The era of a separate women's correctional system, designed to address women's specific needs, was essentially over.

This was not an unwelcome move in the eyes of the administration and staff at CIW who for some time felt they had been treated as the poor cousins of the prison system. But in bidding to be taken more seriously and to be granted what they saw as their fair share of the system's resources, CIW's administrators – like administrators at many other women's prisons – chose to present two apparently contradictory arguments. The testimony of Sylvia Johnson, CIW's superintendent in the early 1980s, before the Joint Committee on Prison Construction and Operations provides an example. On the one hand, Johnson made a claim that a larger share of the system's resources should be directed toward CIW because of what she characterized as the unique needs of female prisoners, especially with regard to their health

---

[46] In the 1970s, female prisoners and prison groups in the U.S. began filing gender discrimination suits in state and federal courts seeking equal rights with incarcerated men in relation to vocational, educational, and recreational programs; health care; classification; condition and diversity of facilities; and visitation rights (see Rafter 1990). Popular interest in women in prison was generated by media coverage of some of these suits and by other kinds of stories on women in prison. For example, in the early 1970s, CIW was occasionally the focus of journalists and popular writers, who highlighted its rehabilitative orientation and "humanizing" environment (see Lilliston 1971; Davis 1973).

care and their roles as mothers. On the other hand, Johnson justified a claim for more resources because female prisoners were becoming more like male prisoners in some respects: "[T]he woman who comes to prison is changing. I believe you can say that the profile is a woman who is acting out more; who has many other problems, emotionally and otherwise . . . It's a new situation for a woman to close her fist, draw back and knock you in the face and draw blood" (Joint Committee on Prison Construction and Operations 1983: 7, 12).[47] In contrast to her predecessors and to CDC tradition, Johnson argued for separating what she believed to be the most threatening and unstable of these prisoners in a special facility designed more along the lines of a men's prison.[48] Her suggestion was not acted upon, in part because of the more pressing demands of simply finding space for the increasing numbers of female prisoners sent to a prison designed for a different era.

Overcrowding was CIW's biggest problem in the mid-1980s but certainly not its only problem. Between 1984 and 1985, the prison lost its American Correctional Association accreditation, the American Civil Liberties Union filed a lawsuit challenging the constitutionality of its overcrowded conditions, a class action suit was filed by Legal Services for Prisoners With Children claiming the prison provided inadequate prenatal care, and a prisoner filed the first in a series of charges alleging sexual abuse by prison staff. In the late 1980s, drug use by prisoners and drug smuggling by guards had also reached unprecedented levels. Between 1987 and 1990, at least twenty-one correctional officers (c.o.s.) at CIW were fired or allowed to resign because of this and other types of misconduct, and at least five were arrested on criminal charges. For prisoners with health problems, the environment at CIW appeared to be particularly dangerous, even by the CDC's calculations. In October 1988, the CDC launched an investigation of the prison's medical department after more than twenty prisoners died in eight years; two years later the prison's chief medical officer was relieved of his duties.[49]

---

[47] Johnson provided little other than anecdotal evidence to back up her claims. As a strategy to gain more resources, portraying women in prison as increasingly dangerous or unmanageable is certainly not new.

[48] The Joint Committee apparently did not concur with Johnson, however, or with her portrayal of the dangers that female prisoners presented. Plans for the Northern California Women's Facility (NCWF), the state's second women's prison, called for a minimum to medium security prison designed, much like CIW, without solid perimeter walls and with four housing units arrayed around a grassy main yard.

[49] For details on the charges of medical mistreatment, sexual misconduct by staff, drug smuggling, and overcrowding at CIW, see a series of stories by Kim Christensen, Donna Wares, and James V. Grimaldi in the *Orange County Register* in late July 1990. Charges of sexual abuse continued to be filed by CIW prisoners throughout the 1980s and 1990s. The first prisoner to file a charge claimed that for three years during the 1980s she was repeatedly raped by two officers – one of them the son of Kathleen Anderson, former superintendent at CIW – and that prison officials had ignored her requests for help. When she laid criminal charges in 1985, she was moved to the administrative segregation unit and kept there for the two years it took to settle the case, and then moved to a federal facility. Both of the accused in this case served prison terms for sexual assault. At least one female correctional officer also

By 1990 even CIW's warden, Susan E. Poole – the fourth since 1980 – was admitting to the media that CIW was "a horrible environment" in which to work (Christiansen, Grimaldi, and Wares 1990: N2). It was presumably no better as a place to live. The opening that year of the Central California Women's Facility, the state's third prison for women, had little impact on overcrowding and its associated problems at CIW. The state legislature responded in a time honored fashion: it appointed a commission. The Senate resolution establishing the commission highlighted two aspects of women's imprisonment. First, it noted that "the problem of the increase in female prisoners parallels the problem of explosive growth in the male prisoner population" despite the fact that women "lend themselves to greater opportunity for rehabilitation and return to society." Second, it acknowledged that "a significant element of the increase in female prisoners has included a disproportionately high number of minority and low-income women" (California Senate 1991: 1–3). The more than thirty recommendations made in the Commission's 1994 final report mirrored those of earlier commissions and investigative committees. The report called for more services for incarcerated mothers, their children and women in need of drug treatment; greater reliance on probation and community-based programs for convicted women; and more effective programs to deal with the transition from prison to parole. Throughout the report, regular reference was made to the "unique characteristics and needs of female inmates." But while these characteristics and needs might justify responding somewhat differently to women's criminal behaviors, they did not in the commission's view obviate the importance of holding women responsible for their actions (California Senate Concurrent Resolution 33 Commission Report 1994).

And so, as we began our research at CIW in 1995, the rate of growth in the state's female prison population had not abated, despite the more obvious failings of the institutions designed to confine that population and an acknowledgment that there ought to be alternatives to imprisonment for many female offenders. What had remained relatively constant over time, however, were both the nature of the problems identified in various official and unofficial investigations of women's imprisonment (inadequate medical care, lack of appropriate services and programs for imprisoned mothers and drug users, sexual abuse of prisoners, and an overreliance on incarceration for convicted women[50]) and the system's inability or unwillingness to address those problems.

---

filed charges against a male co-worker for sexual assault, a case that ended in his conviction in 1989.

[50] These problems continued to provoke legal action, such as *Shumate v. Wilson*, a class action law suit filed in 1995 claiming that the medical care provided to prisoners at CIW and CCWF violated the Eighth Amendment's ban against cruel and unusual punishment. The suit was settled in 1997. The settlement agreement included fifty-seven substantive provisions and provided for assessments of compliance at eight-month intervals. The first of these follow-up

Conclusion

Crime control policies, practices, and discourses altered dramatically over the last three decades of the twentieth century in California. In this chapter, we have outlined some of the political, economic, and social changes in California that penal scholars have associated with a more general shift toward increasing punitiveness in the United States and elsewhere (Caplow and Simon 1999; Petersilia 1999; Pratt 2000, 2002; Zimring and Hawkins 1992, 1994). The intended targets of the get-tough policies and "the revenge rationale" (Hudson 2002: 257) that gave these policies life were almost certainly males, and in particular, the young, violent, predatory males who dominated public imaginings about crime. Nevertheless, an important consequence of California's particular brand of populist punitiveness (Bottoms 1995) was unprecedented growth in the scope of women's imprisonment. Another important and related consequence, which we describe in more depth in Chapters 4 and 5, was a shift away from some of the discourses and practices that had traditionally informed and given a distinctive shape to the imprisonment of women. As the California Department of Corrections was faced with the management of not just thousands more female prisoners but also more prisons for women, it sought to rationalize women's imprisonment and move toward gender equity in its policies and practices. To some extent, then, we see evidence of a trend that Worrall (2002) argues has occurred in the United Kingdom, the United States, and Australia, a trend toward "rendering women punishable." "In the effort to retreat from traditional paternalism and maternalism," she asserts, "the making of the penal crisis in relation to women has been instead the unmaking of 'women' as a category of offender requiring any special attention at all" (Worrall 2002: 64).

But rendering women punishable in late-twentieth-century California was not only, or even particularly, about constructing female offenders as moral and legal equivalents of male offenders. More women became punishable in California in part because of social, economic, and legal changes that raised their chances of coming into conflict with the law. Among these were increasing levels of poverty and homelessness, decreasing access to social services and welfare, and a growing risk of arrest for illegal drug use. Moreover, the statuses that had once given some female offenders legal immunity, or at least partial dispensation – marriage, motherhood, economic dependency on a male – were less common and/or no longer influential in a system characterized by mandatory minimum sentences and reduced discretion.

Women may also have been rendered more punishable through a less direct and subtler process, a process that allowed the public to be at minimum

---

assessments found that the defendants had failed to comply in whole or in part with twelve of the provisions (Justice Now and Prisoner Action Coalition 2000).

indifferent to, if not tolerant or even supportive of, the unprecedented growth in the number of women sent to prison. According to Garland (2001), the restructuring of both the market economy and family life was among the most important changes in the social arrangements of late modernity that fueled the growth of the "culture of control." Women played a critical role in this restructuring, as more and more of them moved into low paying jobs in an expanding service sector and became heads of households and single parents. Whether out of choice or necessity, women in California over the last three decades of the twentieth century moved ever more out of reach of many of the traditional spheres of informal control over their lives. In so doing, they were likely seen as making a particular contribution to what Garland calls "a new sense of disorder and of dangerously inadequate controls." As a consequence, "a reactionary politics has used this underlying disquiet to create a powerful narrative of moral decline in which crime has come to feature – together with teenage pregnancies, single parent families, welfare dependency, and drug abuse" (Garland 2001: 195). Although the public may not have linked women to the crime theme in this narrative of decline, they would certainly have placed women at the center of the other elements of this narrative. In so doing, women became central actors in a late-twentieth-century morality play that featured female failings as the source of social disintegration. If women – especially poor, single mothers, women on welfare, and female drug users – were seen as responsible for this disintegration, they could also be seen as deserving of blame and of punishment. Perhaps, then, the huge growth in the number of women in prison was accepted as an appropriate response to women's contribution to "the collapse of informal norms of restraint" (Garland 2001: 195) and to "the decline in morality and discipline within the family" (Tyler and Boeckman 1997: 237).

Entering the Prisons: Methods

OUR DESCRIPTION OF THE POLITICAL, demographic, and crime trends in California from the early 1960s to the late 1990s provides a framework not only for understanding how the experience of imprisonment may have changed over time but also for understanding how, and under what conditions, prison research occurs today. While the expansion of the crime control industry spawned a new generation of prisons and enough offenders to exceed their capacity, populist crime policies left criminologists and other social policy experts largely on the sidelines (Zimring et al. 2001; Simon and Feeley 2003). Simon (2000: 285) provides a particularly lucid discussion of how "the pathways of knowledge that made the experience of incarceration" visible during the 1950s and 1960s – what, as we have noted, he refers to as the golden age of U.S. prison sociology – have largely disappeared. As a result, researchers are now notably absent from penal institutions in the United States perhaps because, as some have argued, their expertise is seen as less relevant and their work "is virtually all political risk for prison administrators" (Simon 2000: 303). With this in mind, this chapter describes the explicit and implicit connections between Ward and Kassebaum's study of the California Institution for Women (CIW) in the early 1960s and our work there, and at Valley State Prison for Women (VSPW), over thirty years later.

When we embarked on this study, we thought our methodology was relatively well laid out. We knew we wanted to replicate some of the research Ward and Kassebaum conducted at the California Institution for Women and it seemed easy enough to follow in their footsteps. In fact, as we reviewed their methodology we were struck by how relevant it was to much of what researchers often strive for today – the integration of quantitative and qualitative data and an extensive use of narratology.[1] Yet as many scholars have noted, fieldwork entails a host of starts and stops and unplanned journeys in its course of development. Perhaps these events are even more pronounced in the confines of prisons today where prisoners, guards, and staff are hesitant to disrupt their routines or reveal too much. Here we retell our version of this journey, beginning with the framework of Ward and Kassebaum's research and how we extended it in the research we conducted at CIW and VSPW in the mid- to late 1990s. In the process, we also provide relevant descriptive data on the women who were central to these research endeavors.

A Temporal Study of the California Institution for Women, Frontera

Opened in 1952 when California lead the nation in the implementation of new rehabilitative methods, CIW was originally called Frontera, a feminine derivative of the word frontier, meaning a new beginning. The prison's campus design and location in an agricultural area forty miles east of Los Angeles was expected to encourage women to identify with the institution as a home. The 1950s progressive notion of rehabilitation and assumptions about women's needs for a domestically oriented correctional regime were also evidenced in the fact that its 380 residents (as they were called in official publications of the time) wore their own clothing and lived in single rooms in cottages staffed by nonuniformed matrons. Only a cyclone fence surrounded the campus, which was planted with flower gardens.

When David Ward and Gene Kassebaum (1963: 3) entered CIW they had two goals: (1) to determine whether female prisoner types were similar to those reported as characteristic of male prisoners and (2) to examine the interrelation of various roles structuring the female prison community. As we documented in the previous chapter, the population at CIW had more than doubled in the decade since it opened. The superintendent, Iverne Carter, was strongly supportive of the research proposed by Ward and Kassebaum. She gave freely of her time and insights into the institution's operations, history, and problems and she willingly shared her views on the attitudes of staff and the events both past and present that shaped the institution (Ward and Kassebaum 1965: vii–viii). Further, unlike the situation prison researchers often face today, Ward and Kassebaum were given tremendous freedom in the institution and they used this freedom to their advantage by

---

[1] Here we are explicitly referring to the ways in which Ward and Kassebaum used women's accounts of their intimate behaviors and relationships to help us understand how women experienced and made sense of their lives in prison.

conducting extensive interviews with both prisoners and staff and becoming familiar figures within the institution.[2]

Ward and Kassebaum initially conducted unstructured interviews with forty-five prisoners, some selected to provide variation on their criminal histories and some chosen because they held, in Ward and Kassebaum's words, positions of "relative power and prestige" in the prison. The researchers expected that "inmate politicians" would be generally well informed about the activities of staff and prisoners and would be in a position "to provide the researchers (given sufficient rapport) with information and contacts" (Ward and Kassebaum 1965: 229). The first woman interviewed was known to prisoners and prison officials as an inmate politician and she suggested their second respondent. Subsequent interviewees were referred to them either by the staff and other prisoners or by being randomly selected from a list of prisoners categorized by their length of time in the institution; respondents were chosen because they were newly arrived prisoners or because they had been at CIW for over a decade. Ward and Kassebaum (1965: 231) freely acknowledged that they "sacrificed statistical representativeness of the sample in favor of respondents with prison experience and the ability to communicate." The women, thirty of whom were interviewed twice, were asked to reflect on "the major problems of confinement and the general inmate behavior patterns they had perceived" at CIW (Ward and Kassebaum 1963: 5). Looking for evidence of convict identities such as those described by Sykes (1958), Ward and Kassebaum found that these identities were virtually absent among the women at CIW. Instead, as it is now well known, the women interviewed by Ward and Kassebaum talked principally about how sexual relationships among prisoners shaped prison life at CIW. As a consequence, Ward and Kassebaum concluded that "the phenomenon of homosexuality [was] the single most pervasive influence in the prison," affecting virtually all prisoners either because of their personal involvement or because they had to come to terms with its prevalence in the population and the way in which women's sexual relationships structured interaction among prisoners and between prisoners and staff (Ward and Kassebaum 1965: 219). Ward was concerned that his own sexuality was influencing the content of these interviews and, as a result, he employed a female graduate student, Renee Goldman, to determine whether the women would reveal as much about their personal affairs to her. They did. In an interview we conducted with Renee Goldman Ward, she indicated that women's relationships with other prisoners emerged immediately as their central concern despite her and

---

[2] This information was provided to us in an interview we conducted with David Ward and was documented in several of the prisoner newsletters he collected while doing his research at CIW. Articles on Ward and Kassebaum's study appeared frequently in this weekly publication noting the progress and even selected findings from their study.

Ward's efforts to focus on issues most pertinent to the social organization of men's prisons.[3]

To expand the scope of their data on prison life, Ward and Kassebaum used the information they obtained in these interviews to construct a survey that was designed "to confirm or reject a number of propositions dealing with prison life, particularly homosexuality, staff attitudes, and the inmate code" (1965: 253). A respondent group played a particularly critical role in the construction and pretesting of this questionnaire. This group comprised nine women who had been identified by one of Ward and Kassebaum's key informants as prisoners who were "especially perceptive, knowledgeable, articulate, and trustworthy" (1965: 249). Although the researchers again eschewed the notion of obtaining a representative sample of women, they did try to ensure variation in race and offense of conviction. The women in the respondent group, which were drawn from five of the six housing units, included three black prisoners and women with convictions for assault, forgery, and narcotics law violations. These women were, somewhat different from the general prisoner population in that they were relatively well educated (all had at least some high school education) and all but one had been married. In addition, all of the women had histories of prostitution and were conversant with prison life because they had been imprisoned at least once before (Ward and Kassebaum 1965: 250). This respondent group reviewed every item included in the survey to ensure that the wording and prisoner jargon were correct. They also aided the researchers in making critical decisions as to how the survey should be administered and they advocated for the research in their living units. The survey was also publicized in prisoner and staff newspapers. This level of cooperation from both prisoners and staff in the research endeavor stands in stark contrast to what many prison researchers face today (Simon 2000).

Ward and Kassebaum administered the survey to approximately one-half of the prison population at CIW. "Respondents were selected by drawing alternate names appearing on an alphabetical roster of inmates for each cottage" (Ward and Kassebaum 1965: 254). The questionnaire was administered in classrooms that held fifty prisoners. Staff had the responsibility of releasing the women who had been selected as survey respondents. Of the 387 women selected, 314 (81%) appeared and filled out the survey. However, "problems in reading ability, language, misunderstood instructions, and

---

[3] Researchers today who criticize this scholarship for being excessively focused on issues of homosexuality and prisoners' intimate relationships with each other (see e.g., Faith 1993) should consider that in the context of the early 1960s female prisoners perceived these as important to structuring their lives in prison and in the prison social order. Ward and Kassebaum's focus was therefore not just the bias of the two male scholars who conducted the research. In fact, their noted concern for issues of reflexivity at this stage of social scientific development is quite laudable.

incomplete responses resulted in a final sample of 293 "(forty-two percent of the total population)" and 93% of the respondents (Ward and Kassebaum 1965: 255). The data from the interviews, the survey, and other sources served as the basis for their book, *Women's Prison: Sex and Social Structure.*[4]

Collecting Data on CIW Prisoners in the 1990s

In 1994 we gained access to much of the data collected by Ward and Kassebaum, including notes from their interviews with twenty-nine women and with the respondent group, descriptive data from their survey, official publications and documents on CIW from the early 1960s, and working drafts of their book.[5] We also were granted permission by the California Department of Corrections (CDC) to conduct research at CIW, conditional on approval by the warden. Our stated goal was to consider changes over time in how women experience imprisonment by comparing data we would collect with those collected by Ward and Kassebaum.

When we entered CIW in 1995 to begin our study, we were confronted with the remnants of a bygone era in women's corrections. The main body of the prison remained largely as Ward and Kassebaum had found it: seven single-story brick housing units arrayed around a central yard with large trees, lawns, flower beds, and benches that still gave "the impression of a well-kept park," (Ward and Kassebaum 1965: 7). One could mistake it for a high school or hospital. Each of the housing units, named after a former administrator or staff member, faced onto the central yard and although the swimming pool had been paved over, its former site was dotted with umbrella-shaded tables. Yet, despite these similarities, the institution had obviously suffered from almost one-half of a century of use, an expanding prisoner population, and new penal philosophies. Like many aging institutions that have confined too many people in too close quarters for decades, there was a distinct smell to CIW, one that was not disguised by the overlay of harsh disinfectant. In the spring the cooler breezes often covered the odor, but in the heat of the summer, with only portable fans in selected rooms, it was inescapable and frequently joined by the aromas and flies from a neighboring sewage treatment plant. The main reception area was sparsely furnished, circa 1950, and we had the odd sense that it was rarely, if ever, inhabited: the floors had a perpetual sheen and not even a pamphlet or flyer

---

[4] For additional details on the methodology of their study, see Ward and Kassebaum 1965: 228–261.

[5] Notes from Ward and Kassebaum's interviews consist of verbatim quotations from the women being interviewed, paraphrased summaries of the women's comments, and occasional commentary by the interviewer about the interviewee's demeanor or manner. The data we obtained from Ward and Kassebaum's questionnaire were in aggregate form; individual-level data were not available.

appeared to have ever been removed from its allotted space. Administrative offices, for associate wardens and other ranking correctional officers, while often brightened by pictures of family and friends, moved from moderately well equipped to sparse – containing, for example, several old file cabinets, a desk, and a phone – as the distance from the first floor and the warden's office increased.

The change in this prison environment reflects not just a product of wear and tear but also shifts in penal policies. In 1995 the women's cells were double bunked to hold 240 inmates per housing unit and were no longer replete with personally designed curtains and linens or handmade rugs. The roughly 1,700 women imprisoned there had their own clothes replaced by state-issued clothing – muumuus or denim jeans and T-shirts – and uniformed male and female correctional officers guarded them. The custody and support services staff had grown from around 200 in the early 1960s to close to 600 at the time we conducted our research. Towers with armed guards and a perimeter fence reinforced with razor wire also had been added, creating perhaps the most visible depiction of efforts by the CDC to bring this classic cottage-style women's facility into the twenty-first century.

The Gatekeepers

In our initial conversations and meetings with Warden Susan Poole and Associate Warden Ross Dykes, it was apparent that they had many concerns about our project. The warden indicated that she was not averse to having CIW studied but she was concerned about attracting "negative publicity" to the institution. She also felt that prior research (Owen and Bloom, 1995) had documented the needs and concerns of the prisoners and that there was little we could add to the information they already had on their population. Associate Warden Dykes, however, went right to the heart of their concerns by referring to Ward and Kassebaum as two people who wrote the "Black Book" about CIW and to the two of us as the women who were going to write "Black Book II." He revealed that he had given a copy of Ward and Kassebaum's book to some of the prisoners and noted that their reactions were quite negative. We took considerable time to clarify that it was not our intention to replicate Ward and Kassebaum's findings but instead to replicate their methodology to determine how changes both in women's lives and penal policies over the past thirty years may have shaped their carceral experiences.

The focus on the changes in penal policy that were occurring in California was of considerable interest to Dykes. He carefully outlined the ways in which the growth in the prison population had affected CIW, noting in particular his desire to move CIW to a "good girls" institution. The relatively recent opening of both the Central California Women's Facility (CCWF) and Valley State Prison for Women allowed them, at least hypothetically, the luxury of "shipping out troublemakers" and retaining their relatively large population of lifers (290 at that time) whom he viewed as having more interest in maintaining an orderly and predictable environment. He was also concerned about changes in the prison's population given a set of broader shifts in the social and political climate of California. These political changes included both what he referred to as "take aways," or the removal of various services that had been provided to prisoners that were now considered "excessive," and the lack of health services for the poor that resulted in prisons becoming dumping grounds for the mentally ill, drug-addicted, and HIV positive women.

The warden, by contrast, was less focused on the kinds of transformations occurring in corrections and more on the specific transformations that might occur in her prisoners' lives. She was well aware that drug abuse and victimization were central features of these women's lives and she felt that only by taking personal responsibility for their actions would they be able to change. In this process she saw herself as not only a role model but also as motivating women to become involved in service projects that would boost their self-esteem. She believed that the culture of CIW was "twelve hours a day" and she wanted the prisoners to do eight hours of school or work in addition to four hours of "programming" in the evening.[6]

These initial meetings with the warden and associate warden were critical not only for our entrée into the prison but also for our understanding the central role penal administrators play in both the implementation of new penal philosophies and the tenor of an institution. Our next step involved gaining the cooperation of the prisoners themselves.

The Prisoners

The associate warden arranged meetings for us first with five executive officers of the Women's Advisory Council (WAC) and subsequently with all twenty-nine women who were members of the full Council. Women from each housing unit were elected to this council and their charge was to raise

---

[6] The California Department of Corrections strongly encouraged prisoners to create a program of activity during the day by awarding "good time credits" that reduced their prison sentence for participation in activities such as jobs, school assignments or vocational training. Most of the prison jobs were designed to keep the prison running (e.g., food service, cleaning, porter, grounds work, clerical work for staff). Schooling was limited to remedial work in early education and/or obtaining a GED. Vocational training opportunities (data processing, electronics) varied across the two prisons as did the kinds of self-help programs (parenting classes, twelve-step programs, peer counselling) and recreational activities (athletic teams, aerobics, crafts) that were available to prisoners during the evenings.

issues of concern to the prisoners and represent the prisoners' views to the administration. In our initial meeting with the five WAC officers, they told us they had heard about Ward and Kassebaum's book and they assumed that we wanted to study intimate relationships among prisoners. Once we clarified that we were interested in determining how women did time in prison in the 1990s and how that might have changed over time, noting especially the general lack of knowledge about the lives of women in prison, they were extremely interested in, and supportive of, our research. We spent an extended period of time discussing prison life with them, and they facilitated critical contacts for us with women who had been incarcerated at CIW for a substantial proportion of their lives and who could therefore provide insights into the institutional changes that had occurred over the past several decades. Three of these women, all of whom had served between eight and twenty years in the prison, subsequently became important informants and escorts for our journey through CIW. They became advocates for our study, introducing us to an evening meeting of the full Women's Advisory Council and to more skeptical prisoners. They facilitated interviews with women who had different perspectives on the prison and even reassured selected staff about our presence and the necessity of excusing women for extended periods of time from their daily programs for interviews. We scheduled time with them on every subsequent visit and they often wrote to us during our months of absence.

Ultimately, we wanted to interview as diverse a sample of women as possible since, consistent with Ward and Kassebaum's research, understanding the range of women's prison experiences would be critical to the types of questions we included in our survey. We especially wanted to ensure adequate variation in length of time served as prior research has shown this to be one of the more important factors affecting women's responses to imprisonment. We obtained two lists of the women imprisoned at CIW from the California Department of Corrections (CDC): one of all women who had been admitted to the prison (on their current sentence) five or more years ago, and one of all women who had been admitted within the last six months. We then selected twenty-five names from each list using a table of random numbers.[7] An administrator set up the interviews for us. Some women on our lists had been transferred or released before the interviews and so were not available; others, because of administrative problems, did

---

[7] Our goal was to complete at least thirty interviews at CIW. This number reflected the amount of time we had available to do the interviews and a judgment about the minimum number we needed to gather sufficient information for the design of our survey. We omitted names of women in administrative segregation because we were not allowed to interview any of these women; some of the women we interviewed had, however, spent time in ad seg on their current or previous commitments. We also excluded women in the Reception Center because of the brevity of their exposure to the institution.

not receive their notices to appear for an interview or they received notices with incorrect information about when to report for the interview. Eventually, we completed thirty-two interviews with women at CIW.

In the process of conducting our initial interviews at CIW in the summer of 1995, we made some important discoveries that substantially altered the course of our research. A number of the women we talked with expressed concern that they might be transferred to Valley State Prison for Women, which had just opened across the road from the Central California Women's Facility. VSPW was coined "the female Pelican Bay" by women prisoners – a reference to the toughest male facility in the state of California.[8] As a consequence of these comments by women at CIW, that summer we decided to visit VSPW and so drove approximately six hours north into the central valley of California to tour it and its neighbor, the Central California Women's Facility.

Expanding the Research into an Institutional Comparison

From our first visit to VSPW it was clear that it embodied an ideology of imprisonment and a view of female prisoners very different from CIW's, even though, like CIW, it housed women of all security levels. Located on a 640-acre site, the design of the facility was the modular style typical of new men's prisons because CDC wanted to be able to convert it to a men's facility should the female prison population in California decline sufficiently in the future. Multiple perimeter fences (some of which were electrified) foot and vehicle patrols by armed guards, multistory stadium light standards, and guard towers clearly identified this institution as nothing but a prison.

The prison was composed of four separate yards that were fenced off from each other and the main yard. Each had its own set of gray-concrete housing units facing onto a featureless dirt and concrete open space. The housing units contained cells designed for four women, but by the time we completed our research each cell housed eight with the addition of bunk beds; each cell had its own shower and toilet facility. Yards B, C, and D housed inmates from the general population;[9] Yard A held the reception center, administrative segregation (ad seg), and the Secure Housing Unit

---

[8] Pelican Bay State Prison, according to its institutional mission statement, "is designed to house the state's most serious [male] criminal offenders in a secure, safe, and disciplined 'state-of-the-art' institutional setting." Its two Security Housing Units (SHU), the largest in the state, were designed "for inmates who are management cases, habitual criminals, prison gang members and violence-oriented maximum custody inmates." During the 1990s it was under investigation for some of the methods used on its inmates.

[9] At the time we conducted our study, these Yards were used for some classification purposes: Yard B contained mostly women who were on minimum custody and were close to going home, Yard C contained the AIDS cases, and Yard D contained the women who were on psychotrophic medication.

(SHU). To get to any yard, a visitor must pass through multiple security checkpoints and be escorted by a correctional officer. All yards fed into the central yard for the entire facility, which was accessible only during certain times of the day. This central yard had the only visible greenery – treeless grass fields for softball and other recreation – in the entire institution.

VSPW's staff practices and warden's philosophy mirrored the institutional iconography conveying a preoccupation with security, danger, and control. The walled yards, electrified fences, and requirements to line up when walking to and from meals or between different parts of the prison restricted prisoners' movements. Unlike CIW, guards carried batons along with pepper spray and handcuffs. VSPW's Warden Lew Kuykendall also presented a sharp contrast to Warden Poole. In our initial interview with Kuykendall, who had completed twenty years working in men's prisons before moving to a woman's prison, we found someone who welcomed the opportunity to have his new prison as part of a research project and obviously enjoyed talking about the sharp contrasts he found in working with male and female prisoners. Kuykendall was critical of "the system's treatment of women offenders" and its failure to acknowledge the multiple problems they face when they are addicted to drugs and abandoned by family. Yet he was also very clear that his overriding concern was with the safety of prisoners and staff, a concern he acknowledged was somewhat different from that of the wardens of the other prisons for women in California. As a consequence, he had instituted policies, such as restricting the value of personal property to discourage extortion, which some prisoners considered to be harsh, that he felt made the prison safer.[10] The warden's emphasis on safety was also reflected in his belief that VSPW and CCWF were taking the tougher prisoners who got into trouble in other facilities.

We left our initial visit at VSPW realizing that a very significant change had occurred in women's imprisonment and was exemplified in this new high-tech prison for women that, unlike CIW, had yet to develop its own history and culture. We were aware that the differences we observed in some ways reflected the transformations in penality described in recent scholarly work and we began to expand the scope of our research to include not only a study of CIW over time but a study that would compare women's experiences in two very different prison contexts in the late 1990s.

In the following year, we returned to CIW twice to complete the thirty-two interviews with prisoners. And, as previously noted, during these trips we also made a special effort to see women we considered, as Ward and Kassebaum had, to be key informants. These women were bright, articulate, and had

---

[10] As another example of his efforts at making Valley State Prison for Women (VSPW) safe, the warden told us that he had submitted a proposal to the state legislature to have any sex between staff and prisoners defined as rape, because, in his view, it is inevitably exploitative and/or coercive. The proposal was not acted upon.

fascinating insights into both the most mundane and the most "Kafkaesque" aspects of their carceral lives. On one visit, for example, they described to us new prohibitions that had been instituted against wearing shower shoes in the dining room, because a prisoner might slip and fall; against hair dye and makeup, to prevent prisoners from assuming a disguise; and against hair length and style as well as nail length and polish, to prevent contraband from being hidden on their persons.

During this period, we also traveled to VSPW to bring our work at this second institution in line with what we had completed at CIW. The differences we encountered in conducting the research were quite striking. At CIW, we went through a rather informal procedure to get from the main administration building into the building where we conducted our interviews. After signing us in, the correctional officer at the main desk would glance at what we were carrying into the prison – our lunches, tape recorders, and various papers – and then find someone to walk with us to our interview location. In the area they had set aside for our interviews, we were given considerable freedom to talk not just with the prisoners we called up for interviews but prisoners working in the area and on the yard who wanted to talk to us, who either wondered what we were up to, or had heard about our study. Custody staff were relatively relaxed and open and very willing to share their views about how life at CIW had changed over time. By contrast, at VSPW, we soon came to realize that we had to allow ourselves extra time just to get into the institution. The security officers were extremely concerned about our tape recorders and took considerable time to examine them. We were never allowed to roam freely about the prison but were escorted from yard to yard, and through several security checks, before arriving in the unit they had set aside for our interviews. Custody staff were clearly concerned about leaving us alone with prisoners, checking on us repeatedly during the course of our interviews, and making sure that we always knew where a distress button was in any given location. Nevertheless, we were able to complete thirty-eight interviews at VSPW, using the same random selection process from lists of prisoners dichotomized on length of time served.

In both institutions, each interview was conducted by one of the two authors either in a private office (at CIW) or in a conference room, classroom, or chapel (at VSPW); no prison staff were present during the interviews. All but four of the women agreed to have their interviews tape-recorded; handwritten notes were taken during the interviews for these four women.[11] We asked each woman the same four questions, questions that were the focus of Ward and Kassebaum's original study at CIW: (1) What are the most

---

[11] All of the women participated in informed consent procedures as mandated by the University of Minnesota, the University of Toronto and the California Department of Corrections, and all were assured that they were free to refuse to consent to the interview or to refuse to answer any questions we asked them. We were asked by administrators at both prisons not to offer the prisoners compensation for their participation in our study.

difficult aspects of doing time? (2) What are the specific problems of prison life for you? (3) What are the various types of prisoners and how would you characterize relations among prisoners? And (4) what is the nature of prisoner-staff relations? Additionally, women who had served time at both CIW and VSPW were asked to compare their experiences of doing time at the two prisons. Our interviews typically ranged much beyond these four questions, as many women talked at length about various aspects of prison life. While our interviews averaged about an hour for each woman, some went considerably beyond this time period.[12] Many women wanted to talk about their offenses and their relationships with men and drugs and alcohol, all of which they linked to their involvement in crime. Some talked about the abuse they had endured either in their childhoods, with their partners, or both. Still others drew attention to how they felt they had changed since they had been incarcerated as a result of finding Jesus or having time to reflect on a life of addiction, crime, and imprisonment. And still others wanted to talk about their treatment by the criminal justice system – the pleas they felt they were forced to make, their pending appeals, their fear of receiving a third strike, and their fear that their release dates would be pulled by Governor Wilson. The latter was a common theme among women

[12] We were constantly aware of how privileged our existence was relative to the women we interviewed, and how generous they were to share their time, their experiences, their views – and at times – their emotions with us. Of most importance, our ability to simply walk away at the end of the day made it crystal clear that we were not part of their world. We tried to turn these obvious differences into assets by explaining that they were the experts in this setting and we were there to learn as much as we could from them. We found that our distance from their world meant that they were willing to describe many aspects of prison life we could not have been expected to understand. For example, we learned a good deal about their efforts to restore home comforts within the prison context. They instructed us on the art of making "hooch" from orange rinds, the one hundred-and-one ways Ramen noodles could be converted into a gourmet meal with the aid of a "stinger," and the use of sanitary napkins as a cleaning supply. Some women were more open about their lives with one or the other of us, reflecting no doubt our different styles of interviewing as well as our own different life experiences. Yet when we compared notes and stories at the end of the day, we discovered many common life histories and institutional portraits. As our experience interviewing increased, we also became aware of how women's own prison experiences and statuses affected their depictions of the social organization of the prisons. Old-timers were quite critical of what they saw as the boisterously and superficially carefree attitudes of the young prisoners; women with relatively short sentences were often resentful of the control lifers tried to exert over prison affairs; and, women of different socioeconomic backgrounds were often suspicious of each other. Can we know precisely how our own experiences and backgrounds influence our interpretations of their worlds? No, but we have tried to be aware of how our own worldviews have shaped our portrayal of women's experiences in prison and we have not assumed we have reproduced their subjectivities fully in our interpretations. Consistent with Haney (1996: 776), we recognize that reflexivity is best "understood in relation to specific research settings." In this setting, we relied heavily on the practical knowledges of female prisoners, knowledges of which we were largely ignorant. Because we readily acknowledged their expertise, we were able to establish important personal relationships that proved to be critical to the success of our project.

who had been convicted of a domestic homicide; another common theme was perceived gender-based sentencing disparities in spousal murders. For the women experiencing the criminal justice system for the first time, their comments often concentrated on their pretrial detention and their initial experiences in county jail. Many found prison a respite of sorts from jail and were relieved to find it was not as bad as they expected it to be. This was particularly true of the middle-class women who had white-collar jobs prior to their imprisonment and who moved into similar job assignments within the prison. These women believed they had a set of skills that set them apart from the other prisoners and felt they could help the women whose life on the streets precluded them from getting much education or job training.

Some women, of course, found it easier to stay focused on our questions than others, and therefore provided considerable information relevant to our interests; this did not always correlate with social class and education, however. One of our more memorable interviews involved a prisoner with a Ph.D. who wanted to talk exclusively about the problems she observed in the American "prison industrial complex" and who simultaneously failed to realize that she was *a prisoner* serving time in this complex. Other women, for various reasons, found it easier to talk about their lives prior to coming to prison. For example, a woman who had been living in her car with her dog before coming to prison preferred to talk with us about how she managed to find her pet when he ran away rather than about her current relationships with prisoners and custodial staff. Thus, although we witnessed a range of engagement with the interview process, we were amazed at how much of their lives these women – to whom after all were complete strangers – were willing to share with us. This openness included talking about their intimate prison relationships as well as other prisoners' relationships. Yet, in contrast to Ward and Kassebaum, we found the women were neither preoccupied nor particularly concerned with the subject matter; rather, it seemed to be an accepted, if not universally condoned, aspect of prison life. It was rare when someone refused to talk to us, even in the face of language difficulties, and generally we had all of our questions answered.[13]

The characteristics of the women we interviewed are shown in Table 3-1.[14] Similar proportions of the interviewed women at CIW and VSPW were in prison for the first time, had served less than one year on their current sentence, and were serving time for a property or drug offense. The average length of time served on their current sentences was also similar for women

---

[13] There were a few women who were very clear about not wanting to discuss the crime that put them in prison.

[14] Unfortunately, Ward and Kassebaum did not provide comparable information on the forty-five women they interviewed.

Table 3-1. *Selected Characteristics of the Women Interviewed at California Institution for Women (CIW) and Valley State Prison for Women (VSPW) in the mid-1990s*

	CIW	VSPW
Number interviewed	32	38
First-time commitments	73%	68%
Commitment offense		
Violent offense	47%	37%
Property offense	28%	32%
Drug offense	25%	26%
Other		5%
Percent lifers	41%	24%
Average length of time served on current sentence		
– for lifers	158 months	122 months
– for all others	11 months	15 months
Percent who have served <1 year on current sentence	50%	49%
Percent who have served time at the other prison	0% (VSPW)	53% (CIW)
Race		
White	59%	45%
African American	13%	32%
Hispanic	22%	18%
Other	6%	5%
Age		
17–19 years	0%	5%
20–29 years	19%	18%
30–39 years	31%	53%
40–49 years	22%	21%
50–59 years	22%	0%
>59 years	6%	3%

at the two prisons. However, compared to those we interviewed at VSPW, the women at CIW were somewhat older on average, more likely to be serving a life sentence, more likely to be serving time for a violent offense, more likely to be white, and less likely to be African American. More than half of the women at VSPW had served time at CIW, but none of the women at CIW had served time at VSPW, reflecting the fact that VSPW had only just opened when we conducted our interviews at CIW and the fact that CIW was the initial receiving center for most women committed to prison on felonies from southern California.

Finally, it is also important to note that we interviewed a small number of staff at various levels throughout CIW (n = 12). These interviews were not conducted randomly; they were designed to obtain information from administrators and correctional officers who varied in their backgrounds (age, race, and sex), length of service in corrections, and the institutions in which they worked. In these interviews we asked the same four questions we asked the prisoners. We were particularly interested in the fact that many of the staff had spent their entire careers at CIW. We found them to be thoughtful in their responses to our inquiries and seasoned in their views regarding some of the most difficult aspects of prison life for women. At VSPW, it was virtually impossible to conduct any systematic interviews with custodial staff because, we were told, union rules would prohibit staff from taking time away from their jobs to talk to us. Nevertheless, from the somewhat informal information we could gather, it appeared that VSPW had a very different cast of correctional staff than CIW. For many it was their first job in a correctional facility or their first job working with women offenders. Having male offenders most frequently as their point of comparison, their opinions concerning the problems women face doing time were often curt and dismissive, an attitude we observed frequently not only in their remarks to us but in their interactions with the prisoners.

Surveys

Our survey was based on selected items that had been included in Ward and Kassebaum's questionnaire, and questions we designed based on a set of themes that emerged from our interviews. From Ward and Kassebaum's survey we extracted items that pertained to the inmate code of behavior and, more generally, women's perceptions and reactions to staff and prison life (e.g., the difficulty of adjusting to the lack of privacy or the absence of home and family). In addition to these items, we developed questions from the information we elicited about women's perceptions of prison life, their attitudes toward other prisoners and staff, and their experiences with other prisoners and illegal activities. Although some of the items we selected from Ward and Kassebaum's questionnaire matched specific dimensions of these themes (e.g., the prisoners' estimates of the percentage of women in the institution involved in different types of illegal activity) for others we combed the extant prison literature to identify relevant measures. These included, for example, measures of alienation/isolation from other prisoners (Bondeson 1989), measures of self-harm (Shaw 1992b), and a Coping and Difficulties Scale (Richards 1978). The survey included a number of questions about women's background characteristics and prior criminal justice (e.g., age at first arrest, age at first commitment) and related experiences (e.g., drug treatment, mental health treatment). The survey was reviewed by Associate Warden Dykes at CIW and Warden Kuykendall at VSPW, John Berecochea, Chief of the Research Branch at CDC, and two prisoners.

We pretested the survey on three different groups of women at CIW and discussed its wording and content with them. These groups included lifers, parole violators from the reception center, WAC members, pregnant prisoners, prisoners who worked in the fire camp, and a prisoner on medication to control her behavior. In the summer of 1998 we administered the survey to the general population of women at CIW and VSPW. This process had to be tailored to the wants and needs of the particular institutions.

At CIW, John Lee, the Associate Warden for Operations, went out of his way to accommodate us. When we arrived in the reception area the day we were distributing the surveys, there was a notice to all staff announcing the administration of the survey and informing staff that prisoners would be released from their work assignments early for lockdown to fill out the surveys. We proceeded to the warden's conference room and were joined by two WAC members who helped us to stuff the surveys into envelopes. The previous evening WAC sent a general announcement out informing women about the survey. We were allowed to personally distribute 1,224 surveys to the housing units, including the secure housing unit. We returned approximately two hours later with a pushcart and moved from housing unit to housing unit to retrieve the surveys. The correctional officers in each unit varied in their responses to this event. Some had the surveys lined up in a box, with a total count of the number turned in, when we arrived; others could not have cared less whether the prisoners had returned the surveys to them. Ultimately, 887 of the surveys were returned in a completed and usable form, giving us a response rate of 72%.

Our experience with the process at VSPW was entirely different. The warden felt that we would get the best response rate if the surveys were left in the women's units after they were locked in for the night. The administrative assistant to the warden sent out a notice to facility captains in three of the four yards announcing that at 2045 hours the WAC representatives from each yard would pick up questionnaires and hand them out for the prisoners to fill out and, prior to the morning meal release, they would pick up the surveys and return them to the respective program sergeant's office. We left 2,500 surveys at VSPW for distribution by staff to the respective WAC members who would pass them out to the prisoners. We were asked to return the next day. When we returned the next morning we immediately realized that only about one-half of the surveys had been returned. In fact, 1,214 were returned and, of these, 934 were completed and usable, giving us a 37% response rate at VSPW.

We believe that these different response rates are the result of both the differences in how the surveys were administered and the culture of the two prisons. Our ability to personally distribute the surveys at CIW made it visible to the prisoners that this was our research and not that of the

55

administration. It also demonstrated to correctional officers staffing each unit that we had considerable freedom, and administrative approval, to work openly throughout the prison. By contrast, we were absent during this process at VSPW. We met with both the lieutenant, who oversaw this operation, and the warden to discuss the lower response rate at VSPW. They speculated about different reasons for the low return rate. The lieutenant indicated that paper was a valued commodity and many women may not have returned the survey simply because they wanted the envelopes. He also noted that with eight women in a room there was likely to be peer pressure for the women to ignore the survey if anyone expressed a negative view of it. We found considerable support for his second speculation as the surveys that were returned to us often included clumps that had all been dutifully completed followed by a series of blank surveys. The warden, by contrast, laid blame on the staff and the nature of his prison population. He suggested that some of the staff may have been too lazy to hand out the surveys but he was also concerned that the differences across institutions in response rates reflected the fact that the women at VSPW were very different than the women at CIW.

Focus Groups

We returned to CIW and VSPW in 1998 to present selected findings to prisoner focus groups and to correctional staff. We were particularly interested in their interpretations of some of our findings. Consistent with all of our previous encounters at CIW and VSPW, we found marked differences in the administrative and correctional staff's responses to our findings. The staff at CIW demonstrated a genuine interest in our data and tried to account for differences we observed across prisons in response to specific questions. By contrast, at VSPW, it was clear that attendance by a few select administrators had been required and they had little if any interest in our findings. Warden Kuykendall, who retired before our data had been analyzed, represented a notable exception to this pattern. When we called him and asked if he would be willing to meet with us to discuss some of the findings, he was glad to do so and he provided us, in return, with invaluable information.

Survey Respondents

Given the differences in the response rates, it is important to determine whether our respondents at CIW and VSPW differed from each other and whether they were representative of their respective prison populations. In Table 3-2 we present this information.[15] First, comparing the characteristics

---

[15] We are constrained in the variables we can examine because the CDC only publishes limited information on the characteristics of the prisoner populations by prison.

Table 3-2. *Selected Characteristics of the Prison Populations at California Institution for Women (CIW) and Valley State Prison for Women (VSPW) in 1998*

	CIW		VSPW	
	Total Population	Survey Data	Total Population	Survey Data
Inmate population	1,734	887	3,318	934
Commitment offense				
Person offense	30%	38%	25%	30%
Property offense	28%	26%	31%	30%
Drug offense	39%	33%	39%	35%
Other	4%	3%	5%	5%
Parole violators[a]	55%	55%	40%	46%
Race				
White	37%	42%	36%	39%
African American	36%	29%	33%	27%
Hispanic	22%	15%	23%	17%
Other[b]	5%	14%	8%	17%
Age				
17–19 years	<1%	<1%	1%	1%
20–29 years	20%	19%	27%	27%
30–39 years	51%	47%	45%	44%
40–49 years	23%	25%	23%	25%
50–59 years	5%	7%	3%	2%
>59 years	1%	2%	1%	<1%

[a] Survey data includes women in prison for either a parole/probation violation, but only 12–13% reported being currently incarcerated for a probation violation.
[b] Survey data on "other" includes Native Americans, Asians, and women who only indicated that they are of mixed racial origin.
Source: California Department of Corrections, *Characteristics of Population in California State Prisons by Institution,* June 30, 1998.

of the women who responded to our surveys at CIW and VSPW, we find that their distributions across offense, race and, age categories are similar. The most notable discrepancy between the two groups of respondents is the larger proportion of women who are parole violators at CIW than at VSPW. Second, for both prisons the respondents are generally representative of their own larger institutional population on offense of commitment, parole violation status, race, and age. While the survey respondents in both prisons slightly overrepresent women convicted of person offenses (murder, manslaughter, aggravated assault, robbery) and they slightly underrepresent women convicted of drug law violations, the proportion of women convicted of property offenses is quite consistent with what we find in the general population. At CIW more than one-half of the women are parole violators (55%), as are our respondents; however, at VSPW parole violators are slightly overrepresented among our respondents (46%) relative to their actual representation in that prison population (40%). Our survey respondents slightly underrepresent both African American and Hispanic women, and overrepresent women who indicated they belonged to other racial groups, relative to their actual representation in the populations. The over representation of women in the other racial category is primarily an artifact of women reporting they were of mixed racial origin rather than being classified into a specific race by the Department of Corrections. Finally, we find that for both prisons the ages of our respondents represent the actual proportional distributions of women of various ages in the prison populations.

In Tables 3-3 and 3-4, we examine how our survey respondents compare on other background characteristics and criminal histories as well as how they compare to the women Ward and Kassebaum surveyed some thirty years earlier. Ward and Kassebaum's survey did not include questions about women's background characteristics and criminal histories. Instead, they obtained these data by searching the records of the entire population at CIW in 1963 and from comparable work by Zalba (1964).

The 1998 data reveal considerable congruence in our respondents across prisons on the race and age distributions, educational history, marital status, and parental status. The vast majority of women were single with only about one-quarter reporting having been married or living with a man prior to their prison stay. Yet, despite their predominantly single status, roughly three-quarters or more of the women at both prisons had dependent children less than eighteen years of age (78% at CIW and 83% at VSPW). For women at both prisons their chances of being able to support these children are bleak. Almost one-third indicated that they had never graduated from high school nor earned an equivalent high school diploma and less than one-half held a job at the time of their arrest. Chemical dependency, particularly drug addiction, was also prevalent among these women; more than three-quarters of the prisoners reported a drug abuse problem but only about 40% had ever received treatment for their drug addiction. A sizable proportion of women had also received mental health treatment in the past (29% of the respondents at CIW and 31% of the respondents at VSPW). Finally, if family and friends are seen as a critical component of both preprison experiences and postrelease successes (Eaton 1993; Baskin and Sommers 1998), many of these women are at a significant disadvantage as almost two-thirds reported another member of their family had served time in jail or prison, and roughly one-third had a close friend incarcerated.

Table 3-3. *Background Characteristics of Prisoners at CIW 1963, and CIW and VSPW 1998*

	CIW 1963[a] (N = 832)		CIW 1998[b] (N = 887)		VSPW 1998[b] (N = 934)	
	N	%	N	%	N	%
Ethnicity						
White	435	54	350	42	352	39
African American	225	28	239	29	241	27
Hispanic	90	11	128	15	147	17
Other	50	6	119	14	153	17
Age						
21 and younger	86	10	18	2	26	3
22–25	153	17	37	5	84	9
26–35	359	41	347	42	362	41
36–50	226	26	363	44	391	44
51 and older	50	6	54	7	23	3
Education						
No high school	221	30	44	5	44	5
Some high school	296	40	247	30	272	30
High school degree/GED	146	20	233	28	291	32
Some college/college degree	69	9	310	37	292	33
Marital status						
Married	302	35	147	18	198	22
Living common-law	12	1	69	8	67	7
Separated	187	21	86	10	120	13
Divorced	185	21	151	18	168	19
Widowed	53	6	67	8	46	6
Single (never married)	137	16	312	38	293	33
Parental status						
Mothers	594	68	684	83	742	84
Mothers with minor children	516	59	516	78	606	83
Employed when arrested	–	–	321	39	366	41
Substance abuse problem						
Alcohol	244	32	232	30	239	29
Drugs	273	37	583	76	642	78
Drug treatment outside prison	–	–	318	38	361	41
Mental health treatment						
Outside prison	–	–	241	29	273	31
Family member ever incarcerated	403	52	536	65	565	64
Close friends ever incarcerated	–	–	263	33	233	27

[a] The data for the CIW population in 1963 were compiled from different sources. Data on ethnicity are self-reported from Zalba's (1964) survey of women at CIW in 1963. Data on prisoners' ages, and marital and parental statuses were taken from a similar review of prison records by Zalba (1964). Data on education were based on Ward and Kassebaum's (1965) review of prison records for the prison population in 1963. Data on substance abuse and family members' incarceration history were extracted from Ward, Jackson, and Ward's (1969) research for the Task Force on Individual Acts of Violence for the National Commission on the Causes and Prevention of Violence. This research was partially based on the data they collected at CIW in 1963. However, because their analysis of the 1963 CIW data was conducted within offense categories, the data excludes approximately 57 women whose crimes fell outside the scope of their research for the Task Force.

[b] The data for CIW and VSPW in 1998 are based on the surveys.

Table 3-4. *Criminal Histories of Prisoners at CIW in 1963, and CIW and VSPW in 1998*

	CIW 1963[a] (N = 832)		CIW 1998[b] (N = 887)		VSPW 1998[b] (N = 934)	
	N	%	N	%	N	%
Age at first arrest						
16 or younger	188	23	137	17	183	21
17–18	107	13	139	17	125	14
19–20	106	13	83	10	80	9
21–23	147	18	85	11	132	15
24–27	107	13	136	17	129	15
28–34	82	10	124	15	153	17
35 or older	82	10	106	13	84	9
Age at first commitment						
16 or younger	74	9	113	14	148	17
17–18	33	4	110	14	129	15
19–20	41	5	74	9	77	9
21–23	115	14	90	11	124	14
24–27	172	21	138	17	120	13
28–34	188	23	150	19	174	20
35 or older	196	24	123	15	110	12
Prior prison commitments						
0	604	76	364	46	413	47
1	143	18	208	26	222	26
2	29	4	100	13	111	13
3 or more	15	2	122	15	110	13
Number of prior years incarcerated						
0	–	–	217	28	243	28
1	–	–	274	35	249	29
2–3	–	–	129	16	145	17
4 or more	–	–	164	21	224	26
Prior mental hospitalization						
Yes	104	13	137	17	144	17
Offense of conviction						
Forgery or theft	359	44	137	17	190	21
Drug law violation	201	25	271	33	311	35
Burglary	42	5	68	8	68	8
Assault	25	3	49	6	58	6
Robbery	33	4	63	8	69	8
Murder/manslaughter	117	14	184	22	113	13
Other	42	5	49	6	80	9

(*continued*)

Table 3-4 (continued)

	CIW 1963[a] (N = 832)		CIW 1998[b] (N = 887)		VSPW 1998[b] (N = 934)	
	N	%	N	%	N	%
Crime accomplice						
None	–	–	454	58	503	59
Male partner	–	–	201	25	225	26
Female partner	–	–	62	8	66	8
Male and female partner	–	–	60	8	46	5
Other	–	–	12	1	18	2
Time served on current sentence						
0–5 months	82	29	166	21	185	21
6–11 months	88	32	194	24	204	24
12 months or longer	108	39	439	55	479	55
Life sentence	29	4	163	18	64	7
Rule violations on current sentence						
0	522	63	529	66	593	68
1–2	179	22	183	23	187	21
3–4	58	7	44	5	51	6
5 or more	72	9	52	6	40	5

[a] Ward and Kassebaum (1965) compiled data from official prison records on 823 of the prisoners at CIW in 1963. The information reported in Table 3–4 pertaining to CIW prisoners in 1963 is taken from these data, except for the variable "time served." Data on time served were extracted from their surveys (n = 293).
[b] The data for CIW and VSPW in 1998 were taken from our surveys.

The criminal histories of these women are equally grim and comparable across prisons (Table 3-4). Before they turned twenty-one, almost half of the women at both prisons had been arrested, and one-third had been incarcerated. Not surprisingly, then, the majority of these women entered prison on their current sentence with some prior carceral experience. Prior terms of imprisonment for most women were short (one year), however, 21% of the women at CIW and 26% of those at VSPW had been in prison four or more years prior to their current sentence. On their current sentence, these respondents were relatively equally divided between those who had been in prison for less than one year and those who had been serving time for one year or longer. Perhaps the most notable difference between our respondents at CIW and VSPW is the larger proportion of women at CIW who reported having life sentences.

Are the characteristics of these women substantially different from the women Ward and Kassebaum surveyed some thirty years ago? Our data indicate that, over time, the population of incarcerated women in California became more ethnically diverse and older (i.e., the percentage of those aged twenty-five and younger dropped while the percentage of those over thirty-five increased). The aging of the prisoner population likely reflects changes in sentence lengths, including increases in the proportion of women with life sentences and the proportion of women sent back to prison on parole violations. Women's marital and parental statuses also changed. The percentage of married, separated, and divorced women declined over time as the percentage of never married women increased. At the same time, a larger percentage of women at CIW and VSPW had children in the 1990s compared to the 1960s. There are two other ways in which imprisoned women in the 1990s appeared to be particularly disadvantaged: the proportion of respondents reporting drug abuse problems in the 1990s was over double what it was in the 1960s, and prisoners in the 1990s were more likely to have had a family member incarcerated than they were in the past.

Some of these trends parallel those occurring in the general female population (aged fifteen and older) in California over this time period, including the greater ethnic diversity, higher educational attainment, and increase in those who had never married or who were divorced. There is, however, one exception: In the general population, in contrast to CIW's and VSPW's, populations, the percentage of women with children decreased between 1960 and 1990. Other trends may reflect changes in criminal justice policy, such as the increase in the number of women whose family members had been imprisoned. However, regardless of time period, certain types of women – African American women; women who were separated, divorced, or never married; and women with children – were overrepresented in the prison populations compared to the general female population of California.

Differences in the criminal histories of the women imprisoned in the 1960s and the 1990s (see Table 3-4) reflect changes both in women's criminal behaviors and in the criminal justice responses to these behaviors. Women at CIW in the 1960s tended to experience their first arrest at somewhat younger ages but their first incarceration at older ages compared to women at CIW and VSPW in the 1990s. Perhaps in the 1960s the criminal justice system was more likely to respond to early indications of "deviance" by girls by arresting them but then relied on more informal sanctions, stopping short of incarceration. Note that while 49% of the women at CIW in the 1960s were arrested before age twenty-one, only 18% had been committed to a jail or prison before age twenty-one. In contrast, in the 1990s a much larger percentage of the women at CIW who were arrested before age twenty-one

(297 out of 359, or 83%) had also served time before they were twenty-one. These data suggest that young women's criminal behaviors, when discovered, were more likely to be met with carceral responses in the 1990s than in the 1960s. Consistent with this pattern, a much larger proportion of women at CIW and VSPW in the 1990s had served time in prison at least once prior to their current commitment (54% and 53%, respectively) compared to the 1960s (24%). Women imprisoned in the 1990s, then, had more extensive histories of imprisonment, though not of mental hospitalization, than their counterparts in the 1960s.

The offenses that sent most women to prison have undergone a pronounced shift over time and in ways consistent with what we might expect from a combination of the war on drugs and a trend toward the use of alternative sanctions for minor property offenders. From the 1960s to the 1990s, the proportion of women in prison for forgery and theft-related offenses dropped dramatically, whereas the proportion imprisoned for drug law violations increased. This shift could simply reflect changes in the crimes for which women were arrested, and arrest data for these two types of crime suggest this is the case: the percentage of felony arrests of females for drug law violations increased between the early 1960s and mid-1990s (from 15% to 30%) whereas the percentage of felony arrests of females for theft/forgery decreased (from 30% to 19%) (California Bureau of Criminal Statistics, various years).

However, trends in arrest data for three other offense categories are not tracked by similar trends in imprisonment data. The percentage of female arrests for homicides, robbery, and burglary each decreased over time, yet the percentage of women serving time at CIW and VSPW for these offenses increased slightly. In other words, the changes in the offenses for which women were serving time in the 1990s appear to have resulted from changes in both the crimes for which women were arrested and the types of sentences they received if convicted of those crimes. These data suggest that women arrested for drug law violations (and perhaps for some violent crimes and burglary) were more likely to be sent to prison and/or to receive longer sentences in the 1990s than in the 1960s.

There is one other change in women's offending behavior that is worth noting. The information on women's criminal accomplices in Table 3-4 is only provided for the women we surveyed in 1998. These data suggest that well over one-half of the women at both CIW and VSPW committed their crimes alone. While Ward and Kassebaum did not collect comparable data in the surveys they administered to the prisoners in 1963, they did collect it from the women's prison records. Ward, Jackson and Ward (1969: 902, table 35) analyzed these data from the women's prison records within offense categories (homicide, assault, and robbery) for the National Commission on the Causes and Prevention of Violence. They found that while roughly three-quarters of the women in prison for homicide and assault (77% and 75%, respectively) were the sole perpetrators in their offense, only 10% of the females convicted of robbery reported committing the crime alone. We ran a comparable set of analyses (not shown) combining the two prison populations for the same three offense categories. We found that the role of women in assaults has remained virtually unchanged over time: 74% of the women currently doing time for assault reported committing this crime on their own. It is likely that this stability reflects the predominantly domestic nature of this crime. By contrast, the proportion of women reporting that they were the sole perpetrator in a homicide (50%) has declined and, conversely, the proportion of women perpetrating robberies on their own (42%) has risen. These changes may reflect the broader decline in the proportion of homicides involving family members over the past thirty years as well as women's greater involvement in drug-related robberies (Zahn and McCall 1999; Baskin and Sommers 1998).

Women at CIW and VSPW in the 1990s had served more time on their current sentences than had women in the 1960s, with over half having been imprisoned a year or more. Some of this increase in time served was probably accounted for by the larger percentage of women who reported they were serving life sentences in the 1990s – a percentage that mirrors commitments for homicide-related offenses, especially at CIW. In the 1960s, however, the percentage of women at CIW for homicide-related offenses was much greater than the percentage with life sentences, which suggests that in the 1990s women were more likely to be sentenced to life for homicide-related offenses than they were in the 1960s. Violent female offenders appear to have been a particular target of the "get tough" movement of the 1980s and 1990s.

Finally, we find that the use of administrative write-ups for rule violations was remarkably similar in the two periods. About two-thirds of the women at CIW in the 1960s and at CIW and VSPW the 1990s had not been written up for misbehavior, and fewer than 10% had been written up five or more times. Given that the number of write-ups is partly a function of time at risk, one might expect women imprisoned in the 1990s to have more violations since they had served more time on their current sentences.[16]

---

[16] The apparent stability in women prisoner's infraction rates over time may mask changes in the types of acts for which they are sanctioned. For example, based on Ward and Kassebaum's research, and our knowledge of the environment at CIW in the 1990s, it seems likely that women at CIW in the 1960s were more likely to have been disciplined for behaviours that could be interpreted as a sign of homosexuality than they would have been in the 1990s.

Conclusion

This chapter has described our research methods and uncovered some important temporal and institutional differences in the three prison contexts that frame our study. The temporal differences range from changes in the administration and its regard for research; the prison setting; and, perhaps most importantly, the women prisoners themselves. The institutional differences we have documented pertain to penal philosophy, personnel, and even architecture and iconography but seemingly not to the prisoner populations. In the subsequent chapters, we examine what these differences mean for women's carceral experiences and what they can tell us about our evolving practices of punishment.

CHAPTER FOUR

Women's Experiences of Imprisonment at the California Institution for Women in the 1960s and the 1990s

THE AUGUST/SEPTEMBER 1964 ISSUE OF *THE CLARION*, the prisoners' newsletter published through the California Institution for Women's (CIW) educational department "as a medium of self-expression and communication," reprinted a local newspaper story titled "Mrs. Dianne Feinstein: Housewife with a Cause" (Bushman, 1964). It is worth quoting from the story at some length for the sense it provides of penal practice and philosophy at CIW as well as notions about women's roles in the early 1960s.

> "A bright young housewife from San Francisco who looks more like a fashion model has a 120-days a year job which probably would stump the experts on "What's My Line." She's the youngest, certainly the prettiest, and one of the busiest women's parole board members in the United States. Mrs. Dianne Feinstein serves as vice-chairman of the parole board of the California Institution for Women – the largest women's prison in the U.S., located near Corona. This tall, slender brunette, one of three women on the five-member board, is now in her third year on the board "and doing an excellent job," according to its chairman, Mrs. Elizabeth Lewis of Los Angeles. "Behind the delightfully feminine facade there is plenty of thinking going on," points out Mrs. Lewis, a two-term board veteran who is especially proud of her protege.
> Serving as a team they have led the present board through the most spectacular phase in CIW history: In-prison sentence time has been drastically cut in favor of longer and better supervised parole periods, and so far has proved beneficial not only to the prisoner but to the taxpayer and society in general. Understanding the offender's problems and helping them find solutions are the key to CIW's stepped-up rehabilitation program.
> And that's where Mrs. Feinstein is especially valuable, notes Mrs. Lewis, some 20 years her senior. "While all members of the board make it a practice to be guests for meals and 'fireside chats' at various living units, Mrs. Feinstein uses every free moment to stroll around the grounds and chat informally with the girls. She learns things this way we'd never know otherwise, and much

65

to our – and the inmates – benefit." And just seeing Dianne Feinstein – smartly but simply dressed, a poised, friendly, obviously successful young woman – serves as inspiration to those who have been less fortunate, Mrs. Lewis maintains.

In 1962, Feinstein had been appointed to what was then called the Board of Trustees of the California Institution for Women, later renamed the California Women's Board of Terms and Parole, and served until her resignation in 1966.[1] Under the indeterminate sentencing system, the board had broad powers to determine the length of time prisoners would spend in prison before being granted parole, and during the years Feinstein sat on the board the average time prisoners served at CIW dropped substantially. Feinstein's support for community-based halfway houses, rehabilitative responses to convicted offenders, and paroling convicted murderers after a few years in prison reflected the views of many Democrats and progressive correctional officials at that time – including those at CIW. But, as we saw in Chapter 2, Feinstein's views had altered significantly by the time she ran for governor in 1990, when she emphasized her support for the death penalty and argued for increasing the time felons spent in prison through a return to an indeterminate sentencing system. During the race for the U.S. Senate in 1992, when her opponent John Seymour attacked her parole decisions of three decades earlier, Feinstein responded that she had made "mistakes" back then and counterpunched with forceful calls for cracking down on crime and strengthening criminal justice responses to illegal immigrants.[2] In the November 1992 election, she easily defeated Seymour and became the first woman senator from California.

The apparent 180-degree turn in Feinstein's views on criminals and the criminal justice system between the 1960s and the 1990s exemplifies the broader punitive trend in California we described in Chapter 2. In this chapter, we consider how this shift played out in policies and practices at

[1] Feinstein's was largely a patronage appointment by Governor Edmund G. Brown. For a description of Feinstein's work and views on the board, and its influence on her subsequent political stance on criminal justice issues, see Roberts (1994: 51–61, 277–278). Of the "liberal reform ideas" that influenced her decisions on the board and her view that rehabilitation programs should replace punitive approaches to offenders, Feinstein would later say, "In those days I saw the criminal justice arena very differently than I do now. The nature of the problem has changed. I think my perspective is very different. I was very young . . ." (Roberts 1994: 61–62).

[2] Combining a tough-on-crime stance with calls for limiting immigration and strengthening criminal responses to illegal immigration were common features of California politicians' campaign strategies in the 1980s and 1990s, as exemplified by Pete Wilson. In her analysis of late-nineteenth-century discourse on deviance and crime, Leps (1992: 69) identifies a similar theme whereby concerns around national identity are diverted toward criminals: "The exclusion of the criminal served not only to contain certain segments of the population, but also, more importantly, to discern the limits of a consensual 'we,' identified with 'the people of the nation' or that well-known character, 'the public.'"

CIW and in the experiences of women serving time there by focusing on life at CIW in the early 1960s and in the mid-1990s. We compare how imprisonment was practiced and responded to when the rehabilitative model dominated official penal discourse and when the "get tough" era was near its height. The gendered maternal and therapeutic discourses that gave women's corrections a certain coherence and distinctiveness for much of the twentieth century contrast sharply both with the pessimistic penal ideologies of the 1990s and with the move to standardize and systematize penal practices. In this chapter, we examine whether the ways in which women managed their lives at CIW changed as prisons moved toward gender equity and a "penality of cruelty" (Simon 2001: 262). Convicted offenders, as Garland (1990: 262) notes, "form the most immediate audience for the practical rhetoric of punishment, being directly implicated within its practices and being the ostensible target of its persuasive attempts." How were the experiences of female offenders, one segment of this "most immediate audience," affected by the changes in official discourses, ideologies, and practices of penality that we describe both in Chapter 2 and below?

Relationships among Official Philosophies and Practices of Imprisonment and Prisoners' Experiences

A major theme in prison research is that the experience of imprisonment – the ways prisoners think about and relate to other prisoners, to their keepers, and to the prison regime – is shaped by prisons' external and internal environments. With shifts in the political, cultural, and economic climate of the larger society, the relationship of prisons to society as well the relations of actors within the prison changes. Similarly official regimes, structures, and practices inside prisons mold the responses and adaptations of prisoners.[3] In women's prisons, the extent of aggressive behavior, self-harm, collective political action, involvement in prison families, and distrust of other prisoners has been shown to vary in different regimes. For example, in his study of Bedford Hills, New York state's high security prison for women, James Fox (1982, 1984) found that through the influence of the prisoners' rights and feminist movements of the 1970s prisoners' attitudes toward imprisonment and prison life at Bedford Hills underwent considerable change. Prisoners became more political and litigious, their relations with staff grew more

---

[3] For analyses of how external forces influence prison life, see Clemmer (1940), Sykes (1958), and Jacobs (1977). For examples of the effects of internal practices and policies on prison life, see Grusky (1959), Street et al. (1966), Adams (1992), Sparks, Bottoms, and Hay (1996), and Bottoms (1999). Men's prisons provide some of the most conspicuous and well-documented examples of differences over time and among prisons in the experience of imprisonment, such as ebbs and flows in prison riots, the expansion of prison gangs, and trends in prisoner litigation (see e.g., Colvin 1992; Adler and Longhurst 1994; Cummins 1994; Silberman 1995).

adversarial, and the traditional prison social system declined in importance as women reduced their involvement in kinship groups and other close personal relationships. "What was once appropriately characterized as a cooperative and caring community," Fox (1982: 205) concluded, "has slowly evolved into a more dangerous and competitive prison social climate." Rock's (1996: 11) analysis of the redevelopment of Holloway Prison in England provides another example of how the social world of female prisoners can be reshaped: in the case of Holloway, by "the formation and transformation of official typifications of deviant women," changes in the prison's architecture and iconography, and the shifting balance among competing disciplinary modes.[4]

This and other research shows how changes in the expectations that the public holds for its prisons and that prisons hold for their charges, in the ways offenders are defined, and in the techniques prisons use to accomplish their goals alter how prisoners relate to the prison, the staff, and other prisoners. As we saw in Chapter 2 these features of the penal landscape were realigned in California over the last four decades of the twentieth century. What happened in California was part of a nationwide process and this larger process has been subject to considerable scrutiny. Malcolm Feeley and Jonathan Simon (1992), for example, once characterized it as an emerging "new penology," which rejected rehabilitative and normalizing goals, emphasized managerial goals and actuarial techniques, and moved away from individualized interventions based on clinical knowledge (see also Simon 1993; Simon and Feeley 1995). By the 1980s, according to their analysis, prison staff were no longer expected to develop affective relations and open communication with prisoners either for therapeutic purposes or to effect their moral improvement. Instead, prisoners were related to as rational, economic actors who freely chose to commit crime (and likely would continue to do so).[5]

As we alluded to earlier, the extent to which a new or postmodern penology emerged in the latter part of the twentieth century has been widely debated, and Simon and Feeley (2003: 102) themselves have acknowledged that the new penology they described "remains something of a stealth

---

[4] For other examples of how life in women's prisons is affected by external political forces and internal disciplinary regimes, see Mandaraka-Sheppard (1986), Diaz-Cotto (1996), Rierden (1997), and Greer (2000).

[5] Feeley and Simon have since backed away from what Blomberg and Cohen (2003: 17) have termed their "unambiguous announcement that a 'new penology' was emerging." In response to critiques of their work, they state that "To the extent that we were read as trying to predict a new 'stage' of development in crime control techniques to identify a fully realized vision of an alternative to the dominant penal strategies of the twentieth century (anchored in a now old penology of penal welfarism), or to provide a description of and an explanation for a dramatic transformation that had not yet been fully documented let along [sic] understood, the new penology fails" (Simon and Feeley 2003: 77).

policy, and has not captured the imagination of either law enforcement professionals or the public . . . Despite the importance of these new polices anchored in new penology thinking, they are eclipsed by still other policies and programs that are anchored in traditional notions and narratives." That the public and criminal justice administrators lowered their expectations about what imprisonment could accomplish and the extent to which offenders could be reformed over the last three decades of the twentieth century is, however, widely agreed upon. For the public, this was driven by heightened fear of crime and criminal predators; what remained achievable, as well as emotionally satisfying, was to expand imprisonment and make it more punitive. For criminal justice officials operating in a neoliberal climate, transferring the responsibility of rehabilitation from the prison onto prisoners made both political and fiscal sense. And for prison administrators faced with demands for rationality and accountability, effecting behavioral conformity in prison rather than transforming prisoners' attitudes and morals was a less ambitious and more realistic goal (see DiIulio 1987; Bottoms 1995; Garland 1995, 1996, 2001; O'Malley 1992, 1996; Zimring and Hawkins 1995; Caplow and Simon 1999; Tonry 1999; Rose 2000; Simon 2000; Zimring et al. 2001).

What is less clear is how these discursive and ideological trends have influenced the experience of imprisonment. Classic and more contemporary research on prison social organization provides insights into how different prison environments can shape prisoners' adaptations. That research suggest that in prisons with stricter disciplinary and operational regimes, stronger custodial (as opposed to treatment) orientations, and more physically harsh environments prisoners tend to hold more defiant attitudes toward the institution and its staff, choose more individualistic forms of adaptation, and report greater allegiance to a collective inmate social order. In contrast, in more treatment-oriented and less bureaucratic institutions, prisoners tend to form stronger primary group associations and more collaborative relationships with staff (Grusky 1959; Berk 1966; Street, Vinter, and Perrow 1966; Wilson 1968; Mandaraka-Sheppard 1986; Pollock 1986). Thus, to the extent that prisons in California, and CIW in particular, became more austere and more concerned with their security functions and with prisoners as an aggregate rather than as individuals; to the extent that policy and prison practice assigned greater responsibility for rehabilitation to offenders, prisoners may well have become more distrustful of and alienated from the prison and its staff, more self-reliant, and more supportive of a prisoner-based normative system. Fox's (1982, 1984) findings are consistent with this sort of trend, while also highlighting how moves toward standardization, rationalization, and gender equity in corrections compounded these effects for women, encouraging what he characterized as more traditionally "masculine" styles of adaptation to imprisonment.

There are reasons, however, to temper these expectations about transformations in the prison experience, especially for female prisoners. Most importantly, the extent to which a new penal era has emerged and redefined imprisonment is unclear. Prisons have always been sites in which multiple and competing goals and rationales are expressed, even as their logic and function is primarily about the state's power to punish.[6] The goals and rationales for imprisonment ascendant in the late twentieth century were not novel although the political context in which they were deployed might have been. As Garland (1997: 199) has noted, the knowledges guiding punishment often become corrupted and compromised in practice and have unforeseen consequences. Practices developed under different technologies of power can coexist and recombine as these technologies shift (see e.g., Feeley and Simon 1994; Pratt 2000; Hannah-Moffat 2001). And what have been called "the practical complexities of governance" often demand a creativity and flexibility from prison officials and frontline workers that undermine or ignore more abstract discourses and official goals (Valverde 1998: 11).[7]

The discourses and techniques associated with women's imprisonment may be particularly resistant to the types of changes said to characterize late-twentieth-century penality. From its inception, imprisonment has been practiced and justified in different ways for women and men. Assumptions about the nature of the raw materials for women's prisons – criminal women – and about their ideal end products – normatively feminine women – have tended to both soften the regimes imposed upon women as well as deny women's prisons certain resources.[8] Female offenders generally have been seen as more reformable, or at least more tractable, than male offenders; and the female psyche and body have been constructed in ways that have justified gender-specific efforts to control and normalize women. Since the late 1970s, a parity movement in the U.S., while launching equal protection lawsuits to remedy some of the disadvantages faced by women in prison, has also reinforced claims about female prisoners' distinctive life circumstances

---

[6] Carlen makes a compelling argument that the prison's "overwhelming power to punish" overrides the particularities of cultural and political contexts, penal discourses and regimes, or institutional practices. According to her, the punitive power of the prison "has a specificity, which exists and persists independently of the best attempts of (some) prisoners to defeat it ... [and], which grinds both women and men ... independently of the gender-specific modes wherein it is activated" (Carlen 1994: 137).

[7] Lynch's (1998, 2000) research on parole agents and Haney's (1996) study of juvenile justice workers, which show how objectives articulated at a state or regional level can be dismantled at the point of contact with clients in pursuit of individual and organizational ends, provide excellent illustrations of this point.

[8] The history of women's imprisonment is, of course, much more complicated than this statement conveys. Neglect and inadequate resources, punitive treatment of nonwhite and poor women, and long sentences for relatively minor crimes are important aspects of this history (see e.g., Freedman 1981; Rafter 1990; Zedner 1995; Bosworth 2000).

and special needs. As a consequence of obdurate ideological notions of gender, women's imprisonment may therefore still be as Bosworth (2000: 265) observes, "marked by significant continuities in forms and ideologies"; and these may have weakened the extent to which punitive discourses and practices penetrated women's prisons.

In his discussion of why recent penal trends are not best thought of as postmodern, Garland (1995: 204) therefore cautions that "[t]he rapid changes manifest at the level of government representations and rhetoric must not be mistaken for alterations in working practices and professional ideologies, nor should it be assumed that the discrediting of a particular vocabulary (such as 'rehabilitation') means that the practices that it once described have altogether disappeared." Moreover, prisoners are likely to manage their lives in prison not so much according to abstract logics and rationalities of power, or formally stated goals of the prison, but instead through pragmatic rules and habits of doing time. To the extent these rules and habits reflect basic institutional needs, fundamental features of imprisonment, and inherent tensions and contradictions between the goals and practices of imprisonment, the prison experience will probably have at least a core of dreary consistency.

As a consequence of these fundamental features of imprisonment, and of women's imprisonment in particular, there may be considerable continuity in how women experience and respond to imprisonment. Some of the classic and contemporary research on women in prison supports this view (see e.g., Ward and Kassebaum 1965; Giallombardo 1966; Heffernan 1972; Genders and Player 1990; Rierden 1997; Owen 1998; Bosworth 1999; Girshick 1999). In the women's prisons studied since the 1960s, violence, gangs, and overt racial tensions are unusual; intimate and consensual sexual relationships and prison families are common; and relatively cooperative relations with staff predominate. Order and compliance, as Bosworth (1996) notes, are rarely threatened; resistance is typically individual, rather than collective, and covert. These studies suggest that some aspects of the way women choose to do their time may be anchored in basic needs for a measure of comfort and control in a highly restrictive and depriving environment, and therefore may vary little with changes in penal ideologies or a prison's regime.

Official Philosophies and Practices of Imprisonment at the California Institution for Women in the Early 1960s

If Dianne Feinstein's first exposure to CIW in 1962 was anything like other people's, she would have been struck by its campus-like appearance and rural location, both of which were intended to "create a nonpunitive environment in which, it was believed, true rehabilitation could take place" (Bookspan 1991: 86). When the original CIW at Tehachapi, a remote site in central California, was devastated by an earthquake in 1952 its 380 prisoners were moved to the just completed CIW at Frontera. In the decade since it had opened, CIW's population had grown to more than 800 women, and the California Department of Corrections (CDC) had been bringing more and more aspects of its operations under its control.[9] Nevertheless, as we saw earlier, CIW was still allowed to administer programs and develop regulations in ways that were distinctly different from men's prisons.

The rural isolation of the site was specifically chosen to encourage prisoners – or, as they were called at the time, residents – to identify with the institution as a home and to obviate the need for concrete walls, barred windows, and guard towers. State law mandated that a female superintendent head CIW and virtually all of the 220 employees at CIW, in the early 1960s were female. A handful of males worked as perimeter guards; as medical, dental, technical, and maintenance staff; and as chaplains, but male correctional officers rarely held positions in which they had regular contact with prisoners until the 1970s. Because it was the only prison for women in California, CIW imprisoned female felons of all types and security levels who were housed, one to a room, in six housing units or cottages arrayed around a central lawn and flower beds planted with roses.[10] As part of the domestic disciplinary regime, each housing unit had its own kitchen and dining room where prisoners prepared meals under the tutelage of women's correctional supervisors (WCSs). Because treatment and custody functions were not differentiated at the time, WCSs, most of whom had college degrees, were responsible for both. Cottages were also assigned female correctional counselors who were expected to develop individualized

---

[9] Until 1932, female prisoners were held in the state's two prisons for men, San Quentin or Folsom, except for a brief period (1922–1923) when the state ran an "industrial farm" in Sonoma for women convicted of vice crime. In 1929, in response to pressure from California clubwomen who had taken on the role of penal reformers, the legislature authorized the construction of a prison for women at Tehachapi, which opened in 1932. Four years later, responsibility for female prisoners and parolees was moved from San Quentin to a separate Board of Trustees, which allowed CIW at Tehachapi to be run for many years independently from the correctional system for men. As Richard Morales (1980) describes it, the clubwomen who had lobbied to run this separate system for women soon found themselves overwhelmed with the responsibilities of the reform program they had hoped to institute. With the reorganization of the state's prison system in 1944, and the appointment of Richard McGee as first director of the California Department of Corrections, a long and very gradual process of bringing CIW under the complete administrative control of the CDC began, a process that would not be fully complete until the 1980s. As part of this process, in 1957 the institution's Board of Trustees ceded control over the administration of the parole program to the Women's Parole Office, and in 1963 responsibility for female parolees was shifted completely to the CDC. Also, see Bedrick (1993) for a useful analysis of CIW's origins and early administration, and especially the philosophy guiding the women reformers involved in its development.

[10] In addition to the entire range of state felons, a small number of recalcitrant tuberculars, sexual psychopaths, psychopathic delinquents, Youth Authority wards, and federal prisoners were also imprisoned at CIW (California Department of Corrections 1961: 2).

treatment programs for the prisoners based on their consultations with them and various psychological and scholastic tests. As part of the effort to encourage interactions between staff and prisoners and to foster a free-world feel, staff wore street clothes instead of uniforms.

The daily lives of prisoners were regulated by a set of local institutional rules that subjected them to somewhat different and generally less severe restrictions than men in prison, which created what some observers considered to be a "benign atmosphere" at CIW (Zalba 1964: 14).[11] While subject to count three times a day, women could move around the prison with relative freedom and were allowed to wear their own clothing, as long as it was "simple in style and made of inexpensive materials" (California Department of Corrections 1960: 40).[12] A minimum of four hours a day of work was required, either at jobs necessary to maintain the prison or in the garment factory, which was part of the State Correctional Industries. Women were also required to participate in twice-weekly "living group" problem-solving sessions in their cottages, and those younger than fifty-five had to enroll in a homemaking course. High school courses, vocational training in cosmetology, laundry, sewing, quantity cooking, and group counseling and individual therapy sessions were available on a voluntary basis. The demand for individual therapy, however, outstripped what the clinical staff could supply.

Prisoners' daily lives were also regulated through the use of indeterminate sentences. Their release dates were set by the Board of Trustees of the Women's Parole Division, which, as noted earlier, had both sentencing and parole authority over adult female felons. Only after their initial appearance before the board did prisoners know when they would be considered eligible for parole; their actual release could occur months or years after initial eligibility. Decisions to parole were based not just on the woman's crime but also on evaluations of her behaviors and attitudes while in prison as well as on her participation in prison programs. Women convicted of the same crimes could therefore serve very different sentences, a practice justified in the name of rehabilitation and prisoners' need for individualized treatment.

CIW's administration viewed rehabilitation as its responsibility but also as a formidable task because of what it saw as the inadequacies of both the prisoners and the resources available to the prison. In a 1963 issue of *The Correctional Review,* Superintendent Iverne Carter wrote that "[t]he challenge at CIW is to provide, with its limited means, resocialization for emotionally unstable, culturally dependent, physically and sometimes mentally

---

[11] For the local institutional rules at CIW, see California Department of Corrections (1960).

[12] Restrictions on underclothing were carefully spelled out, however. For example, only white or pastel underclothing was allowed. According to Ward and Kassebaum's (1965: 10–11) conversation with a staff member, red underclothes were seen as a "symbol of homosexuality."

ill women" (p. 12). The women imprisoned at CIW then were not seen as particularly dangerous or evil, nor were they considered fully responsible for their circumstances. The staff training manual developed specifically for CIW in 1957 by Carter's predecessor, Alma Holzschuh,[13] reflects this view:

> We deal with people who have been buffeted by fate, the rejected, the unwanted, the inadequate, the insecure. They are looking to us for help, for guidance. When they rebuff us because of the authority we represent, they need our understanding the more...Unless our relationship is one of genuine professional interest, seasoned with warmth and friendliness, it has no value (California Department of Corrections 1957: 21).

CIW administrators also strongly believed that their charges, compared to male prisoners, "had different problems and consequently, they needed different treatment" (Ward and Kassebaum 1965: ix). These assumptions justified the use of a combination of at times discordant methods to prepare the women to "assume various adult roles as a mother, a wife, or a self-supporting individual" (Buwalda 1963: 14).

Along with the coercive power that derived from the system of indeterminate sentences, CIW also relied on maternal and therapeutic methods in its efforts at rehabilitation. Interactions between WCSs, or matrons, and the girls, as the prisoners were commonly called, were intended to mirror as well as model a nurturing maternal relationship.[14] WCSs were to present themselves as role models and confidants for prisoners, and like the ideal mother, they supervised prisoners' training in homemaking, deportment, dress, and grooming. The disciplinary aspect of their maternal role included the moral regulation of prisoners, particularly as this related to their sexuality. When women were discovered in what were termed immoral situations, however, they were not treated to a motherly heart-to-heart talk or sent to speak to the psychiatrist. Instead "[h]omosexual behavior brought to official attention is handled as a disciplinary matter and not as behavior requiring case

[13] Holzschuh was appointed superintendent of CIW in 1942 and resigned (under pressure) seventeen years later. She was, according to Morales (1980), the first professional in penal administration to head CIW, but also considered herself a humanist and a reformer. According to some of her detractors in the CDC, however, Holzschuh ran CIW as if it were her personal fiefdom. Iverne Carter, her replacement, was "a professional career correctional officer" who had "started with the Department of Corrections, was a product of the organization, and was a perfect fit in the system...She inherited a prison that...was trying to succeed with newer scientific methods than those perceived by the California Institution for Women's founders" (Morales, 1980: 378).

[14] The hope that being nurtured could help women become better nurturers was more implicit than explicit in official documents but apparent from other sources. For example, *The Clarion* reported the story of a prisoner who had been nursing a bird back to health, but who lost it when the bird was blown over the fence by a gust of wind. Iverne Carter called a local radio station to alert residents near the prison about the bird. When the bird could not be found, the prisoner was given another injured bird to nurse back to health.

work and clinical attention" (Ward and Kassebaum 1965: 217). For example, according to notes taken at a day's disciplinary hearings at CIW, a case of immorality received much harsher sanctions than all but one of the other cases heard that day. The women charged with this offense had been found on the same bed, kissing. Neither had disciplinary records. The sanction for each included one week in lockup, and one of the women was told that she had probably lost her parole date.[15]

Therapeutic methods were also central to CIW's rehabilitative program. These methods assumed that prisoners would learn "responsible adult roles" not just by being trained in them, but by gaining "self-esteem, self-knowledge, and self-realization" through individual and group therapy (Cassel and Van Vorst 1961: 22). Self-knowledge required sharing one's thoughts and feelings as well as considerable personal information with the psychiatrist and psychologist on staff. But individual evaluation and intervention by professionals were only one element of the therapeutic approach. In group therapy and living group sessions, prisoners were expected not just to take responsibility for their own behaviors but also to demand the same of other prisoners. As in other therapeutic communities, peer-group pressure was seen as an important tool in the rehabilitative enterprise (see e.g., California Department of Corrections 1962).[16]

Tensions between the therapeutic and maternal strategies that coexisted at CIW were apparent to at least some of the staff. May Buwalda (1963), CIW's assistant superintendent, blamed what she called CIW's "protective" and "parent decision-making role" for creating a "child-adult culture" at the prison. This culture, which encouraged "handling problems with just sympathy, arbitrary decisions, or a 'pill' prescription," was in her view antithetical to learning personal responsibility in a group culture. In addition, Buwalda (1963: 14) worried that easy adjustment to the prison's domestic regime was probably a predictor of "repeated failures in assuming socially acceptable roles in the community." Staff were also aware, at least at some level, of the conflict between the softer, more feminized disciplinary techniques they were encouraged to rely on and the coercive techniques that underpinned these. Ward and Kassebaum (1965: 8), for example, noted that when tear gas equipment was issued to male correctional officers, who

---

[15] The notes taken by the researcher who had observed the day's hearings state that "this was the most severe punishment of the day's session, except for a woman" who "had set fire to her room and generally raised havoc." Another case heard that day, which involved one prisoner "pummeling" another in a dispute over some loaned coffee, was resolved by giving each a suspended sentence.

[16] Peer pressure was exerted in other ways, as well, including through *The Clarion*. For example, an editorial in the August 13, 1962 issue admonished women to dress and conduct themselves "in a more ladylike manner," refrain from holding hands, and comply with rules about visiting in each others' rooms, lest prisoners lose the privileges that made the atmosphere at CIW "not that of a prison, but more like a rehabilitation colony."

were the only staff allowed to use physical force on prisoners, female staff reacted with "giggles and lack of interest in handling the weapons.... Our impression is that female staff members willingly delegate these [coercive control] responsibilities which are inconsistent with their roles as ladies."

For prisoners at CIW in 1963, then, the administration held a wide-ranging and not entirely consistent set of expectations. At a time when official discourse expressed considerable optimism about the prison's capacity to rehabilitate, being a good prisoner at CIW meant many things. One should be normatively feminine in behavior, appearance, manner, and attitude but not overly dependent on the institution. One should have an attitude of openness to staff and other prisoners, as a means to self-knowledge, and through peer pressure should encourage other prisoners to acquire their own self-knowledge. Compliance with prison rules was important, but compliance without attitude change was insufficient; and compliance that came too easily could signal weakness or immaturity. These were exacting expectations for women viewed as inadequate and unstable, and they encouraged the use of methods that were themselves discordant. Maternal and therapeutic approaches coexisted, albeit uneasily and within the shadow cast by the prison's punitive and coercive capacities. However, these capacities went largely unacknowledged in official discourse because they were antagonistic toward the goal of creating a nonpunitive rehabilitative environment.

Official Philosophies and Practices of Imprisonment at the California Institution for Women in the Mid-1990s

In 1995, CIW's physical plant looked much the same as it had when Dianne Feinstein walked the yard and chatted with prisoners in the early 1960s. However, as we noted in Chapter 3, additional security (a perimeter fence reinforced with razor wire and four towers staffed with armed guards) had been added, and the prison population of about 1,665 women was over twice the size it was in 1963. Although three other prisons for women had been built, the state did not differentiate them according to security classification as it did with its men's prisons. As a consequence, CIW still held prisoners of all security levels.

While no longer mandated by law, CIW was still headed by a woman, although her title had changed from superintendent to warden. Equal rights legislation had helped to alter the composition of staff working in the housing units and other positions requiring regular contact with prisoners. Of the 320 or so uniformed custody staff, half were males and many previously had worked in men's prisons. CIW no longer provided its own specialized training. Instead, its correctional officers, like those at other state prisons, were drawn from the state's training academy and were members of the

California Correctional and Peace Officers Association, one of the largest unions in the state. According to some staff we spoke with, these changes had lead to greater distance and detachment in staff relations with prisoners.

In 1995 CIW was governed not by local institution rules but by Title 15 of the California Code of Regulations. The shift away from a rehabilitative model toward a managerial model is apparent from the CDC's (1994: 11–12) list of the seven major functions of its prisons, which began with custody, classification, and case record management; education and other inmate services were at the bottom of the list. Group counseling and individual therapy were no longer required of prisoners at CIW, and the few groups offered were run either by volunteers from the community or by the prisoners themselves. A drug treatment program, limited to those within six months of release, had space for only 120 prisoners and a long waiting list. While vocational training had expanded to include word and data processing, electronics, and plumbing, work opportunities were also limited. More than one-third of the prisoners were "involuntarily unassigned" to jobs and therefore unable to earn half-time credits.[17]

With the abolition of both indeterminate sentencing and the separate parole division for women, CIW had lost an important instrument for regulating prisoners' behaviors.[18] In contrast to the 1960s, in the 1990s most prisoners – with the exception of those serving life sentences – knew their release dates when they entered prison. Only life sentences continued to be indeterminate sentences, and lifers remained subject to the parole board's discretion in setting release dates.[19] As we noted earlier, with the opening of three other prisons for women, CIW's administration had gained a new control mechanism: the threat of transfer. Administrators told us they hoped to turn CIW into an "informal level two or 'soft' level three[20] institution" by transferring "troublemakers" to one of the newer prisons, which were built according to a prototype used for men's prisons and rumored by prisoners to be stricter and "military-like." In this sense, administrators were subverting the official policy of not differentiating women's prisons by

---

[17] Unless they have received a life term, prisoners who work at prison jobs or who studied could earn a day's credit for every day they work (or studied), reducing their sentence by as much as one-half.

[18] Parole remained important in regulating the lives of prisoners: about one-third of the women at CIW in the mid-1990s were there for violating parole conditions. The expanded use of parole is an important feature of late-twentieth-century penality (Feeley and Simon 1992). One of its consequences at CIW and elsewhere was "the emergence of two new prison profiles, short-term, and long-term inmates" (Senate Concurrent Resolution 33 Commission Report 1994: A-8).

[19] In the mid-1990s fewer than five of the approximately 300 lifers at CIW had been given a parole date.

[20] At the time of our research, prisons for women in California were classified as level one through level four, meaning each held minimum to maximum security prisoners.

security classification. However, they were doing so not through statistically based risk assessment tools – one of the hallmarks of Feeley and Simon's new penology – but rather through subjective and personalistic assessments about the type of women they wanted at CIW.[21]

Despite the obvious de-emphasis of rehabilitation in CDC publications and documents, in the mid-1990s CIW's administration still talked about rehabilitation as a goal of imprisonment. But in contrast to the 1960s, rehabilitation had become an individual not an institutional responsibility. As Warden Poole said to us in 1995: "We're not rehabilitating anyone. We're creating an atmosphere in which women can change themselves . . . We have a culture of responsibility here." Thus, CIW's work, educational, vocational, and volunteer programs were offered as ways for women to empower themselves,[22] boost their self-esteem, and accept personal responsibility for their lives in order to change them. The prisoner was no longer expected to rely on clinical experts to design her route to rehabilitation but had been responsibilized and rendered a rational actor, "an agent in his [sic] own rehabilitation, and . . . an entrepreneur of his [sic] own personal development" (Garland 1996: 42).[23]

Poole's emphasis on personal responsibility was in keeping with official and popular discourse on imprisonment and the neoliberal environment of the 1990s. However, her belief that women could best learn this responsibility in a prison context modeled after a therapeutic community and attentive to women's distinctive needs harkened back to the 1960s. Her personal style and approach to her job did as well, at least in some respects. Like the superintendents and matrons of CIW's early years, Poole presented herself as a role model for prisoners, as someone who, having used life's adversities to become stronger, could motivate her charges to do the same. Her efforts to encourage prisoners to personally identify with her recalled those of female prison reformers and administrators who sought to establish a woman's regime at CIW in the 1950s (Morales 1980). Thus, CIW's warden, while embracing elements of the penal ideology of the 1990s, also drew on more traditional gendered discourses and techniques in her work.

---

[21] See Lynch (1998) and Hannah-Moffat (1999) for other examples of criminal justice officials taking "an individualistic approach to their clientele and an intuitive approach to their management" (Lynch 1998: 839) in ways that undermined efforts to implement actuarial techniques of risk management.

[22] Hannah-Moffat (2001: 173) argues that "[i]n the prison context, empowerment becomes a technology of self-governance that requires the woman to take responsibility for her actions in order to satisfy not her own objectives but rather those of the authorities."

[23] For more on how this responsibilization process has infiltrated the criminal justice system, see O'Malley (1992, 1996), Simon (1994), Garland (2001), and Hannah-Moffat (2001). This trend has been linked to what O'Malley (1992) terms "prudentialism" a process occurring not just in the criminal justice system but, more broadly, in modern forms of government.

Our interviews with other administrative staff and frontline workers at CIW indicate that many of them also took an eclectic approach to their jobs, an approach that balanced system wide official concerns over accountability, efficiency, and public safety against their own sense of women's particular needs and natures and, specifically, the character of women at CIW. Like their 1960s' counterparts, staff we spoke to tended to see female prisoners not as particularly dangerous or deserving of punishment but as generally inadequate, weak, emotionally needy, and dysfunctional. Efforts in the 1980s and 1990s to demonize certain types of female offenders, particularly drug users (see e.g., Gomez 1997; Campbell 2000), were not strongly reflected in the views of CIW's staff. Similar to Ward and Kassebaum's (1965: 53) portrayal of women at CIW as "criminally immature," CIW staff in the mid-1990s blamed women's criminal involvement on their relationships with criminal men, their susceptibility to drug addiction, and their histories of physical and sexual abuse. While state law might treat female and male prisoners as equal, CIW staff rarely saw them that way. As one senior administrator told us, "95% of the women here wouldn't try to escape if you took away the fences."

Given the official stance that rehabilitation was the prisoner's responsibility and the prevailing view among staff that women at CIW suffered from numerous deficiencies, it is not surprising that staff generally held low expectations for the women and for what the prison could accomplish. This pessimism may also have been fed by the contrast between the rational actor assumed by the rhetoric of responsibilization and what staff saw as the emotionally unstable character of the prisoner population. What staff strove for, then, was neither normalization nor remolding of women's psyches but behavioral conformity within the prison, a less ambitious and more immediate goal oriented toward institutional needs. The shift away from the expansive discourse of normalization and moral regulation toward a constrained one of security and custodial control is exemplified in the justifications for rules about personal appearance and the approach most staff took toward women's sexuality. In the 1960s, rules regarding clothing and hairstyles expressed concerns with creating normatively feminine-looking women who could more easily assume normatively feminine adult roles on release. In the 1990s, these same rules were presented not as serving women's needs but the prison's need to reduce opportunities for smuggling contraband, extortion, and escape through misidentification. Similarly, women's sexual activity in prison was a preoccupation of staff in the 1960s in part because the prison was expected to morally reform its charges. In the 1990s, staff expressed concern over women's sexual activities to the extent that these caused conflicts among prisoners and disrupted prison order.

Summary

The differences we have described in penal objectives and policies in California and in penal practices at CIW are easily interpreted as evidence of some of the macrolevel shifts in criminal punishment highlighted by scholars of punishment. Compared to the 1960s, CIW in the 1990s imprisoned more women in a more apparently prisonlike and impersonal setting; its programs were oriented less toward individualized treatment, normalization, and rehabilitation; and it regulated prisoners according to more bureaucratic and gender-neutral policies. CIW's goals had narrowed and shifted toward organizational ends of security and order. As such, it expected less from its prisoners and from itself.

Despite these changes, there were important continuities in the practices of imprisonment at CIW. Rehabilitation figured in official discourse in both periods. The 1990s neoliberal ideology was not opposed to prisoners rehabilitating themselves or was the correctionalist ideology of the 1960s incompatible with prisoners taking personal responsibility for their rehabilitation. In both periods, an eclectic mix of disciplinary modes and control techniques was available and drawn on to serve officially stated goals as well as more pragmatic institutional purposes. Moreover, imprisonment at CIW remained gendered in a number of respects. Because the vast majority of female prisoners in the 1990s, as in the 1960s, were not seen as particularly dangerous and disruptive, the CDC's and many prison officials' view was that they did not need to be housed in prisons differentiated by security level or did staff need to be armed as they were in men's prisons. And administrators and staff still viewed prisoners at CIW as having distinctive needs and requiring different treatment from male prisoners. Ideological notions of gender differences, then, continued to play a role in how imprisonment was practiced at CIW and may have shielded it from greater infiltration by the penal ideologies and punitive discourses of the late twentieth century.

What remains to be seen is whether and how these similarities and differences in penal discourse and practice were reflected in prisoners' experiences of imprisonment. The interviews conducted at CIW by Ward and Kassebaum in 1962 and 1963, and by us in 1995, 1996, and 1998, provide evidence as to how women viewed and related to the prison regime, to staff, and to other prisoners. (Brief biographies of these women and the pseudonyms we assigned to each of them to protect their confidentiality are presented in the Appendix.) We begin by comparing these women's views on and reactions to the prison regime and staff in the 1960s and 1990s, and then turn to a comparison of their relations with and attitudes toward other prisoners.

Prisoners' Views on and Responses to the Prison Regime and Staff at the California Institution for Women

In the 1960s CIW's stated goal was to provide women with an individually oriented and therapeutically informed rehabilitative program, whereas in the 1990s it had delegated to the women themselves the task of their rehabilitation. The women interviewed in both periods generally agreed on their need for rehabilitation but most questioned the extent to which this could be accomplished whether through the prison's guidance or on their own within the prison context. In both periods, women noted how various routine practices of imprisonment as well as the existence of contradictory goals and conflicting logics subverted efforts at rehabilitation. In both periods, women also questioned whether the prison had the resources and will necessary to achieve – or to allow them to achieve – rehabilitation. And in both periods, women pointed to fundamental characteristics of imprisonment that they felt would inevitably prevent rehabilitation whether by the prison or by prisoners.

Prisoners' Views on CIW's Regime in the Early 1960s

For women serving time at CIW in the 1960s, these issues are particularly well illustrated by their views on how CIW's rehabilitative program was practiced. Several pointed to the conflict between the program's emphasis on open communication and prisoners' concerns with how information shared with staff could be used against them, in particular in their appearances before the parole board. For example, as she was telling the interviewer of her intention to live with another prisoner when they left prison, Wanda added, "I never talk to anyone on staff like I'm doing today – if the board knew I was going to live with [her lover] on the outside, they might make me do the whole fifteen years." Vicky echoed this in explaining why she did not talk to clinical staff: "because if you tell them anything, you'll hear about it at the board." Concern over the consequences of sharing personal information was at times combined with criticism of clinical staff for a lack of professionalism in the types of information they sought and how they used it. Ursula said she avoided talking to the psychiatrist because "he just wanted to pat you on the butt ... [and] blab one's problems about." In describing one of her sessions with the psychiatrist-in-training, Ginger complained that

> [he] found out I was a prostitute and call girl on the outside and that started him off. He wanted to know if I reached a climax every time, what position I took, what about oral contact, how many times a night. He slouches under the desk. I think he was playing with himself ... What business has he of asking

how many times I reach a climax? . . . He asked my roommate these questions and she told him to mind his own business, but he wrote a bad board report on her.

A number of other prisoners noted that the staff's preoccupation with and punitive responses to their sexual relations with each other all but ruled out open communication. Any sign of affection between prisoners, the women claimed, was read as an indicator of homosexuality; once labeled a homosexual their behaviors and attitudes were, they felt, interpreted largely through this identity.[24] As more than one woman observed, such labeling appeared to run counter to the official emphasis on individualized diagnosis and treatment.

Several prisoners also questioned whether key elements of a therapeutic community could be implemented within prison, by nature a hierarchical and authoritarian environment. Efforts to reduce distance between prisoners and staff were seen as unrealistic and inappropriate by many prisoners. For example, Kay remonstrated about staff who danced on the yard or played their bongo drums with prisoners: "staff should know their place – they're not inmates." Similarly, Ward and Kassebaum (1965: 24) noted that prisoners were often frustrated that staff would not accept greater responsibility for their role as authorities and experts: "There is so much emphasis on the efficacy of 'treatment' and the advantages of having decisions made by experts that inmates wonder why treatment specialists ask the 'patients' what they think would be best for their ills." Several women also observed that the voluntariness upon which treatment supposedly relied so heavily was an illusion at CIW. After "a string of curses directed to [the psychiatrist] for his tests for prereleases," Faye (who objected to a test question asking if she had slept with her father) described what had happened to a friend of hers. When Faye's friend inquired if the test was voluntary, she was told "We'd like you to take it voluntarily, but if you don't then it's mandatory."

The group-based aspect of CIW's therapeutic program, which emphasized peer pressure and confrontation, was also seen as problematic within a prison context. Women worried that it discouraged solidarity among prisoners and encouraged women to collaborate with staff in policing other prisoners. Barbara, for example, disparaged the prison psychologist who "points to a girl and tells her to answer and (if you don't) the other kiss asses start in on you. I really hate it." Given the value placed on open communication, group techniques were seen as rewarding women who snitched and creating distrust among prisoners. Relative to group therapy, individual counseling, and therapy were perceived more positively by the women. But prisoners, as well as some administrators and observers (Buwalda 1963;

---

[24] An "H" on one's file was the formal way of labeling a woman homosexual, but prisoners noted that informal labeling was more common.

Zalba 1964: 12; Ward and Kassebaum 1965: 224), noted that the clinical staff could not meet the demand for individual sessions and prisoners worried about expressing opinions in individual therapy sessions that counselors might interpret as signs of poor attitude adjustment.

Prisoners' Views on CIW in the Mid-1990s

Although the philosophy guiding CIW's program and the practices intended to implement it had changed in some respects, women at CIW in the 1990s, similar to those in the 1960s, did not contest the prison's stance on rehabilitation. That is, on the whole, the women we interviewed agreed that accepting personal responsibility was necessary. Carla, who was in prison for the first time, was one of several who voiced such a view:

> I'm trying to do everything that I can do, the best that I can do it . . . There's a lot of self-discipline, because either you're gonna do it or you're not. It's entirely up to you, because they're not going to make you do it . . . They don't care if you want to do it or not. But if you want to do it, it's a self-want.

Similarly, when asked if "anything they do here helps people change," Tara said "Nothing. It's all up to the individual. It has to be." However, she went on to observe, more cynically, that "[t]hese people aren't willing to help you do anything. They're here to punish you and that's all."

As this suggests, women at CIW in the mid-1990s saw the prison as posing a number of constraints and contradictions that made their quest for personal transformation very difficult. Given what they characterized as the punitive and highly controlling nature of the prison context, and the cutbacks in funding for prison programs, many women questioned whether self-want was a sufficient condition for rehabilitation. As Hilary said, "There's less and less options for people. There's less ways in which they can help themselves . . . You can want to change but if they don't give you ways to do it, it don't matter." Others who had tried to take advantage of what the prison claimed to offer pointed out the difficulties of doing so. Belinda described how enrolling in the fire camp program, which she thought would help her get a job after prison, had made her ineligible for the drug treatment program. She knew that getting custody of her child would be impossible without drug treatment, so when preparing her parole plans she inquired about live-in, postrelease drug programs but could get no information on their availability. Instead, she said, the parole planning sessions "just teach you how to do resumes . . . [and] ask you questions about what your goals are – one-year goal, ten-year goal, five-year goal . . . I mean, I don't even know what I'm gonna do when I get out, let alone ten years from now what my goal's going to be, you know?"

The administration's emphasis on making adult choices was also seen by many as unrealistic in an environment that they believed was essentially about negating that ability. Nina said, "They try to break us... They've done that to me already. I guess I'm ready to just say 'here, you can take it. I'm tired of fighting'... It's just, 'OK, tell me what to do and I'll do it.'" Despite having taken the initiative to establish a battered women's support group at CIW, Tina felt much the same: "You lose how to think, you lose how to make decisions. You don't have to make decisions... The only decision you have to make is wrong." Because CIW was experienced as both highly restrictive but also nondirective, some prisoners felt particularly frustrated in their efforts to take responsibility for their lives. As Pauleen stated, "So you don't know what to conform to, you know? So it's kind of hard, you know? It's like you're a puppet or something... You don't know what they want from you half the time. And it's to me like no control." A few women, however, refused to see their situation in this light, even as they acknowledged, as Carol did, that "The system has given up on rehabilitation; it's warehousing, not rehabilitating." Carol, a lifer, had accepted the responsibility for her own rehabilitation as part of her philosophy of doing time, and noted that "We all have choice, even the inmates here. I've always felt like I had the choice to do my time in certain ways."

For others, one way of demonstrating that they were responsible and could make what the prison defined as good choices was through complying with prison rules. At the same time, they typically recognized the coerced nature of this compliance. Andrea said she and her co-workers "work real hard because we have to show the responsibility, we have to do what we need to do. We have to put ourselves out... because if we don't we can get fired." Losing her job meant going off of half-time, which would have added months to her sentence. Bonnie expressed a similar sentiment in explaining why she stayed out of "the mix":[25] "There's certain rules, you're gonna listen to 'em because I want to go home to my boy, you know, my family." Because the prison's capacity to punish provided the context and impetus for their conformity some women questioned the value of such choices. As Eva observed, "what's so adult about always trying to follow their rules, not thinking for yourself? About asking permission to do every little thing, having to act like you're a kid? How's that gonna make me more of an adult when I get out?" The tendency for prisons to infantilize, rather than empower, is of course not a recent development and was recognized by administrators at CIW in the 1960s. What perhaps is new is the contrast

[25] The term "the mix" referred to a grouping of women who, according to prisoners, "get in people's business," are "always in the middle of something – gossip, drugs, fighting, playing games, homosecting [homosexual relations]," and "stir up trouble."

between what women saw as the realities of prison life and the assumptions behind the responsibilization discourse of the 1990s.

Among these assumptions, as we saw earlier, is that the prisoner is a rational actor, making choices based on knowledge of the costs and benefits of potential actions. The women we interviewed at CIW in the 1990s saw this assumption as faulty in important respects. They claimed, for example, that many prisoners did not know what security classification they had been assigned, were unsure whether they had any strikes (or how many they had), and did not know how decisions to transfer women to other prisons were made. Regardless of the length of time they had served or had left to serve, women consistently noted how difficult it was to get information they deemed important for making decisions about their lives after prison.

Similar to women at CIW in the 1960s, then, women at CIW in the 1990s typically expressed a desire to cooperate in the prison's rehabilitative regime but identified a series of barriers to doing so, barriers they attributed to particular institutional failures or limitations as well as to the nature of the prison as a total institution. What differed to some extent between the two periods were the types of constraints and contradictions emphasized by the women. How, given these, did women manage their lives? And to what extent did their ways of managing their lives reflect similarities and differences in the prison regimes?

Prisoners' Responses to CIW's Regime in the 1960s and 1990s

The interviews with women convey the impression that there was considerable consistency over time in their approaches to doing time, despite what prisoners and staff acknowledged was the more punitive and austere character of imprisonment at CIW in the 1990s.[26] As Margo, a woman who had served more than fifteen years at CIW, put it in an interview with us:

the faces have changed, the words have changed, the clothes have changed. But the way women do time has not changed that much. The way the institution offers what should be done with time and society's expectation of what happens when the person comes out has changed completely, and it's sad.

Ward and Kassebaum (1965: 78), similar to other prison scholars of the time, characterized women's approaches to doing time as "adaptations to imprisonment," noting that "inmates may utilize more than one adaptation at any given time or at various stages of their confinement." Psychological withdrawal, colonization, rebellion, and, in particular, homosexuality

---

[26] For a more detailed analysis of continuity and change in women's approaches to doing time at CIW in the 1960s and 1990s, see Gartner and Kruttschnitt (2004).

were the adaptations they identified among women at CIW in the 1960s. The women we interviewed described patterns of behavior and approaches to doing time that parallel Ward and Kassebaum's categorization. But our reading of both sets of interviews suggests that in the 1960s and the 1990s few women adapted by submissively resigning themselves to prison. Instead, women in both periods developed approaches to doing time that both took advantage of and were shaped by the regimes to which they were subject. Because those regimes had much in common, we see some important similarities in how women managed their imprisonment.

Efforts to distance themselves from their surroundings and from staff were mentioned by virtually every woman interviewed as a means to escape the strains of prison life and to protect themselves from its toll. If some of the more obvious and public forms of disorder, rebellion, and resistance were infrequent at CIW in both periods, concerted efforts to negotiate and at times challenge power relations and to maneuver around rules were not. For example, in the 1960s and the 1990s women admitted to using and dealing in drugs or other contraband, and to appropriating items from the prison for their personal use. These activities were characterized by prisoners in a variety of ways: as resistance, as efforts to exercise some control in their highly restricted lives, or as simply ways of easing the pains of prison life. Zoe told an interviewer in the early 1960s that occasionally refusing to follow rules was an important end in itself: "It keeps me from getting so tight inside. I kind of check myself and find out that my soul is still my own. I have a little freedom within myself and so if I get punished for the things I do, I get punished." In contrast, for Yvonne, who was also at CIW in the 1960s, dealing drugs and stealing from the state was rewarding but only in a material sense: "It's a hassle with the money...you have to deal in pills and come into contact with all these people, wheel and deal, scheme and connive and I'd never done that before. But you learn to do it in here or else you don't survive."

Women's involvement in such illicit activity did not, according to the interviews, appear to vary much between the two prison contexts. What did vary over time was the extent to which prisoners characterized these activities as resistance.

Resisting the Prison Regime in the Early 1960s

Intimate sexual relations among prisoners were prohibited and subject to disciplinary proceedings in both the 1960s and the 1990s. They were also, according to Ward and Kassebaum, the predominant adaptation of prisoners in the 1960s, who were much more likely than their 1990s counterparts to portray these as efforts to challenge the prison's authority. In talking about her current relationship, Joanne pointed out that she had no "H" [indicating she was a homosexual] on her record and that "they [staff] know, but it makes them very angry because they can't catch us together." Nora, who said she was not interested in women "that way," commented that "the girls on campus engage in homosexual behavior... because it aggravates the supervisors."

Rules that required women to have hair of a certain length and fashion – an effort to curb what many staff believed were overt signs of homosexuality in the 1960s – therefore became a resource for contesting the administration's preoccupation with prisoners' sexuality. According to Lana, who worked in the cosmetology department, the policies were

> money down the drain. They [the butches] think it's funny. You see them one day in cosmetology, and the next day they've washed it out or cut their hair off... One girl had the operator leave the permanent wave solution on too long. When it was finally removed, the hair was so badly burned it had to be cut even shorter.

Joanne called the rules "ridiculous," and flouted them by wearing "a DA[27] in back, [but] very feminine in front... and nobody's gonna make me change the DA." Other women chose less public ways to challenge these rules. Xena, for example, asked the prison rabbi what the Bible had to say about homosexuality. He told her "to read the prophets: 'No man shall lie with another man.'" She then went to the Bible herself and found "other justifications for [homosexuality]" that questioned the rabbi's interpretation.

Interviews with women at CIW in the 1960s revealed a number of other ways in which they challenged the rehabilitative regime and the relations of power that accompanied it. Among those mentioned were refusing to disclose personal information to counselors, fabricating "juicy answers" to questions about their preprison lives in hopes of getting the psychiatrist to write a good report on them, and mocking certain therapeutic procedures. For example, because of the silence in her therapy group, Wanda "told them it was so quiet you could hear a pin drop and the other day I brought a pin and dropped it. And boy did they [staff group leaders] have a fit." Some women chose less apparent but more subversive methods. Despite the counseling she had received at CIW, Rhonda said she was a "born prostitute" and expected to return to hustling when she got out because of the easy money and exciting lifestyle. Similarly, Faye, who had decided to give up "regular" prostitution, nevertheless planned to get a secretarial job as a "front" for being "kept by a man" and expected to return to her drug habit, saying she "would like to stay out [on drugs] all the time."

---

[27] A "duck's ass" – a hair style the administration viewed as masculine and a sign of homosexuality.

Resisting the Prison Regime in the Mid-1990s

Efforts to defy or evade elements of the prison regime in the 1990s appear to have been at least as widespread, but less varied than they were in the 1960s, according to our interviews. Women at CIW in the 1990s did, however, have one important means of contesting aspects of their imprisonment that was not part of the repertoire of women at CIW in the 1960s. The extension of a wider array of civil rights to prisoners in the 1990s fostered more collective or organized activities, such as a class action lawsuit aimed at the prison's medical services and a battered women's group that sought clemency for women who had killed abusive partners. But if collective action was potentially more available in the 1990s, our interviews suggest that women at CIW in the 1990s, compared to their counterparts in the 1960s, generally had fewer avenues for challenging the prison regime in individual and more private ways, in part because the prison was interested and intervened in fewer aspects of their lives in the 1990s. Consistent with Garland's (1995: 194) portrayal of prison officials in the late twentieth century, CIW's administration had shifted its concerns from depth to surface.

In other words, because the rehabilitative regime of the 1960s gave greater scope to authoritarian demands for normalization, it also opened up a wider range of opportunities for resistance through behaviors, attitudes, appearance, and so forth. But in the 1990s, when behavioral conformity in prison had replaced normalization as a priority, the range of ways to challenge the prison's authority was more constrained. Conversely, and perhaps ironically, being seen as a good prisoner – or at least, not being seen as a troublemaker – may have been easier in the 1990s compared to the 1960s, even as the responsibility for rehabilitation was shifted onto the prisoner precisely because the prison expected less from its charges. As we noted earlier, an important reason for CIW's minimal expectations was the widely shared belief that while prisoners were not particularly dangerous or evil, they were unlikely to change as a result of their carceral experience. Additionally, with full knowledge of the diminishing resources available to these women, maintenance – or what Feeley and Simon (1992: 470) have termed the "waste management function" of prisons – was gradually replacing any remaining notions of transformation.

Prisoners' Views on and Relations with Other Prisoners at the California Institution for Women

How prisoners view and interact with each other is likely to reflect broader public views of and official discourse on criminals, the ways in which prison regimes structure the activities of prisoners, and characteristics of the prison population. In the 1960s compared to the 1990s, the public viewed female prisoners more sympathetically, CIW encouraged prisoners to view each other as resources for personal transformation, and the prison population at CIW was smaller and more homogeneous. As a consequence, we might expect women serving time at CIW in the 1960s to have more positive attitudes toward and relationships with each other compared to women at CIW in the 1990s. While the interviews provide some evidence for this expectation, they also reveal considerable continuity over time in prisoners' views on and relations with other prisoners. By far the most common response to questions about the best way to do one's time, regardless of time period, was a variant of the description given to us by Eva: "Mind your own business. Stay to yourself. Have a few friends. Don't trust anyone." In other words, most of the women interviewed in the 1960s and the 1990s said they preferred to limit the extent and nature of their contacts with other prisoners and did not expect loyalty from each other. But the extent and strength of these views, the interviews suggest, was greater in the 1990s. Because of the similarities between the two periods, we do not discuss them separately as we did in our previous discussion of women's responses to the prison regime.

In what the interviewer in 1963 characterized as an effort to put up a "tough girl" front, Barbara asserted that "I just like two or three friends, but you can trust no one . . . Why should I be interested in others?" This sentiment was by no means limited to the youngest or newest prisoners at CIW in the 1960s. Corinne said she didn't care much for "the girls" at CIW, "with a few exceptions . . . [T]here's no love lost on either side." Women who had several prior commitments to prison were no more tolerant of other prisoners. After claiming that "everyone at CIW is crazy [inmates and staff]," Faye acknowledged that she had two friends inside. Patty held a similar view: "I don't like to associate with any of them [prisoners], but need a few friends to talk to." But, as these statements suggest, women did make friends with and at times confide in prisoners. For example, after three weeks at CIW in 1963, April observed that "the girls aren't rough and tough. We can talk to each other, knowing it will go only that far."

The women we interviewed at CIW in the 1990s expressed a similarly restricted range of attitudes about relations with other prisoners. Some, such as these two women in prison for the first time, described detachment and caution toward but not complete rejection of other prisoners. "I've made a few friends, you know," said Joyce, "but I don't really buddy up with 'em too much." Similarly, Julie observed that "there are a few other people in here I've met who I really like . . . but I'm talking about 2% of the people in here." Immoderate and highly critical views of other prisoners were more common in the 1990s, however, as these excerpts indicate: "I've worked hard at projecting that I just don't give a shit, get away from me . . . " (Charlotte); "you make one friend, you know what I'm saying, out of all the people here and that friend turns out to be just as scandalous as the rest of them" (Elizabeth); if you make a friend, "then when you least expect it they fuck your ass up, straight up" (Andrea).

Frustration over lack of loyalty among prisoners was also a common complaint in both periods but was more frequently and strongly voiced by women at CIW in the 1990s. Despite being keenly aware of how prison constrained and structured their own lives, the women we interviewed in the 1990s tended to attribute the lack of solidarity among prisoners not so much to the nature of imprisonment but to the nature of women.[28] Women were seen as essentially fickle at best, disloyal and conniving at worst, and unlikely ever to stand up for each other: "Women do not stand together in what's wrong and what's right . . . A woman will turn against you in a heartbeat just because she has a PMS [premenstrual syndrome] day" (Tina); "we don't cooperate as a group to get things done. I think women don't want to lose their little creature comforts" (Carol); "Women don't [get organized]; they're pitiful about it. They're too busy getting jealous or upset about something" (Tara). Essentializing notions of gender, then, shaped the ways women understood their prison experience and their relations with other prisoners in both periods. But in the 1990s, women's more negative views of other prisoners may also have mirrored the low expectations that their keepers held for them.

As decades of research in prison would predict, informants were singled out for censure in both periods. Virtually all the interviewed women expressed disdain for snitches and said that they had been schooled in the importance of turning a blind eye (or the other cheek) to the illicit activities of other prisoners, even if they were the target of these activities. A handful of women admitted they had been hit or threatened by other prisoners but had not reported this to staff because, as one stated "then I would have got a snitch racket, you know, a jacket on me." In both periods, however, some women described circumstances that they felt justified informing, for example, if one prisoner was being beaten seriously by a group of other prisoners or if someone was using a dirty needle to tattoo prisoners. But for most others – such as Rhonda who was doing time at CIW in the 1960s – even if "someone is going to be hurt, you can tell another inmate, but never staff."

What differed somewhat between the two periods were the reasons women thought snitching occurred and the reasons they disapproved of it; these reflect differences both in penal regimes and in the extent of women's distrust of other prisoners. Women interviewed in the 1960s tended to

---

[28] There was one exception to this tendency to attribute women's lack of loyalty to their natures. Penny, who had several previous commitments on charges related to her substance abuse, blamed "the warehousing orientation of the prisons now" for the lack of respect among prisoners: "People don't learn how to take care of themselves and don't learn to respect others. It used to be that prison could instill habits, but it doesn't now because it's just warehousing . . . "

attribute snitching to prisoners' beliefs that cooperating with staff would lead to an earlier release, greater identification with staff than other prisoners, and envy toward weekenders – prisoners with very short sentences.[29] The group-based aspect of the therapeutic program at CIW in the 1960s, which emphasized peer pressure and confrontation, was also blamed for discouraging solidarity among prisoners and encouraging women to collaborate with staff in policing other prisoners. Women in the 1960s most often disapproved of informing because they felt it made the staff's job too easy and blurred the line between prisoners and staff. Snitching "helps the staff do their jobs," observed Lana in 1963. "When they [prisoners] start that, they should get a badge and a paycheck." In the 1990s, however, women were more likely to attribute snitching to a general lack of morals among prisoners and their disapproval was directed more at the damage informing did to other prisoners. As Marina said, "if you say anything, you know, then everybody goes to jail... So you just don't get into it, you just don't, you know?"

Despite women's alienation from and suspicion of others, serious violence, racial conflict,[30] and gang activity were rare at CIW, even in the 1990s as the criminal justice system sent more women to CIW and masculinized (a term some staff and prisoners used) its regime. When conflicts between prisoners did arise, interviewees in both periods explained, they were typically short-lived and interpersonal, rather than related to or expressive of different group affiliations – a pattern characteristic of conflict in men's prisons. Initial fears about being attacked or threatened by other prisoners that arose from popular depictions of women's prisons were acknowledged by many women, who said they set these aside after a few days at CIW. The predominant explanation for confrontations among prisoners was based

---

[29] Ward (1982), in her study of a woman's prison in England, argues that the high degree of snitching among prisoners was a product of their lack of power over their release dates, and not, as some prisoners claimed, due to women's essentially devious natures. Informing, then, was for these women – like women at CIW in the 1960s – a commodity, something to be traded for a chance to influence staff and, through them, their release dates.

[30] Ward and Kassebaum largely ignored whether and how race influenced women's relationships with each other, and so we are not able to compare the views of women on this issue in the 1960s and 1990s. A few of the women interviewed by Ward and Kassebaum volunteered opinions about other racial groups or how they thought race influenced women's relationships, although these comments were brief and largely in passing. Two white women commented that black prisoners were prejudiced toward whites, and a third suggested the prison ought to be segregated because prisoners tended to associate with others of their own race anyway. Another white prisoner stated that whites were prejudiced against black prisoners and would stir up racial conflict by informing on them. In contrast, a black prisoner interviewed for Ward and Kassebaum's study stated that she saw no race problems at CIW and pointed out that "the staff have a policy of no favoritism." The problems with interpreting these comments are many and include the issue of how interviewers' race affects women's willingness to discuss their views on relations among the races and the nature of what they said.

on an essentialized notion of women's nature and similar to that given for prisoners' apparent lack of solidarity: women are emotional, high-strung, and volatile, interviewees claimed, which makes them prone to outbursts. "It's difficult living with women," observed Tina. "They're miserable, they're catty. They look for anything to fight about, and then once they fight they can be your best friend. And then all of a sudden, they get pissy at you again . . . " But consistent with the generally more adverse attitudes toward criminals of the 1990s, the women we interviewed were more likely than their 1960s counterparts to read predatory motives or amoral mind-sets into these conflicts. Disputes were attributed to women who were "treacherous, dangerous, and out for themselves," especially younger ones, who "have no morals, no code or anything they live by" (Margaret).

The generalized detachment from other prisoners that most women in both periods preferred was not incompatible with the development of affectionate and intimate relationships with particular individuals. Ward and Kassebaum (1965: 80) considered intimate sexual relationships the predominate adaptation of prisoners in the 1960s and devoted much of their book to describing the dynamics of these relationships and their effects on "role differentiation in the female prison." According to women we interviewed, sexual relationships among prisoners were also "just a part of life in here" (Maxine) and "involve pretty much everybody in one way or another" (Deedee), even though, as in the 1960s, these violated prison rules. Some of the women we interviewed had read or heard about Ward and Kassebaum's description of sexual relations among women at CIW in the 1960s and said, "I would say that's very accurate" (Julia), and "It sounds like life in here" (Tara). Probably because of the public's greater acceptance of same sex relationships more generally, and the prison's shift away from a preoccupation with the moral regulation of many aspects of prisoners' lives, homosecting did not emerge as a major topic of concern in our interviews with women in the 1990s.

Conclusion

In this chapter, we relied on interviews with women at CIW in the 1960s and 1990s to shed light on the practices and experiences of imprisonment at two key points in the recent history of penality in the United States. Much scholarship on criminal punishment has focused on macrolevel shifts in discourses and logics, or on legislation and policy, with little attention to whether and how these shifts are translated into practice or experienced by those subject to criminal punishment. But, as Garland (1997: 207) has noted, "[t]he question of how prisoners engage with [imprisonment] practices and the ways in which these practices do or do not actually shape prisoners' subjectivity and behavior is . . . [an] issue of great importance."

In addressing this issue, we found that imprisonment did change and in ways that are perhaps predictable given the growing punitiveness and pessimism of the criminal justice system and the public over the last twenty-five years of the twentieth century. Evidence of this change can be seen in how women responded to the prison regime and how they characterized their relations with other prisoners and staff. In the 1960s, CIW's stated goal was to provide women with an individually oriented and therapeutically informed rehabilitation program. Official discourse was optimistic about prisoners' capacities for reform and encouraged close relations among prisoners and staff. In contrast, in the 1990s penal rationalities that emphasized self-reliance and individual responsibility were more hostile to a prison social order based on collaborative relationships and familiar interactions. Prisoners did not expect to be guided toward reform by benevolent others. The prisoner as an economic actor had replaced the inmate, or resident, as a social actor who was a member of a prison community. As the prison became less ambitious in its goals and lowered its expectations of prisoners, prisoners in turn came to expect less from the prison and from each other. In a penal regime characterized by greater austerity, greater emphasis on custody and security, and less attention to individuals, prisoners appear to have responded by becoming more self-reliant and more detached from and distrustful of other prisoners and staff.

However, women's experiences at CIW also suggest that changes in penality – both in the practices of imprisonment and in who was subject to them – did not fundamentally alter how they did time or how they dealt with the problems imprisonment presented them, even though some of those problems and their responses were regime specific. In important respects, the ways in which women in the 1960s and 1990s managed their lives in prison and related to those around them were quite similar. In both periods, most women sought individual and private solutions to the problems imprisonment presented them – by distancing themselves from and negotiating their relations with others so as to buffer the pains of imprisonment. Even those who served time under the ostensibly more benevolent and less punitive regime of the 1960s did not, by and large, embrace or expect open and trusting relations with others. In this respect, our findings resonate with those from Hannah-Moffat's (2001: 197) study of the federal imprisonment of women in Canada: "Prisons are governed by material structures, cultural sensibilities, and mentalities that limit the extent to which the content of a regime can be changed. Regardless of the form and content of a woman-centred regime, it is still in many respects about punishment, security and discipline."

This suggests that while discourses, practices, and people come and go, important realities of imprisonment persist, as do certain gendered assumptions about the nature and needs of criminal women. The stabilizing influence of ideological notions of gender and assumptions about women's criminality were an important source of continuity in both the practices and experience of imprisonment at CIW. Staff and officials in both periods shared the view that their charges were not, on the whole, dangerous or predatory but disabled and deficient, and that women prisoners' particular needs required a gender-specific regime. These views reflected and reinforced prisoners' attitudes toward and relations with each other, which were often distrustful and suspicious but also intimately affectionate at times.

Whether subject to the maternal, therapeutic regime of the 1960s that promoted rehabilitation through individualized treatment or to the neoliberal regime of the 1990s that shifted responsibility for rehabilitation onto prisoners, women at CIW lived with and negotiated fundamental features of imprisonment that shaped their experiences in comparable ways. Penal regimes, O'Malley (1999) argues, often incorporate elements of different and conflicting rationalities, albeit in an uneven and negotiated fashion. The experiences of women at CIW in the 1960s and the 1990s show that an apparent concern with rehabilitation of offenders can coexist with punitive, disciplinary, and managerial preoccupations, in part because the definition and means of accomplishing rehabilitation, like many other goals of imprisonment, are not fixed. As such, changes in imprisonment at CIW over the last four decades of the twentieth century are perhaps best described as a "refigurement" rather than a transformation (Garland 1995), as a continuation of a reformist project that has a long history of resurrecting and repackaging old practices under new labels and justifications.

Variations across Time and Place in Women's Prison Experiences

A PROFILE OF EACH OF CALIFORNIA's thirty-three state prisons is provided on the California Department of Corrections (CDC) website, and each profile includes a brief "Institution Mission Summary." The mission summary for the California Institution for Women (CIW) reads as follows:

> CIW accommodates all custody levels of female inmates and functions as a reception/processing center for incoming female inmates. In addition to its large general population, CIW houses inmates with special needs such as pregnancy, psychiatric care, methadone, and medical problems such as HIV-infection.

The "Special Historical Note" that follows this summary and concludes CIW's profile highlights the prison's link to an earlier, more explicitly gendered penological era:

> Until 1987, CIW was California's only prison for female felons. It was originally called "Frontera," a feminine derivative of the word frontier – a new beginning. The campus-like design was in keeping with the 1950s "progressive" notion of rehabilitation.

The "Institution Mission Summary" for Valley State Prison for Women (VSPW), in contrast, is readily interpretable as representing a very different penological era, an era in which "system management, resource allocation, cost-benefit calculation, and organizational efficiency" (Garland, 1995: 190) are the predominant goals. It reads:

> At design, Valley State Prison for Women provides 1,980 women's beds for California's overcrowded prison system. VSPW is designed as a work-based,

95

fully programmed prison that provides legally mandated programs and services. The work, educational and vocational opportunities available to eligible inmates are designed to enhance inmate productivity, emphasize self-improvement and reduce idleness and recidivism.

VSPW's mission, then, is to serve the wider prison system by alleviating the burden the system – not the female prison population – faces from overcrowding. The statement indicates that prisoners are to be provided beds, but apart from that only those programs and services that the law requires and only those prisoners deemed eligible are to be given opportunities for work or training. There is no allusion here to the particular needs of women, or to accommodating prisoners, as there is in CIW's statement. Instead, productivity, self-improvement, and avoiding idleness are emphasized in language that harkens nostalgically if sternly back to the goals of the nineteenth century prison. For those who have not visited CIW and VSPW, this may seem to read too much into these statements. But our interviews with prison administrators and prisoners and our surveys of prisoners at the two prisons suggest otherwise, as we will see.

In the previous chapter, we compared the experiences of women serving time at CIW in two different penal eras and found evidence of substantial continuity in the ways women responded to other prisoners, the staff, and the different penal regimes to which they were subject. On this basis, it may be tempting to conclude, as some scholars have (e.g., Sykes 1958; Bondeson 1989; Hannah-Moffat 2001), that the prison's capacity for punishment and deprivation override the particular goals, discourses, techniques, and practices that constitute the experience of imprisonment in any specific time and place. We believe that conclusion would be premature, if it were based solely on women's experiences of imprisonment at CIW. As the first and longest-standing women's prison in California, CIW has an extensive history and a distinctive culture that may have helped it withstand change even as its population more than doubled and its gendered rehabilitative framework was dismantled. At the time we did our research, Valley State Prison, by contrast, had no history and was in the earliest stages of developing its own culture. It was built at the height of a very different penal regime, one informed by neoliberal politics and a more punitive public mentality, both of which were embodied in VSPW's design. In other words, as our comparison of their mission statements suggests, the newest prison for women in California is dramatically different in many respects from the state's oldest prison for women, and from many other prisons for women across the United States. The questions we address in this chapter are whether and how those differences are reflected in the ways in which women experienced and responded to imprisonment at VSPW.

Official Philosophies and Practices of Imprisonment
at Valley State Prison for Women in the late 1990s

When the Central California Women's Facility (CCWF) was built amid pistachio and almond orchards outside of Chowchilla, California in the late 1980s, it was to be the first of four prisons located at what was referred to as Four Corners. After VSPW was built across the street, the plans for more prison construction were put on hold, and so VSPW and CCWF, the largest and second largest women's prisons in the world, sit facing each other, the only buildings in sight on two dusty corners of a crossroads in the midst of the Central Valley, about 150 miles south of Sacramento. The prisons are mirror images of each other, both having been built according to a prototype modular design typical of the state's new men's prisons. At least as early as the eighteenth century, when Jeremy Bentham developed his blueprint for the panopticon prison, penal observers have recognized the significance and symbolism of what Garland terms "the actual fabric of penal institutions." As Garland goes on to observe, "One of the most important instances of this symbolism of physical appearance . . . is contained in the external imagery of the prison, and in the iconography of institutional architecture" (Garland 1990: 258).[1] If CIW might still be mistaken for a high school campus, VSPW – with its multiple perimeter walls and fences (some electrified), thousands of yards of coiled razor wire, foot and vehicle patrols by armed perimeter guards, and multistory stadium light standards and guard towers – could only be read as a prison and as an institution in which security and control are of primary importance.

Paralleling the many physical markers of control and containment at VSPW were institutional rules and staff practices that limited prisoners' movement and conveyed official preparedness to respond to disorder. Unlike at CIW, VSPW's custody staff carried batons along with pepper spray and handcuffs. When alarms sounded, prisoners were required to "hit the ground" to allow correctional officers (c.o.s.), in the words of one sergeant, to "quickly gain control of any disturbance." Also unlike CIW, prisoners at VSPW were not permitted relatively free access to their cells during the day. Instead, for the general population of prisoners at VSPW cell doors were unlocked every hour for ten minutes, then locked again.[2] Pat down

---

[1] Paul Rock's (1996) examination of the reconstruction of Holloway Prison for women in England provides a powerful illustration of this point. Similar to Foucault (1979), Rock argues that the architecture of a prison is inscribed with the official typifications of prisoners. It is this recognition that encouraged the redesign of Holloway from a radial structure designed to emphasize control, containment, and discipline to what he calls a therapeutic structure, which had vague and permeable boundaries.

[2] Some women, such as newly admitted prisoners with sentences of life without parole, were given "closed-A" classifications, which limited their movements considerably more than this.

searches were part of the regular routine of life at VSPW. In moving between their yards and their work or educational sites, prisoners lined up at work exchange where each was searched and her destination verified. Prisoners were also prohibited from visiting in different yards or housing units, and so they had contact with women from other yards only when the main yard was open.

Many of VSPW's restrictive practices were unique among the state's prisons for women and reflected the philosophy of the prison's first warden and his handpicked associate wardens. Lew Kuykendall, the first male to head a women's prison in California, had been warden of VSPW for just over two years when we began our research at the prison. After twenty years working in men's prisons and another ten years at the Northern California Women's Facility (NCWF) and across the street, at CCWF, Kuykendall came into the job with a no-nonsense attitude about the importance of safety and security, an orientation he openly and somewhat proudly acknowledged was different from other wardens of the state's prisons for women. In stark contrast to his colleague Susan Poole's self-help rhetoric that urged women, as she told us, to use the "adversity in their lives to try and turn themselves around," Kuykendall's goals were much more limited. In our interview he did not mention rehabilitation, and when questioned about the biggest challenges facing corrections for women in California he quickly replied "Finding places to put all of them." One could read this and other statements by VSPW's warden as exemplifying both a managerial approach to his job and the "de-centering of the criminal justice system," whereby criminal justice organizations and officials "have become less confident of their ability to produce positive 'outcomes' in the external world, and increasingly preoccupied with internally deliverable 'outputs'" (Loader and Sparks 2002: 87–88). If the prison cannot reform its charges, it can at least strive to house them safely and efficiently, and this appears to have been the core of Kuykendall's philosophy.

This philosophy was not, however, accompanied by either an uncritical acceptance of what Kuykendall referred to as the system or lack of empathy toward women prisoners. Indeed, the system was failing women, in his view, by sending them back to the streets unprepared to deal with their histories of drug and alcohol use. Life after prison was often more difficult for women than men, he said, because women are more likely to be cut off from sources of financial and emotional support when they go to prison. Recalling his experience working in men's prisons, Kuykendall noted that male prisoners' families often moved to be near them while they served time, whereas he said he knew "of only two families that have moved to the area around VSPW" to be near their wives or mothers. As a consequence of being poor, single parents and of the lack of services for parolees, high recidivism rates were to be expected for female ex-convicts, according to Kuykendall. And so, faced with large and growing numbers of prisoners, too few resources, and a bureaucracy that prevented experimenting with innovative programs, prison officials in his view necessarily had to focus their expectations on what they could reasonably hope to accomplish.

While Kuykendall's views on imprisonment and female prisoners had clearly been shaped by his ten years' experience working in women's prisons, those of many of the c.o.s. at VSPW had not. As we noted in Chapter 3, we were not able to conduct formal interviews with c.o.s. or staff at VSPW, but we did have a number of casual conversations with them as they accompanied us around the prison. Our impression, which Kuykendall subsequently confirmed, was that c.o.s. at VSPW tended to be younger and more recent graduates of the state's training academy compared to c.o.s. at CIW. As a consequence of VSPW's newness and in contrast to CIW, neither a strong organizational culture nor staff subculture that shaped the attitudes and the actions of new staff toward prisoners had yet developed. Thus, we heard a much wider range of views on female prisoners and observed more variation in the treatment of prisoners, from custody staff at VSPW. Some staff emphasized the daily dangers that the women posed for them while others expressed a mixture of relief and frustration that women were much less likely to be violent but much more likely to complain than male prisoners. Some were quite professional and even courteous in their interactions with prisoners while others were verbally abusive and often derogatary (see Kruttschnitt, Gartner, and Miller 2000: 706–707). Thus, while it appeared that custody staff were aware of Kuykendall's emphasis on control and safety, what these words meant for how they conducted their work seems to have differed depending on how new they were to the job or to working in a woman's prison.

The range of activities available to prisoners at VSPW in the late 1990s was, as its mission summary conveys, quite limited compared to CIW. Legally mandated educational programs and vocational training were provided, and the variety of vocational programs was greater than at CIW.[3] But support and counseling programs run by prisoners or volunteers were almost nonexistent, as were the kinds of prisoner organizations, sports teams, and handicraft groups common at CIW. The newness of the prison no doubt was partially responsible for this. That VSPW's warden did not emphasize the potential of such activities to encourage self-esteem and empowerment, as CIW's warden had, must also have played a role. And this illustrates again a fundamental difference between the two prison regimes: at least some of the key officials at CIW continued to express faith in the power of personal

---

[3] Vocational training programs at VSPW included auto mechanics, dry cleaning, eyewear manufacturing, graphic arts, landscape gardening, small engine repair, refrigeration and air conditioning repair, and welding.

transformation whereas for those we spoke with at VSPW, prison was not a place that could be expected to encourage such changes, or were the problems female prisoners faced likely to be overcome simply by the force of their own wills.

Summary

In several respects, VSPW lived up to its reputation among prisoners at CIW – it was a much stricter and bleaker place to do time. Several prisoners tried to capture the distinctions between the two prisons by pointing out that CIW was an institution, whereas VSPW was a prison both in name and reality. Many of the features of a more pessimistic and austere approach to imprisonment were immediately apparent in VSPW's physical structure and practices, and reinforced by official discourse about the prison's purpose. These conveyed the impression that CIW and VSPW existed, to some extent, in different worlds – one the world of women's corrections of the past, the other the world of women's imprisonment of the future. In Chapter 4, we described a number of ways in which CIW in the 1990s differed from CIW in the 1960s, and we see many of the same types of differences between CIW and VSPW in the 1990s. VSPW's regime was more impersonal, more concerned with organizational imperatives of control, security, and order, and less expansive in its expectations than was CIW's regime.

But there were also important similarities between the two prisons. Externally, they shared the sociopolitical context described in Chapter 2 and internally both were governed by Title 15 of the California Code of Regulations, which specifies prisoners' behaviors, appearances, and activities, along with their rights and privileges. Core features of women's day-to-day lives were the same at each prison. So, for example, at both institutions prisoners were lockeddown and subject to multiple counts throughout the day, were required to line up for meals at cafeterias where they had little time to eat, had their mail and telephone calls monitored, and were not eligible for overnight family visits if they were serving life sentences. In addition, both prisons housed women of all security levels, and, as we saw in Chapter 3, the populations of the two prisons were similar in their background characteristics, and in their crime and criminal justice experiences.

To explore the extent to which prisoners' views on VSPW's regime, its staff, and its prisoners reflect the similarities and differences in penal regimes and practices we have described, we turn to the interviews we conducted with thirty-eight women at VSPW. Following this, we present data from surveys of the general population in each of our three prison contexts – CIW in the 1960s, CIW in the 1990s, and VSPW in the 1990s – to test the conclusions we have drawn from the interviews about the experiences of doing time.

Prisoners' Views on and Responses to the Prison Regime and Staff at Valley State Prison for Women

I've done twenty-six years at CIW, and when I came up here, I cried (Christine).

It sucks. It's hard. It's mentally draining to the person . . . CIW, the staff over there was very cooperative . . . Whereas, here . . . they don't want to help you (Toni).

This is the hardest time I've ever done . . . They're just tougher here (Mandy).

I don't like it. They're too strict against women. They don't try to help us in no shape, form or fashion. I'd rather be at CIW (Jackie).

When I came here they said that the warden said this is not CIWonderful or Madera [CCWF]. This is a prison, and will remain a prison, you know. Yeah, it is . . . it is a prison (Jill).

This [VSPW] is really scary looking, huh? And I understand that the warden here is the warden for the men's Pelican Bay Prison.[4] That's why it's run so strict (Ivy).

It's like, being in Valley State Prison, it's like – hell. Which I don't know what hell is like, but I can imagine. It's like a nightmare. . . . I've never been in an institution that has nothing positive for you (Dawn).

Our conversations with women at CIW and our own reaction on walking into VSPW for the first time had prepared us for these sorts of responses to the question "What's it like doing time here?" Every one of the thirty-eight women we interviewed at VSPW made reference to what they saw as an, overriding concern with control and security, and limited interest in helping women. The restricted range of programs and activities were also a source of concern to most of the women we interviewed. "I need help, I know," said Mandy. "I desperately need help . . . [but] the counselors here, they . . . all they do is paperwork. They don't call you in. They don't get personal." Support and self-help groups, drug treatment, group counseling, all were seen as absent or inadequate – "it's been, you know, two years since this prison's been opened," said Sally, "and there's really no groups in here for us . . . there's nothing for us to do." Nothing, perhaps, except to follow the rules and it was clear to most women that this was really all that was required of them, that the administration's orientation was fundamentally aimed at institutional maintenance and discipline. "I tell you, it's a control issue. I think the warden has a control issue," is how Lindsey summarized it.

Women interpreted the motivation behind the administration and staff's approach in different ways, however. A few put the strictness of the regime down to an intentional punitiveness. "I really do think he hates women," said Lindsey about the warden. "It's as though emotionally and physically they feel we will never get out of prison, so they can do whatever they want to us," Miriam stated and then noted, "You would swear that they think we were rabid dogs or something." Other prisoners believed that the prison, like the

---

[4] Kuykendall was not, of course, the warden at Pelican Bay or had he ever worked there.

wider society, simply did not think or care about them. In Clair's opinion "there are officers that don't care whether you learn or not. This is their job, and if you're gone, they lose their money... Without us they have no job, and that's the attitude they'll throw off to some of us." But a few prisoners saw the kind of logic behind the strictness that the warden had described to us. As Jill put it, "he wants to keep certain things down and if he gives [us] too much maybe we'll go crazy or take advantage or whatever." She went on to note that "They are really concerned about their male staff. Tell you the truth, there have been fourteen walked off since I've been here."

For the nineteen or so women who had also served time at CIW, there was little doubt that VSPW's regime was more rigorous and restrictive. Women commented on the greater freedoms they had at CIW, the wider range of programs and activities, the more cooperative relations with staff and other prisoners, and what some called CIW's proinmate style. "At CIW, the staff there was very, um, cooperative as far as trying to help you, giving you options of things," commented Toni and then stated, "Whereas here they don't want to help you... Everything is military here... I got along really well at CIW with inmates as well as staff. There wasn't a bunch of animosity towards everybody, like there is here." Lindsey, who had done two terms at CIW, noted that prisoners there, unlike at VSPW, held what she called "critical jobs" in the institution's bureaucracy. In contrast, VSPW "is the only prison that I know of that is run by officers." But not all of these women agreed that the apparent differences between the two prisons were of much significance for prisoners' lives. Evelyn, who had been transferred to VSPW after two months at CIW and two months at CCWF, noted that women often complained that staff at VSPW "don't care." "Well, caring is not their job," she observed. "We don't even know whether they're people who can care... and it really doesn't make any difference whether it's here or CIW or across the street." Miriam, who had served part of her twenty-two years at CIW and CCWF before coming to VSPW, also saw a fundamental commonality among her experiences: "It is different depending upon the prison that you're in. But in any of the three prisons, it's very emotionally painful."

Although the thirty-eight women we interviewed were unanimous in their description of VSPW as bleak and severe, their evaluations of it were more varied than we had anticipated. Darlene acknowledged that doing time at CIW or CCWF would be easier but said that the harder time she was doing at VSPW "doesn't bother me. It doesn't, really." A half dozen other women, including short-termers, first-termers, and lifers, agreed. Janeen's description was typical of this group: "It's not that good that I want to come back, you know? But I'm saying it's like, I, like I'm at ease. It's cool, you know, you just keep your own nose clean... " Frida also seemed not to be particularly disturbed by the regime – "The strictness of this place doesn't really bother me.

You know, I've never been incarcerated anywhere else so I've gotten used to it." The warden would have been pleased to learn that some of the women appreciated the tighter controls because they believed, "it keeps down a lot of gangs, racists, fights, crimes" (Jocelyn) and made VSPW not as "wild and messy" (Sarah) as CIW. A few women who had been in prison before also saw a deterrent value in VSPW's regime, noting that if they had first done time there they "would have never probably been back" (Colleen). After four months inside on a parole violation, Diana agreed:

> I don't want no easy time... Because, see it makes a person know if you got to go through a life like this, it makes you not want to come back, you know?... Everybody keep talking about time bein' easy... Prison is not supposed to make it easy for you. It's supposed to make it hard for you so you don't go out there and do wrong again, you know?

What these comments do not and cannot be expected to reflect is the overwhelming research evidence indicating that recidivism has very little to do with the strictness of a prison's regime.[5]

The nature of women's specific complaints about life at VSPW suggests that they, like the administration, had lowered their expectations about what the prison could do for them and, as a consequence, women concentrated these expectations around such basic needs as self-maintenance and privacy. Similar to our interviews at CIW, women interviewed at VSPW commented at length on what they saw as inadequate medical care, and many said that the food was poor.[6] Concerns about privacy were expressed more often by women at VSPW than women at CIW, which is not surprising given that women at VSPW were housed eight per cell. But these concerns were focused more on staff behavior than the behavior of their "bunkies," with several women noting that the privacy screens in the showers did not adequately shield them from the view of officers walking by their rooms, or that it was difficult to change clothes without being visible to people in the hallways. Obtaining basic necessities such as soap, toilet paper, and feminine hygiene products was a source of frustration and humiliation for many prisoners. As Lindsey said, "In the worst of my addiction, the lowest of my addiction, the lowest point I've ever reached in my addiction, I've never run out of toilet paper, or sanitary supplies, and then, yet I come to prison and I have to worry about running out of toilet paper."

---

[5] For research on the relationship between the nature of prison regimes and recidivism rates, see McGuire (1995).

[6] We chose not to focus our interviews or our analysis around the critical issue of women's access to adequate medical care at VSPW and CIW, because this issue has received considerable coverage in the media, by academics, and by prisoners' rights groups (see e.g., Stoller 2000; Justice Now and Prisoner Action Coalition 2000).

Women's diminished expectations for their time at VSPW also appears to have influenced or perhaps reflected their evaluations of custody staff. In contrast to women at CIW, some of whom praised the assistance they had received from c.o.s. there, the half dozen or so women at VSPW who said anything positive about c.o.s. did so within strict limits, as the following statements illustrate: "They're OK, they're just doin' their job" (Janeen). "I mean, they're all we got, and most of them are pretty decent . . . But we all know, you know, some of 'em are . . . some of 'em are just assholes" (Dana). "They're pretty strict here, but our guards act pretty reasonable" (Ivy). "You know, like I said, you talk to them, they'll talk to you and stuff, but they're never, you know, out of control and stuff" (Rosa). Critical comments about staff were much more common and more extreme than we encountered at CIW, however. Darlene described how staff "make you feel like you're a failure and you're not gonna' make it out there. They'll say 'Oh, you'll be back.' I've heard them say that when somebody's paroled. 'Oh, I'll see you next week.'" Three women at VSPW who talked about their histories of abuse – two were abused by their male partners, one by her mother – compared their treatment by staff to their earlier abuse, including Nicole. After describing her embarrassment at having to ask for and being denied extra sanitary pads, Nicole said

> I was in an abusive relationship for lots of years and it led to a night where this tragedy happened and that's why I'm here. And I feel sometimes that I'm still getting abuse, you know? [T]here's a lot of males, mostly male c.o.s. here, you know? . . . They have this attitude where you know they have full control over us, you know? . . . [W]hen I lived with an abusive man, you know, full control. And these men have that same attitude. They make me feel the same way.

The consistency with which prisoners described VSPW's regime was striking, especially given the range of background experiences and criminal justice histories of our interviewees. How these women evaluated the regime, however, did vary somewhat. But when we consider how women responded to the regime, that is, how they chose to relate to its requirements and constraints as well as to its staff, we see little evidence of variation.

Prisoners' Responses to VSPW's Regime

In the previous chapter, we argued that women's predominant response to CIW's regime, whether they served time there in the 1960s or the 1990s, involved distancing themselves from their surroundings and from staff. This was even more pronounced among the women we interviewed at VSPW, who talked about avoiding contact with staff except when absolutely necessary, trying not to draw attention to one's self, staying in "my own little world," and focusing on getting out. A few women acknowledged that they had initially been assertive or argumentative but had learned that holding back and following the rules was preferable because, in Clair's words, "I'm powerless. I can't change the way officers treat me." Following rules was not, in many women's opinion, easy, in large part because they seemed to change so often. But one learned to adapt to different staff by listening and watching. "If they move, you move, and you got to obey the rules. That's what prison's all about," observed Diana.

The regular references, whether out of frustration, bitterness, or resignation, to the importance of following the rules set women at VSPW apart in some respects from women at CIW. At CIW, at least some women responded to a regime that stressed taking responsibility for one's rehabilitation by organizing and participating in self-help groups and prisoners' organizations. Women at VSPW could not see this happening there, because, as Wilma put it, "here, the women are so scared, because now they take away so much time from you. They take time away from you for . . . for anything." At VSPW, because of "all the tension and pressure we're up against behind custody," said Dawn, women were more likely to withdraw and turn inward, if not bitter, a characterization that accorded with our impressions from our interviews. As a consequence, the ways in which women talked about doing time at VSPW seemed to us more homogeneous, less patterned by women's background characteristics and experiences.[7] Some of the women we interviewed at VSPW drew a similar conclusion, such as Hanah, a self-described "gang banger" who had "grown up": "I would say everybody in this place hurts. I don't care how bad they are. I don't care how big they are. I don't care what they're about. They all hurt, you know what I mean?"

Just as VSPW's administration had de-emphasized the potential for reforming its charges, fewer women at VSPW than CIW talked about rehabilitation, although when they did, they agreed with their counterparts at CIW that it was their responsibility. But the relative silence about rehabilitation by VSPW's prisoners suggests that they, like the prison administration, had lowered their expectations for what could be gained from their time in prison. Their goal was, in most respects, the short-term one of endurance: few women talked about either their hopes or fears for life after prison, beyond their anticipation of being reunited with their families. Keeping one's head down and away from all but the most necessary contact with staff made enduring easier and reduced the chances of either sharing too much in a way that could be used against one or coming into conflict with staff and losing time as a result. On this issue, younger and older prisoners,

---

[7] For a fuller analysis and comparison of how women's background characteristics and experiences shaped their prison lives at CIW and VSPW, see Kruttschnitt, Gartner, and Miller (2000).

short-termers and long-termers agreed, as illustrated by the statements of Stacey and Clair:

> "You know, it's like when you have a problem, or you just need to talk to someone for advice, there's nobody you can go to . . . You can't trust anybody. You can't trust a teacher; you can't trust your boss; you can't trust a C.O. . . . There's nobody you can trust, because it's always going to come back and get you, you know?"
>
> "There's a lot of things that I don't agree with, but I have to live and learn to accept it . . . I haven't really even talked to too many of the officers, you know? They don't really know nothin' or they don't want to hassle with you. So I just stay away . . . Rejection is a let down, and when you're in here you have a bunch of it."

Prisoners' Views on and Relations with Other Prisoners at Valley State Prison for Women

Research on prison social organization, as we noted in the previous chapter, suggests that prisoners choose more individualistic forms of adaptation in prisons with stricter disciplinary regimes, stronger custodial orientations, and more austere physical structures, and this certainly seems to describe how prisoners chose to respond to VSPW's regime and staff. Moreover, the ways in which women related to other prisoners at VSPW compared to CIW also appears consistent with this pattern. As we saw in the previous chapter, women at CIW in the 1960s and 1990s typically kept their distance from and expressed distrust of most other prisoners, preferring to limit the number and depth of any friendships they had. Our interviews suggested that this tendency was more marked at CIW in the 1990s than in the 1960s and reached its fullest extent at VSPW. These comments about relations with other prisoners are from seven different women and are representative of the views of almost all of the women we interviewed at VSPW.

> There's not many that offer friendship, and if they do they want something in return. That's why I stay to myself (Darlene).
> I stay to myself. If I don't know you from the streets, I'm not botherin' with you in here. I don't want no friends. You don't take care of me; you don't do nothin' for me. Leave me alone . . . I don't care what happens to you. They can kill you, I don't care. I'm not gonna' help you . . . I don't even speak to my bunkie (Jackie).
> You learn in here that you have no friends and nobody likes you . . . As long as you keep that in mind, you can go about your business. There's a lot of people who are fakes and frauds, you know (Toni)?
> You don't have a friend here . . . There's no closeness. I don't have anyone I hang around with. I'm just, you know, by myself (Colleen).
> As far as having anyone you can trust, inmate or staff, very, very rarely can you trust anyone (Miriam).

I don't want none of these friends in here ... I don't trust anybody in here, you
know? I'm a private person (Tanya).

Everybody's trying to knock each other's ego down. You know, you're lucky if you
get one or two good friends. That's what will keep you [from coming back],
dealing with other inmates, not the police. You know, it's horrible to say for
our own kind ... it's pretty awful here (Sarah).

Avoidance of and withdrawal from other prisoners were, according to the
interviews, clearly more common responses to imprisonment at VSPW, and
the women who had done time at both prisons elaborated on this apparent
difference in prisoners' relationships with each. Christine, who had spent
twenty-six years at CIW before being transferred to VSPW, noted that many
of the people she knew at CIW changed when they came to VSPW. At CIW,
she said, "lifers stick together, you know. If a brand new one came in and
they knew that person was doing a long time, they would take 'em and
learn under their wing and, you know, just try to guide them ... and just
how you're supposed to do time, you know? Around here, they don't do
that ... They don't tell you nothing in here." Given the widespread sense that
women were more distrustful, distant, and solitary at VSPW, explaining this
difference required women to look to the way imprisonment was practiced
at VSPW, rather than to women's essential natures. Consequently, unlike the
accounts we heard at CIW of the basic fickleness and deviousness of women,
at VSPW women attributed the poor relations among prisoners to what they
saw as overcrowded conditions, too few programs and activities, the generally
harsher regime, and the negative attitudes and seemingly arbitrary behavior
of staff, that affected how prisoners saw each other. Christine explained the
lack of trust and friendship among prisoners at VSPW very simply: "It's the
surroundings."

Despite what were characterized as more anomic relationships among
prisoners at VSPW, the interviews did not convey consistent evidence that
racial tension, physical confrontations, or overt conflicts were of greater
concern to women there. With regard to relations among racial groups, we
heard essentially the same comments from women at VSPW as we had from
women at CIW. While a few women – mostly white women in prison for
the first time – believed that racial tension was a general problem or said
it was of concern to them, the majority agreed with the statements of these
three women, the first an African American woman, the second a Hispanic
woman, and the third a white woman:

Well, there's no hostility between women. It's not, no I can't say that there really
is. You might find a one or two that are ... that don't like a black, or a black that
don't like whites, but basically in prison, in women's prison, there's nothing,
there's really no hardship as far as color is concerned (Colleen).

No, I don't see that [race problems among prisoners] at all here. Um, in
this prison I see the most interracial social friendship, you know ... you see

everybody, every type of race in one group . . . it's not a problem in here I don't
think, as far as I can see (Mona).

For the most part, white girls hang out with white girls, blacks with blacks, Chicanas
hang out with Chicanas. But there's not a lot of racial problems. There's really
not (Dana).

Women at VSPW also talked about intimate relations among prisoners
in much the same fashion as had women at CIW. Some women discussed
their relationships with other prisoners as among the few opportunities
they had to let down their guard and feel close to another person. Others
noted that, with eight women sharing a cell, the chances for private assigna-
tions were quite limited. Rarely did women express condemnation of such
relationships, though some pointed out that they were one source of the
few physical confrontations that occurred in women's prisons. And despite
the greater strictness and preoccupation with control at VSPW, none of
the women we interviewed suggested that staff were particularly zealous in
policing this rule violation, particularly if "you keep it private and out of
their faces" (Stephanie). Hanah, who had been with her girlfriend for eight
months shrugged when asked about this and said "like me and my girlfriend,
we're out on the yard all the time . . . but we don't give the cops no problems,
you know? They all know we're together . . . They haven't told us one thing
yet." Under a regime relatively uninterested in either morally regulating its
charges or transforming them into normatively feminine women, prisoners
who did not overtly challenge the rules or create disorder were largely left
to their own devices.

Survey Data on Prisoners' Experiences of Doing Time

In our analysis in this and the previous chapter of interviews with women
at CIW in the 1960s, women at CIW in the 1990s, and women at VSPW
in the 1990s, we have described similarities and differences in how women
managed their relations with staff and other prisoners, developed pragmatic
rules and habits of doing time, and negotiated around the particular constraints on and possibilities for action that each regime presented them.
The question we now turn to is how representative of the wider population
of prisoners were the views of the interviewed women? To address this, we
begin by comparing responses to a set of ten items that appeared on both
Ward and Kassebaum's and our surveys. The number and range of items
we can compare across all three contexts are not as great as we would like,
because Ward and Kassebaum's research focus was different from ours. We
will, however, elaborate on this analysis by next comparing the responses of
women at CIW in the 1990s with those of women at VSPW in the 1990s on
a more extensive range of survey items tapping their views of each prison
regime, its staff, and other prisoners.

Survey Data from CIW in 1963, CIW in 1998, and VSPW in 1998

The ten items asked on each of the three surveys are listed in Table 5-1 and are divided into two sections, one tapping women's attitudes about prison staff, the other tapping women's attitudes about other prisoners. Our interviews suggested that prisoners at CIW in the 1990s were more distrustful of and detached from staff than prisoners at CIW in the 1960s, and that prisoners at VSPW in the 1990s were the most distrustful and detached of all three groups. The survey data largely confirmed this conclusion. Approximately three-quarters of respondents at CIW and VSPW in 1998, compared to more than half at CIW in 1963, agreed that if they revealed too much about themselves to staff, the information would be used against them; and the proportion agreeing with this statement was greatest at VSPW. Similarly, the proportion of women agreeing with the statement that correctional officers have to keep their distance from prisoners was smallest at CIW in 1963 and largest at VSPW in 1998. Equivalent proportions of women at CIW in 1963 and at CIW in 1998 agreed that it was best not to let staff know they were down, perhaps reflecting the continued influence of features of a therapeutic culture at CIW; whereas a significantly larger proportion of the women at VSPW – more than three-quarters – agreed with this statement.

These differences appear to reflect both the general trends in penal ideology and discourse since 1960 as well as institutional changes at CIW that we described in Chapters 2 and 4; and the institutional differences in prison regimes and staff-prisoner relations that we described in this chapter. As we saw in the previous chapter, the administration at CIW in the early 1960s sought to reduce barriers between prisoners and staff by encouraging staff to develop relations of warmth and friendliness with prisoners, and by encouraging prisoners to share their feelings with staff in individual and group therapy sessions. These efforts were at least partially successful; some women interviewed in the early 1960s acknowledged receiving useful advice and help from at least some staff members. As April, who had recently arrived at CIW, told her interviewer in 1963: "I don't feel that I can't come to them for help. I appreciated that [advice from a woman's correctional supervisor (WCS)] and kept it in my mind. I'm going to have to turn to one of them at one time." At the same time, and reflecting the majority view that information would be used against them, many women at CIW in the early 1960s pointed to the conflict between the official emphasis on open communication and prisoners' concerns with how this might affect their appearances before the parole board. While the indeterminate sentencing system no longer governed the length of time women served in the 1990s, distrust of staff was even greater in the 1990s probably because of women's perceptions that, in the words of Tara who was doing time at CIW, "These

Table 5-1. *Prisoners' Views on Doing Time, Staff, and Other Prisoners, 1963 Survey Data from CIW, 1998 Survey Data from CIW and VSPW*

	CIW 1963 (N = 293)	CIW 1998 (N = 887)	VSPW 1998 (N = 934)
% agreeing[d] with the following statements:			
Attitudes about prison staff			
If you reveal too much about yourself to staff the information will be used against you	53%[b,c]	72%[a,c]	78%[a,b]
Correctional officers have to keep their distance in dealing with inmates	32%[b,c]	51%[a,c]	57%[a,b]
The best way to do time is grin and bear it, and not let staff know when you're down	61%[c]	61%[c]	76%[a,b]
Staff here have made clear how they expect you to behave if you're to stay out of trouble	68%[b,c]	78%[a,c]	73%[a,b]
An inmate should stick up for what she feels is right and not let staff set her standards	92%	92%	93%
Attitudes about other prisoners			
The best way to do time is to mind your own business and have as little to do with other inmates as possible	72%[b,c]	88%[a,c]	93%[a,b]
When inmates stick together, it's easier to do time	77%[c]	80%[c]	84%[a,b]
Most inmates aren't loyal when it really matters	72%[b,c]	83%[a]	84%[a]
In some situations, it's OK to inform on another inmate	43%[b,c]	35%[a,c]	23%[a,b]
A good rule to follow is to share extra goods with friends	56%[b,c]	38%[a]	39%[a]

[a] Significantly different ($p < .05$) from respondents at CIW in 1963.
[b] Significantly different from respondents at CIW in 1998.
[c] Significantly different from respondents at VSPW in 1998.
[d] "Agree" and "strongly agree" were collapsed in this analysis.

people aren't willing to help you do anything. They're here to punish you and that's all." This view was even more prevalent among women interviewed at VSPW and is reflected in the survey results.

The statement that staff made clear their expectations about how prisoners should behave received strong but significantly different levels of support across the three prison contexts. The interviews shed light on these differences. In the 1960s, prisoners often expressed frustration over "wishy-washy" staff who would not accept greater responsibility for their role as authorities and experts, according to Ward and Kassebaum (1965: 24). And there were many complaints in the early 1960s that staff were nondirective. For example, when asked "What do you find most annoying about doing time?" one prisoner responded: "The confusion of never getting a straight answer – I don't mind strict rules if supervisors would enforce them." In contrast, in the 1990s with greater standardization and bureaucratization, women more often complained about the strictness of the rules and their enforcement, especially, as we saw, at VSPW. "There's a certain way you do things, a certain way you gotta dress," observed Hanah. "So your best bet," she continued, "is to find out from staff what is really going on. They give you a Title 15 rules book with all the rules and regulations. Everything's in there." Another reason more prisoners in the 1990s agreed that staff made expectations clear may be that, as we argued in the last chapter, the prison had a narrower range of expectations to make clear; following rules had become one of a limited range of indicators of being a good prisoner. There is a small but significant difference between the responses of women at CIW and VSPW on this item. We suspect that this reflects two things. First, staff at VSPW were younger and less experienced than staff at CIW; and second, VSPW had been in operation for only a short period and was still working the 'bugs' out of some of its institutional procedures.

The one item that received virtually identical levels of support across all three prison contexts refers to the importance of prisoners standing up for what they feel is right and not letting staff set their standards. Regardless of differences in prison regimes and penal discourses, over 90% of survey respondents agreed with this statement, which Ward and Kassebaum (1965) took to be an essential indicator of "the inmate code." In interviews, women regularly endorsed taking what they saw as a principled stance in their relations with staff, even knowing it would get them nothing. "You tell the staff that a supervisor is wrong, you know it's a losing game, but you must anyway," said Kay at CIW in 1963. Debbie, serving time at CIW in 1995 for sales of methamphetamines, similarly asserted "I'll do whatever it takes when it comes to one of my rights or something in here, because we have very little rights. But what little rights we have we need to stick by them, you know?" Even at VSPW, where our interviews suggested women were more resigned to the power the prison held over them, nine out of ten survey respondents agreed on the value, in Ohlin's words, of asserting one's "autonomy and rightness." (Ohlin 1959: 10).

Paralleling the differences in attitudes toward staff across the three prison contexts are difference in attitudes toward other prisoners and these, too, reinforce the conclusions we drew from the interviews. Across all three contexts, the vast majority of women surveyed agreed that the best way to do time was to mind one's own business and have little to do with other prisoners, and that prisoners are not loyal when it really mattered even though doing time is easier when prisoners stick together. Consistent with our analysis of the interviews, the extent of agreement with these statements was greater in the 1990s and reached its height at VSPW, where, as we saw from the interviews, women were uniformly critical of other prisoners and grimly resigned to doing their time on their own. Here it is worth repeating the statement of Jackie from VSPW who described how she related to other prisoners this way: "Leave me alone . . . I don't care what happens to you. They can kill you, I don't care . . . I don't even speak to my bunkie."

A negative response to the statement about informing on other prisoners is considered an important indicator of endorsement of what classic prison research termed the inmate code of ethics – a code which pits prisoners against staff. The significantly different levels of agreement with this statement suggest that women at VSPW felt the most strongly about not cooperating with authorities, whereas women at CIW in the 1960s were the least concerned about such cooperation. An important element of the inmate code is a prohibition on providing information about prisoners to prison staff. In interviews, when the topic of snitching was raised, virtually all of the women, regardless of when and where they served time, expressed disdain for snitches. However, a few of the women interviewed at CIW in the 1960s and 1990s described circumstances that they felt justified informing on others, and women interviewed in the 1960s were more likely to see instrumental reasons for snitching – cooperating with staff, they felt, might help earn an earlier release date. In contrast, none of the women we interviewed at VSPW described circumstances that might justify informing. Indeed, when asked to name "the lowest form of inmate" on our survey, women at VSPW were significantly more likely than women at CIW to respond "a snitch."

The final item common to all three surveys asked about sharing goods with one's friends, and here women at CIW in the 1960s appear more generous toward others than women at either prison in the 1990s. This reflects, in large part, a change in CDC's rules that have curtailed the exchange of personal property among prisoners. As Marcy, who had served sixteen years at CIW in 1995 stated " . . . now it's a little bit different. I share less . . . It's in the DOM [Department Operations Manual]. We're not supposed to borrow each other's things." Women's greater distrust of other prisoners in the 1990s presumably also contributes to this difference. The potential for conflict was cited by women we interviewed at both CIW and VSPW as a reason not to share with others. "If you loan somebody something, it's hard for you to get it back. And the next thing you know, you're gonna' be boxin' for it," said Elizabeth.

Summary

There are at least two interpretations of the responses to the ten items shown in Table 5-1, one that would highlight the extent to which women's responses differ across the three prison contexts, the other that would point to the similarities in these responses. The former interpretation is supported both by the statistically significant differences in support women in the three different prison contexts expressed for most of the statements. The second interpretation would argue that the data in Table 5-1 do not portray a picture of either major transformation over time or major differences between prisons in prisoners' relations with and attitudes toward staff and other prisoners. Rather, the differences shown in Table 5-1, while statistically significant, are primarily ones of degree and not kind. That is, women's attitudes did not so much shift in direction as coalesce toward greater consensus about doing one's time in a way that kept staff and other prisoners at a distance. Our analysis of the interviews is most consistent with this second interpretation and suggests that while the pains of imprisonment were more sharply etched at VSPW in the 1990s, they were fundamentally the same regardless of prison context.

Survey Data from CIW in 1998 and VSPW in 1998

By drawing on our 1998 survey data from both prisons, we can evaluate this conclusion more fully for women serving time at CIW and VSPW in the 1990s. Tables 5-2, 5-3, and 5-4 present women's responses to questions about their experiences and perceptions of doing time, their views on c.o.s. and staff, and on other prisoners, at each of the two prisons.

Prisoners' views on the experience of doing time at CIW and VSPW are shown in Table 5-2. When asked to indicate how difficult it was to adjust to various aspects of prison life, women at VSPW were significantly more likely than women at CIW to identify medical care, overcrowding, lack of privacy, lack of programs, and rules and regulations as problems. Of course, one explanation for this pattern is that women at VSPW were so generally dissatisfied with imprisonment that they simply complained more than women at CIW. However, note that when asked about aspects of imprisonment that were not specific to a particular regime – such as absence of home and family, or absence of friends – similar percentages of women at each prison identify these as difficulties. Similarly, complaints about food, which is fairly

Table 5-2. *Prisoners' Views on the Prison Experience and on Doing Time, 1998 Survey Data from CIW and VSPW*

	CIW	VSPW
	(N = 887)	(N = 934)
How difficult has it been to adjust to the following: (% responding difficult, very difficult, or extremely difficult)		
Absence of home and family	90.2%	92.0%
Medical care	80.9%	88.1%***
Overcrowding	73.1%	90.2%***
Absence of friends and a social life	71.8%	73.3%
Lack of privacy	71.5%	85.7%***
Food	59.0%	63.3%
Lack of programs	55.6%	68.0%***
Rules and regulations	23.7%	37.5%***
No one likes doing time, but there can be some good things that come out of it. What are some of the things that have been good about doing time for you? (Check all that apply)		
Having time to think about my life	79.4%	75.5%*
Getting off of drugs	55.5%	51.8%*
Boosting my self-esteem	45.0%	27.2%***
Getting more education/learning to read	44.1%	51.0%***
Finding a religion	35.6%	28.6%***
Establishing important, personal relationships	34.3%	23.3%***
Nothing good has come out of doing time	5.8%	9.2%**
What do you think this place is about? (Choose one)		
It's a place that helps women in trouble	6.3%	1.6%***
It's a place to send women who get in trouble	24.2%	21.3%
It's a place to punish women for something they did wrong	69.5%	77.1%
% agreeing or strongly agreeing with the following statements:		
Doing time here hasn't been as bad as I expected	66.4%	38.6%***
I don't expect the prison to rehabilitate me; it's my responsibility to rehabilitate myself	88.5%	86.9%

* $p < .05$
** $p < .01$
*** $p < .001$

Table 5-3. *Prisoners' Views on Correctional Officers and Staff, 1998 Survey Data from CIW and VSPW*

	CIW	VSPW
	(N = 887)	(N = 934)
% indicating the following are very or extremely annoying aspects of doing time at this prison		
Being treated like a child by staff	58.4%	69.3%***
Staff acting like they are always right	56.8%	65.6%***
Staff won't give inmates a straight answer	58.3%	71.6%***
In what ways have the c.o.s. and staff here helped you?		
Treated me with respect	40.3%	24.6%***
Listened to my problems	26.3%	12.3%***
Provided good advice on how to do time	21.2%	13.0%***
Increased my self-esteem	14.0%	5.7%***
They haven't helped me at all	39.4%	60.5%***
% agreeing or strongly agreeing with the following statements:		
Most staff don't care about what happens to us. They're just doing a job	77.5%	86.3%***
When dealing with prisoners, most c.o.s. go by the rule book	53.9%	44.7%***
If you obey staff most of the time, they're willing to look the other way when you mess up on small things	56.7%	58.9%

* $p < .05$
** $p < .01$
*** $p < .001$

standardized across prisons, do not distinguish women at VSPW from women at CIW. In other words, women at VSPW appear to have found elements of their prison's regime, as opposed to general consequences of imprisonment, more onerous than women at CIW. Even so, there was general agreement across prisons as to which aspects of prison life were the most difficult to adjust to: absence of home and family, medical care, and overcrowding.

A question about good things that had come out of doing time received a similar pattern of responses. Women at VSPW were significantly less likely than women at CIW to identify any of the options as benefits of doing time, with the exception of getting more education or learning to read. The greatest differences in responses were for items that tapped elements specific to

Table 5-4. *Prisoners' Views on Other Prisoners, 1998 Survey Data from CIW and VSPW*

	CIW	VSPW
	(N = 887)	(N = 934)
How difficult has it been to adjust to other prisoners here? (% responding difficult, very difficult, or extremely difficult)	46.0%	59.4%***
Do you have any good friends among the prisoners here?		
None	12.1%	12.9%
1–2	46.3%	45.7%
3–5	24.0%	23.6%
More than 5	17.6%	17.9%
If you could decide for yourself, would you want more chance to be alone here or more chance to be with other inmates?		
More chance to be alone	45.6%	68.0%***
% agreeing or strongly agreeing with the following statements:		
I often go to prisoners who've been here a long time for advice on how to get along in here	55.0%	53.9%
If you know a prisoner is OK, it doesn't matter what color she is	82.4%	86.8%*
A prisoner's race is more important than anything else in determining who hangs together here	26.0%	23.3%

* p < .05
** p < .01
*** p < .001

what each prison offered women, as opposed to what imprisonment might offer regardless of where one served time. So, for example, having time to think about one's life and getting off of drugs are potential benefits of imprisonment generally and do not depend on where one serves time. In contrast, boosting self-esteem, establishing important relationships, or getting access to particular educational or religious programs depend more on the particular prison context. Note, too, that more than three-quarters of the women at both prisons said that prison had benefitted them in one way or another, indicating that their generally negative views on imprisonment did not prevent them from seeing something positive about the experience. In large part, this reflects many women's general understanding of their personal problems and failures, most frequently an addiction to drugs. As Maxine recounted: "I have a drug problem in the street; so I know that that was something that needed to be resolved all my life, so that I could put it behind me and become productive as a person ... " Others identified a lack of education or an inability to read as contributing to their life on the streets. Margo, a relatively well-educated prisoner, observed that "it's a huge amount of dysfunctionalism that leaves some with a fifth-grade education ... but if you can get beyond that and redefine it, then most people want to be able to be self-staining ... not many want to stay that way." Thus, it is the disabilities and disadvantages that these women have disproportionately experienced that contributes to their almost uniform ability to identify at least one aspect of their carceral experience – which involves addressing such disadvantages – as important to how they imagine their future lives.

When asked to choose among three statements describing their prison, we again see significant differences between the prisons in the distribution of responses as well as substantial agreement about the nature of imprisonment. Most women at both prisons viewed their prison as a place of punishment, rather than a place that offered them help or that simply incapacitated them. But consistent with the statements of our interviewees, there was greater consensus among women at VSPW that punishment was what their prison was about. Not surprisingly, then, women at VSPW were significantly less likely to agree with the statement that doing time there was not as bad as they expected. However, what did not differ between the two prisons were women's attitudes about rehabilitation. When asked to reflect upon the purposes and expectations of imprisonment generally, similar proportions of women at VSPW and CIW agreed that it was their responsibility to rehabilitate themselves; in other words, they had internalized the neoliberal rhetoric of responsibilization (O'Malley 1992; Garland 1996). Where women differed was in their evaluation of the particular regime to which they were subject.

Table 5-3 presents the responses of women at CIW and VSPW to a series of questions about prison c.o.s. and staff. The conclusions we drew from our interviews are strongly supported by these survey data. Compared to women at CIW, women at VSPW were much more likely to be highly annoyed by different aspects of their treatment by c.o.s., and much less likely to identify ways in which c.o.s. and staff at the prison had helped them. In fact, 60% of survey respondents at VSPW said c.o.s. and staff had not helped them at all, compared to 39% of respondents at CIW. More than three-quarters of the women at each prison thought that staff cared little about them; women at VSPW were significantly more likely to voice this opinion than were women at CIW. Despite the emphasis on rules and regulations at VSPW, significantly fewer women there thought c.o.s. "go by the rule book" in their dealings with women. Nevertheless, most women at both CIW and VSPW acknowledged that staff would ignore small indiscretions if they behaved most of the time, the only issue on which women's views did not differ significantly between the two prisons. In all other respects, the picture portrayed in Table 5-3 of greater dissatisfaction with and distance from staff among women at VSPW parallels what we heard in our interviews.

Differences between women at CIW and VSPW in their views on other prisoners were less pronounced, according to survey responses shown in Table 5-4. Despite the fact that significantly more women at VSPW reported having difficulty adjusting to other prisoners, their friendship patterns mirrored those of women at CIW. About 40% of women at both prisons indicated that they had at least three good friends inside; fewer than 15% said they had no friends – a smaller proportion than we might have expected based on our interviewees. Nevertheless, a substantially larger proportion of women at VSPW, compared to women at CIW, indicated that they would prefer to spend more time alone rather than with other prisoners, a pattern that parallels what the interviewees at each prison told us. In contrast, there was no difference in women's willingness to seek advice from long-term prisoners; more than half of the women at each prison reported they often did so. Over all, women's responses to these survey questions about relations among prisoners were perhaps not as strongly differentiated by prison as the interviews suggested they might be. The conclusions we drew from our interviews about the negligible extent to which race affects women's relations with other prisoners are upheld by the survey data, however, and show little variation across the two prisons. For the vast majority of women at both CIW and VSPW, who one chose as a friend or saw as trustworthy did not depend on race.

Summary

The survey responses of women serving time in the 1990s suggest there were distinct differences between VSPW and CIW in the experience of imprisonment, differences that are consistent with our analysis of our interviews with women at both prisons. The interview and survey data suggest that where administrators were preoccupied with the security and management of prisoners – as they were at VSPW in 1998 – rather than with transforming them, prisoners were particularly disaffected, suspicious, and isolated. VSPW's warden had worried that staff might become too complacent and "let their guard down," which likely conveyed a message to prisoners as well as staff that this was not a safe environment. Whether intended or not, this may have had the consequence of pushing prisoners at VSPW to rely largely or solely on themselves in managing their imprisonment and to see others – both staff and other prisoners – as threatening, exploitative, or untrustworthy. Even so, the pattern of responses suggests a conclusion similar to the one we drew in our comparison of survey responses from CIW in the 1960s, CIW in the 1990s, and VSPW in the 1990s. That is, a larger proportion of women at VSPW voiced negative views about the prison regime, about prison staff, and about other prisoners compared to women at CIW in the 1960s and 1990s. But the nature of women's views on their imprisonment – their experience of prison life as painful, anomic, and punitive – was essentially the same over time and between the two prisons.

Conclusion

According to the interview and survey data we have presented in this and the previous chapter, both the practice and experience of women's imprisonment in California underwent substantial changes between the early 1960s and the late 1990s. The domestic disciplinary regime and therapeutic community model of the 1960s were dismantled and replaced with a more punitive and seemingly degendered approach to imprisonment. The women's "institution" (as in CIW) was superceded in name and in practice by the women's "prison" (as in VSPW). The rate at which women were imprisoned increased so dramatically during this period that by 2000 it was equivalent to the combined male and female imprisonment rate of the late 1970s. And while the public and prison staff may still have viewed female offenders as less dangerous than men, they had lowered their expectations regarding women prisoners' ability or willingness to be reformed, or, given the rise of responsibilization strategies, to reform themselves.

The ways in which women perceived imprisonment and related to other prisoners and to prison staff to some extent reflected these and other changes in the discourses, goals, and practices of imprisonment. As the findings from the previous chapter indicated, in the 1960s, when the rhetoric (if not always the practice) of individualized treatment reigned, women's attitudes toward other prisoners and staff were more varied than they were in the 1990s, when a managerial strategy that focused on governing aggregates had emerged. Indeed, at VSPW, the prison where this managerial approach was most fully realized, women's attitudes were the most crystallized – as if their treatment as members of a group had homogenized their subjectivities.

If differences in institutional context are as important to understanding women's experiences in prison as we have argued, why haven't these differences figured more prominently in the sociological research on women's imprisonment? One explanation is that the women's prisons that have been studied have provided relatively little variation in their institutional contexts. The classic studies of women's imprisonment (Ward and Kassebaum 1965; Giallombardo 1966; Heffernan 1972) and some of their more contemporary counterparts (Bondeson 1989; Rierden 1997) may have been conducted in institutional contexts still strongly shaped by more traditionally gendered notions and practices of women's imprisonment, notions and practices much less apparent at VSPW in the 1990s. It may also be that the contextual yardstick for these studies was men's prisons. In searching for variations between the experiences of women and men in prison – and, in particular, in their preoccupation with women prisoners' greater involvement in intimate relationships – these studies may have neglected more subtle intragender variation in the experience of imprisonment, variation due to the different institutional, political, and cultural contexts in which women have served time. Thus, one important implication of our analysis of women's experiences in these three prison contexts is the recognition that these experiences are not monolithic, but contingent. They reflect discourses and practices of power and control that are to some extent common across prisons, but in other respects are the distinctive products of particular historical contexts.

Negotiating Prison Life: How Women "Did Time" in the Punitive Era of the 1990s

(With the assistance of Ross Macmillan and Kristin Carbone-Lopez)

TO THIS POINT, our analysis of women's imprisonment in California has concentrated on how temporal and institutional factors shape prisoners' responses to their carceral environments. We found that both factors are important. The California Institution for Women (CIW) in the 1990s had only partial success in translating the goals of the new punitive era to its inhabitants largely because of its tenure and legacy in California's imprisonment history; but at Valley State Prison for Women (VSPW), an institution whose tenure began in the 1990s, the effects of the recent transformations in penalty are clearly more discernable. In this final chapter, we consider the extent to which the kinds of institutional distinctions we have drawn remain important for how women do time once we take into account women's personal attributes and life experiences. To do this, we expand our analysis, which to this point has largely relied on interviews, to incorporate information we obtained from our respondents to the surveys we administered. We develop a measure of, or operationalize the concept of, "doing time" by using latent class analysis. While less nuanced than our previous analyses, in what follows we hope to provide both a more representative picture of how women do time in the 1990s and a more complete description of the factors that help to determine their different responses to imprisonment.

Our analyses draw on two different but related traditions in prison research and they incorporate some insights from feminist work on punishment that have helped us to think in new ways about how women react to the deprivations of imprisonment. The first tradition emerges from what, as we noted, has been referred to as "the golden age of U.S. prison sociology" (Simon 2000: 285) – the point at which sociologists made it their business to draw analytic attention to the prison social order and inmate subculture and, in the process, vigorously debated the merits of the functionalist and importation models. During this era, only a handful of scholars ventured into women's institutions determined to find out if women's reactions to the pains of imprisonment were similar to the reactions that had been observed among men. They documented a social order very different from that in men's prisons – one dominated by consensual sexual relationships and prison families – that served to demarcate the female prison subculture for most of the rest of the century. While today we realize that female prisoners have diverse carceral experiences that extend beyond these relationships, we have relatively little understanding of what factors, both within and outside of prison, shape them.

The second tradition emerged from a shift in prison discourse from one that privileged the prisoner culture to one that was intended to serve the needs of prison management (Simon 2000). Prisoner's characteristics and the prison setting still figure prominently in this research, but the outcome of interest has shifted from the values and attitudes of the prisoners to their behaviors and what are seen as their adjustment and coping skills. Most commonly, this research examines disruptive behaviors (violating prison rules, interpersonal violence) or emotional problems (psychosis, depression, self-injury, and suicide) among male prisoners (Adams 1992). Research on indicators of women's coping and adjustment typically has been an afterthought to the work on male prisoners (cf. Liebling 1999), particularly when the implications of the findings turn to questions of risk identification and prison management. Although we examine this limited body of quantitative research in our consideration of the different ways in which women prisoners' do time, it is not our exclusive focus. We also draw attention to the recent qualitative feminist research on women prisoners, that applies a different set of concepts and uses a different analytic framework for assessing women's responses to imprisonment. Rule breaking, self-harm, and sexual relationships with other prisoners are no longer seen as coping mechanisms but instead as a means of resistance, as indicators of prisoners' agency (Worrall 1990; Faith 1993; McCorkle 1998; Bosworth 1999).

In the analyses to follow, we cast aside the earlier readings of women prisoners that depict their behavior primarily as a function of their sex roles in the larger society and the more recent analyses that tend to read women prisoners' behaviors primarily as a function of agency. As Maher (1997: 1) so eloquently states in her critique of the literature on women offenders, both perspectives engage in oversimplifications on the one hand by denying women agency and on the other by overendowing them with agency. Instead, we begin by identifying a common set of responses to prison, or styles of doing time, based on women's attitudes and behaviors toward other prisoners, the staff, and the institution itself. We then move to consider how women's life experiences and current prison setting affect these responses to incarceration. We also consider a different set of indicators of how prison time is managed, which tells an equally important story about women's prison lives – actions labeled as rule violations or mis-behavior and self-reported mental health. In our consideration of these rule violations and mental health indicators, we do not attempt to privilege adjustment or agency rhetoric. Instead our effort is directed toward pro-viding an empirical assessment of these different research traditions and, ultimately, a varied and multilayered picture of how women respond to prison life.

The Pioneers: Prisonization, the Inmate Code and Argot Roles

The forerunners of the first large-scale studies of women's prisons emerged from the detailed studies of prison social organization in the U.S. during the first half of the twentieth century, most notably Clemmer's (1940) study of Menard in the 1930s – the maximum-security prison in southern Illi-nois – and subsequently Sykes (1958) study of the New Jersey State Prison. For Clemmer (1940: 294), the prison culture was comprised of "the habits, behavior systems, traditions, history, customs, folkways, codes, the laws and rules which guide inmates." Inmates submerged in this culture were "pris-onized" – a status that deepened their commitment to criminality and dis-rupted their reentry into society. Although his ethnography of prison life also included a description of the hierarchy of prisoners and their roles, it was his concept of prisonization that became central to the field.

Twenty years later, building on the work of Talcott Parson (1951), the prison emerged as an adaptive fully integrated "social system" where the inmate social system was seen as a conscious or unconscious attempt to deal with the deprivations of prison life (Irwin 1980: 32; Sykes 1995: 80). As Sykes (1995: 82) recounts:

> the behavior patterns of inmates sprang from a set of values, attitudes and beliefs that found expression in the so-called inmate code couched in prison argot. This code held forth a pattern of approved conduct . . . an ideal rather than a description of how inmates behaved.

Although Sykes (1958) envisioned the inmate code only as an "ideal" type of prisoner interactions, its tenets – for example, "never rat on a con, be cool, do your own time, and don't exploit inmates" – and the functional paradigm that spawned them became central to the study of prisoner behavior.

The prominence of the functionalist model, however, may not reflect its empirical validity as much as its generation of both complementary and competing paradigms that significantly widened scholars' ability to explain inmate adaptations to incarceration. According to the situational version of the functionalist model, the nature of prisoners' responses to imprison-ment is not just a consequence of the fundamentally coercive character of total institutions but instead depends on specific institutional characteristics such as the nature of the disciplinary regime, size and physical layout, or organizational objectives of the prison (Grusky 1959; Berk 1966; Street et al. 1966; Wilson 1968). The competing paradigm, the importation model, argued that the prison is not a completely closed system, as prisoners' responses and adaptations to incarceration are shaped by preprison experiences, originating in and sustained by subcultures outside of the prison (Irwin and Cressey 1962; Cline and Wheeler 1968; Irwin 1970). Together these models dominated the literature on responses to imprisonment for the next several decades (see e.g., Garbedian 1963, 1964; Wellford 1967; Jacobs 1974; Thomas 1977; Bukstel and Kilmann 1980), including the work on the imprisonment of women.

While it may not be surprising that Sykes' explication of an ideal type of inmate behavior found little currency in women's penal facilities, it is surprising that until relatively recently scholars of women's imprisonment have taken a rather narrow approach to documenting the attitudes and beliefs that might find expression in women's conduct and modes of adaptation to prison life.

As we have described, Ward and Kassebaum's (1965) study of CIW was the first large-scale study of a women's prison that was explicitly concerned with the ways in which females responded to imprisonment. Looking for evidence of convict identities such as those described by Sykes, Ward, and Kassebaum found that they were generally absent among the women at CIW and, as we have seen, that support for the tenets of the inmate code was relatively modest among this population. These scholars did not identify a complementary set of attitudes relevant to how female prisoners do time, but they did provide an extensive account of women's primary and intimate relationships within the institution. As a result their research was heavily criticized for an apparent preoccupation with the homosexual activity of prisoners (Elliott 1966) and a rather one-dimensional view of women's experiences of imprisonment (Messinger 1967). Nevertheless, this study became the template for research on female prisoners both because of its contemporaneous challenge to the male tradition of prison scholarship and because the findings resonated with the emerging integration of importation and functional theories. The formation of primary relationships among female prisoners was "rooted in social roles played in the free world" and emerged because of "psychological needs unsatisfied in the prison world" (Ward and Kassebaum 1965: 74).

Two other studies are critically important in this early scholarly history of women's adaptations to imprisonment: Giallombardo's (1966) study of the Federal Reformatory for Women in Alderson, West Virginia and Heffernan's (1972) research at Occoquan, Washington D.C. Giallombardo framed her research with the obvious puzzle women's adaptations to prison posed for functional theory. If the inmate social system develops as a response to the conditions of imprisonment, why does the "informal group organization developed in the female prison differ markedly in structure from that which has been described in the male prison" (Giallombardo 1966: 6)? Consistent with Ward and Kassebaum, she found female argot roles were numerous but revolved primarily around homosexuality and prison family relationships, and these prison experiences could be understood by employing deprivation and importation paradigms. Specifically, women attempt "to resist the destructive effects of imprisonment by creating a substitute universe within which the inmates may preserve an identity relevant to life outside the prison" (Giallombardo 1966: 129). Heffernan (1972) also drew attention to the unique character of the female inmate social system and early on rejected the classic models of inmate adaptations offered by Clemmer and Sykes. Instead, she turned her attention to the propositions of Irwin and Cressey (1962) that asserted that preprison identities are critical to understanding how inmates do time. On the basis of her study of various dimensions of prison life, she argued that women have three different ways of doing time: the "square" who adhere to conventional norms; the "cool" who are the more sophisticated criminals and who know how to manipulate the prison environment to their advantage; and, the "life" whose identities are influenced by their petty criminal activities (e.g., prostitution, theft) on the street. Although her research also contained a heavy dose of descriptive data on sexual relationships among prisoners, it remains more notable perhaps for the explicit attention she devoted to understanding women prisoners' adaptations to prison life outside of the realm of their traditional gender role identities.

Research documenting the nature and extent of same sex relationships among female prisoners and institutionalized delinquents continued well into the last decade of the twentieth century (see e.g., Mahan 1984; Leger 1987; Genders and Player 1990; Alarid, 1997). To a lesser extent, this is also true of the empirical assessments of the relevance of prisonization and the inmate code of ethics for female prisoners. Although this latter body of empirical research has been heavily criticized for evaluating female behaviors with outdated male behavioral norms (Pollock-Byrne 1990: 138–140), it is important to remember that this research was instrumental in drawing attention to a different aspect of female behavior, one that did not involve gender roles or women's sexual behaviors. In so doing, it shed much needed light on the attributes and life experiences that shape women's responses to incarceration. For example, a heightened opposition to staff was commonly found among women with prior prison experience, as well as among younger women, nonwhite women, and single and childless women (Jensen and Jones 1976; Alpert, Noblit and Wiorkowski 1977; Zingraff and Zingraff 1980; Kruttschnitt 1981; Mandaraka-Sheppard 1986).

How phase of institutional career and specific aspects of the prison environment inscribe themselves on women's carceral experiences is much less clear from this body of prior research (see e.g., Tittle 1969; Jensen and Jones 1976; Alpert et al. 1977; Hartnagel and Gillan 1980; Kruttschnitt 1981; Mawby 1982; Larson and Nelson 1984; Mandaraka-Sheppard 1986; Bondeson 1989; Craddock 1996) and the more recent scholarship that speculates about the effects of overcrowding, long sentences, and more diverse prison populations on women prisoners adaptations (Rierden 1997; Greer 2000). Owen (1998: 63), in her ethnography of the Central California Women's Facility (CCWF), maintains that crowding has become "a defining feature of institutional life," affecting virtually every aspect of women prisoners' daily experiences. Her analysis of women's adaptations, which harkens back to the classical era of prison scholarship, draws on Schrag's (1944) concept of the "axes of life" to describe what she sees as the three central elements of the prison culture: negotiation of the prison world, which is achieved through respect and reputation, commonly found among lifers and "longer-termers"; styles of doing time, which are determined by adherence to the prison code and career phase; and, the "mix" or the degree to which women are involved in prison hustles for drugs and sexual liaisons. As interesting as these descriptions of women's prison life are, it is not clear whether these axes are unique outcomes that are independent from what Owen identifies as their central determinants (phase of institutional career, prior prison experience and commitment to a convict or conventional identity, as well as preprison experiences) or how they are affected by the specific characteristics of this prison.

Rule Breaking and Mental Health

The focus on prisonization, the inmate code, and argot roles in prison research generally declined over the last third of the twentieth century and was replaced by interest in a broader range of adaptations – misbehavior, interpersonal violence, and mental health (Goetting and Howsen 1986; Adams 1992; Bottoms 1999; Liebling 1999). Although certainly the racial and political conflicts that erupted in American prisons during the 1960s and thereafter turned scholarly attention towards violence in prison (Irwin 1980), the more general movement over the last half of the twentieth century to effective prison management, including prisoner classification and risk assessment, also fed into a desire for information about prison adjustment and coping. Women prisoners, for whom issues of racial and interpersonal violence were not of central concern and whose populations are smaller and generally have been perceived as being more manageable than their male counterparts, remained largely on the periphery of the research on adjustment and coping (see, Kruttschnitt and Gartner 2003).

Nevertheless there is a small body of research that attempts to predict prison misbehavior and mental health among female prisoners. It shares much in common with the earlier scholarship on inmate subculture that saw characteristics of the individual and the prison environment as critical determinants of prisoner adaptations. Women cited for misbehavior, according to this research, share many individual attributes with their counterparts who report having emotional problems. They tended to be young and to have had disadvantaged preprison lives, which include little schooling, unemployment, few if any family responsibilities, and a history of maltreatment and substance abuse problems (Roundtree, Mohan, and Mahaffey 1980; Wilkins and Coid 1991; Adams 1992; Liebling 1992, 1999; McClellan, Farabee, and Crouch 1997; Boothby and Durham 1999; Bottoms 1999; Loucks and Zamble 2000).

The prison environment and phase of institutional career also appear to influence these behaviors. Disciplinary infractions and mental health problems are reported to be greatest at the beginning of a prisoner's sentence. Some scholars have hypothesized that this is a function of the stressful process of transitioning into the prison (Adams 1992; Bottoms, 1999). Prisoners in close custody also score higher on depression, stress, and misbehavior than those who experience less restrictive conditions (Ruback and Carr 1984; Mandaraka-Sheppard, 1986; Rock 1996; Boothby and Durham 1999). The effects of specific prison environments may also be contingent on female prisoners' biographies (Adams 1992; Bottoms 1999) but based on prior research it is unclear how this interaction plays out for female prisoners. It could be that in more secure and coercive institutions, individual biographies may be less important than in less secure facilities because the deprivations prisoners experience serve to equalize any cultural and individual distinctions among them (Goodstein and Wright 1989). Or it may be, as Jacobs (1983) suggests, that in especially austere institutions prisoners have fewer distractions, and so cleavages to external sources and modes of identification become more important than they would in less austere institutions.

Recasting Concepts of Women Inmates' Responses to Prison

Over the past decade a group of feminist scholars have approached women's prisons and women's responses to both punishment and prison life from conceptual frameworks that differ substantially from those that informed earlier scholarship. Although to various degrees they acknowledge that both women's biographies and the prison environment help to shape the institutional culture and the way prisoners adapt, their research fundamentally alters prior conceptions of female prisoners' experiences and behaviors. Not only are the behaviors that received so much attention in earlier work, such as sexual relationships, seen in a new light, but a broader set of behaviors that indicate how imprisonment is experienced are considered. Most commonly, women's responses to the carceral setting are seen as critical aspects of their attempts to retain a sense of self, an identity, in an environment over which they have limited control and in which they have few means for expressing active resistance. For example, Faith (1993) and Diaz-Cotto (1996) draw attention to the role women's cultural heritages plays in the efforts of some prisoners to create politicized responses to incarceration. McCorkle (1998), observing women in a prison drug treatment program, suggests that specific rule violations, including smuggling contraband, are women's means of defending their own definitions of self and identity. Bosworth's (1999) research in three English prisons for women also focuses on women's prison identities. She singles out sexual orientation, age, history of abuse, and sense of alienation as important determinants of women's prison identities (see also Jones 1993). Appreciating the complexity and intersectionality of identities, however, she also draws attention to the ways in which religious and ethnic practices – pertaining to diet, education, and dress – interfaced with images of femininity and presentations of self. Women used these constructed identities to thwart the mundane and alienating aspects of prison life on largely private and individual levels. For Bosworth, then, women's attention to their physical appearances and their sexual relationships with other prisoners are central aspects of resistance to carceral regimes, rather than reactions to the deprivations of, and accommodations to, prison life (see also Dirsuweit 1999).

Others, while acknowledging prisons as sites of constant power negotiation and resistance, see women's experiences and responses as more varied. Eaton (1993), for example, used female prisoners' recollections of coping with various periods of confinement to draw attention not only to resistance and retaliation but also withdrawal, incorporation and self-mutilation as common adaptations. Withdrawing from the prison community, and women prisoners' preference to alternate the bonds that keep them connected both to the free world and to other prisoners, are emergent themes in this line of scholarship (Girshick, 1999; Mandaraka-Sheppard, 1986). Some scholars speculate that the increasing distrust and even fear of close interpersonal relationships may be tied to changes in the prisoner population and the longer sentences that are being executed within a custodial, as opposed to rehabilitative, framework (Greer 2000; Kruttschnitt et al. 2000). Withdrawal has also been linked to prisoner self-mutilation, a phenomenon that has been of more concern and better documented in the United Kingdom and Canada than in the United States. Self-mutilation appears among female prisoners who are more likely to describe themselves as having problems interacting with other prisoners and who prefer to remain isolated from the general population (Liebling 1999: 314). Finally, the notion of incorporation refers to women who are actively involved with the prison regime and prison authority. Although variously described as "street smart" or "organizationally smart" (Owen 1998) these women recognize and rely on prison authorities to get through their period of incarceration with minimal hassles (see also Mandaraka-Sheppard 1986).

Conceptualizing "Doing Time"

Research on responses to prison life has evolved from a concern with how the deprivations imposed by prison life, and conditioned by life experiences, shape behavioral outcomes to a concern with specific misbehaviors and mental health broadly conceived as indicators of prisoners' coping and adjustment. Although we have always known far more about these responses in male prisoners than female prisoners, selected ethnographies and qualitative studies of women's imprisonment are producing new perspectives and new conceptualizations of women's adaptations and resistance to the pains of imprisonment. There are a range of ways in which women respond to prison but also distinct forms of adaptations that may have different etiologies and different correlates both within and across various penal institutions. The transformations in women's imprisonment over the last half of the twentieth century, we believe, may have produced particularly profound effects on what are considered to be important behavioral reactions to prison life.

To gain a broader understanding of how the women at VSPW and CIW approached their time in prison we began by reviewing the questions in our survey that addressed their attitudes and actions toward other prisoners and toward staff, as well toward the prison itself. Independently we each selected questions that we thought would be valid indicators of how prisoners approach doing their time in the context of these relationships and the exigencies of prison life. The items we selected and the distribution of responses to them appear in aggregate form in Table 6-1.

The first two items reflect how women feel about their fellow prisoners. While a majority of women (61%) disagree with the statement that they do not care to "associate with the kinds of women who are" imprisoned with them, they clearly limit these associations to a relatively small circle of friends. Reflecting the kind of wariness toward other prisoners we found in our interviews, the largest proportion of women (42%), indicate that they spend their free time with only one or two other prisoners when they are not locked in their cells; a surprisingly large percentage (39%) spends most of their time by themselves. Women's attitudes toward and interactions with staff appear to reflect the realities of having to contend with both good and bad staff and the feeling they derive from being constantly subject to

Table 6-1. *Response Distribution for Items Used to Model How Prisoners Do Time*

Attitudes and actions toward other prisoners	
1. I don't care to associate with the kinds of women who are in this institution.	
Strongly agree/agree	38.9%
Disagree/strongly disagree	61.1
2. When you are not locked in, how do you spend your free time?	
Mostly with one group of inmates	6.7%
With one or two inmates	42.2
With many different inmates but no one group	11.8
Mostly alone	39.3
Attitudes and actions toward correctional staff	
3. How difficult has it been for you to adjust to the correctional officers?	
Not at all difficult/a little difficult	48.7%
Difficult/very difficult/extremely difficult	51.3
4. Earning the respect of staff is more important to me than earning the respect of other inmates	
Strongly agree/agree	32.8%
Disagree/strongly disagree	67.2
Attitude toward the prison	
5. I feel like I have no control over my day-to-day life in here.	
Strongly agree/agree	53.0%
Disagree/strongly disagree	47.0
Total Number of Respondents	1821

custodial control. Specifically, while they seem to be relatively evenly divided in their assessment of how difficult they find it is to adjust to correctional officers, the majority (67%) feel it is more important to have the respect of their colleagues as opposed to the respect of the staff. Finally, we also asked them whether they felt they had control over their daily lives in prison. Considering the restrictions imprisonment places on daily choices and movements, it is perhaps surprising to find that almost one-half of these prisoners (47%) do feel they have some control of their day-to-day lives.

We used latent class analysis to model the item responses that appear in Table 6-1.[1] Latent class analysis is a technique that allows us to use this

---

[1] Latent class analysis defines a latent variable as unobserved but as accounting for the relationships among the observed measured variables (Clogg 1995). In this respect, latent class analysis is similar to factor analysis. However, unlike factor analysis, latent class analysis uses information from observed variables to produce qualitatively distinct categories or subsamples rather than a ranking of the sample based on subscales. Latent class analysis describes the distribution of the sample in categories and the conditional probability of variable items in these categories.

Table 6-2. *Response Distribution for Items Measuring Styles of Doing Time by Latent Class Analysis**

	CIW			VSPW		
	I Adapted	II Convict	III Isolate	I Adapted	II Convict	III Isolate
"How do you spend your free time?"						
With 1 group	**.08** (.07)	**.09** (.10)	**.02** (<.01)	**.08** (.11)	**.09** (.08)	**.02** (.02)
With 1 or 2 inmates	**.44** (.46)	**.48** (.41)	**.24** (.22)	**.44** (.43)	**.48** (.50)	**.24** (.31)
With no special group	**.14** (.14)	**.13** (.12)	**.07** (.07)	**.14** (.15)	**.13** (.14)	**.07** (.06)
Alone	**.34** (.32)	**.31** (.37)	**.67** (.72)	**.34** (.32)	**.31** (.28)	**.67** (.62)
"I like to associate with other inmates."	**.75** (.81)	**.68** (.71)	**.17** (.05)	**.75** (.77)	**.68** (.68)	**.17** (.19)
"I have difficulty adjusting to correctional officers."	**.21** (.11)	**.81** (.85)	**.48** (.38)	**.21** (.06)	**.81** (.93)	**.48** (.54)
"It is more important to earn respect of inmates than the respect of staff."	**.65** (.65)	**.87** (.78)	**.31** (.42)	**.65** (.66)	**.87** (.89)	**.31** (.33)
"I feel like I have no control over my life."	**.26** (.27)	**.70** (.60)	**.68** (.50)	**.26** (.41)	**.70** (.67)	**.68** (.76)
Probability of class membership, by prison	**.47**	**.33**	**.20**	**.29**	**.48**	**.23**

* Results of homogenous model appear in **bold** and the results of the heterogenous model are in parentheses.

	L^2	df	P-value	ID
Homogeneity	137.65	101	.010	.099
Heterogeneity	109.50	80	.016	.083
Δ	28.15	21	.136	–

variable information to produce distinct categories of respondents; as such, it permits us to describe the various ways in which women at CIW and VSPW do time in substantive terms. The results of this analysis appear in Table 6-2. The latent variable was defined by three classes; the latent class probabilities indicate the expected distribution of the sample across these three classes. The conditional probabilities of item responses within each of the three classes define the characteristics of each latent class by showing variation in the style of doing time across classes.

In the first class, or style of doing time, the women have a high probability of associating with other prisoners and they enjoy these associations. While about two-thirds of the women in this class agree that it is more important to earn the respect of inmates than it is to earn the respect of staff, few of them report having had problems with correctional officers. Perhaps not surprisingly then, these are also the women who have the highest probability of disagreeing with the statement, "I feel I have no control over my life in here." We refer to these women as "Adapted" because they seem to have figured out how to manage the contradictions and constraints of prison life. Margo, who had spent a substantial proportion of her adult life incarcerated, provides a particularly vivid account of her take on correctional officers, which reflects the kind of confidence the women in what we have called the Adapted class demonstrate in this environment.

> These people that are officers now are coming in very, very young...they're not overly paranoid, but they're very business-oriented. I don't have prob-lems...And I make a point when I want my door opened or whatever I want, and I know how to defer to authority, and so I'll just, I'll just say words like 'please' and 'thank you' and those simple things go a long way. So sometimes if I'm in a jam and I need to make a quick phone call, I can usually ask and get it, because I have not violated that person or challenged their authority or in any way caused their eight-hour stint to be more difficult.

As a lifer, Margo's approach to other prisoners was also indicative of this style of doing time. As she described to us, lifers often find it difficult to associate with other prisoners who will be released and who cannot possibly understand their situation. By contrast, Margo preferred to stay in touch with the assemblage of prisoners and prison life.

> They have a unit in here called the 'honor unit' and it's loaded with women who have probably done anywhere from ten to twenty years and I've made a point of not being in that unit...I like to feel like I can walk out on the yard and know what's going on and not fall into that bag of being fearful. You're always fearful of what you don't know, and if you live in the isolated situation, it's sort of like if your car broke down in South Central, but you're living in Beverly Hills, you're scared to death, and I don't like that idea. And also, I think that having a unit full of women that have done so much time, they complain a lot. They're very nitpicky and they focus in on this prison too much for me.

Similar accounts of how to approach staff and how to get along were voiced by other lifers, like Alice who acknowledged having "no problem saying 'please,' 'thank you,' 'yes sir,' 'no sir,' 'ok sir,' whatever. It's in my best in-terest to obey whatever your little rules are, and get along." But this talent for learning how to deal with staff was not associated exclusively with having done long periods of prison time. Rather, as Owen (1998) found, there were some women who just knew how to work the system. Carla, who had been incarcerated for less than one year at CIW, reported not only that it was her first time in prison but also her "first time in trouble, period." She exem-plifies the approach of those in the Adapted class to their relationships with staff and other prisoners. With regard to the staff, she indicated that

> you learn real quick, real quick, really quick. One conversation with them and that'll tell ya' what kind of staff they are. But the female officers are really...they're really easy going, all of them. I don't know any angle that they're bad...none, not one, not one. Whether they're younger or older, it doesn't matter. They're all really, really easy to get along with. Then there's these little robocops that come from God knows where. I have no idea where they come from...we make fun of them all the time. We say maybe if we put you in the men's prison they'll straighten you up, and then you can come back. 'Cuz guys don't put up with that stuff...They'll beat some of 'em before long.

Carla's confidence in being able to interpret staff is matched by an acceptance of the wide range of behaviors and personalities she encounters among her colleagues.

> When I came here, I look at these people and especially a lot of the lifers, you know. A lot of 'em are real older, you know. They look like they could be somebody's grandmother. You kind of wonder, wow, what did they do to get here, you know. They look like real caring people, you know. But everybody's got their own little obnoxious behavior, and then there's people here who are really, really nice. Really, really super nice people you would never met them out there anywhere, never. And you wonder what could they have possibly done to get here, you know. Nobody really knows what each other's here for; we just know we're all here and we gotta' get along. And we can get along. Some people try to make it just really obnoxious. I guess they feel bad 'cuz they're here, you know. And so they got to take it out on whoever they can take it out...some of them take it out on the police, some of them take it out on the other inmates, and are hard to get along with...I myself happen to be one of the best people to get along with. I get along with everybody; I don't care. I didn't come here to get along with people. I didn't come her to make anybody happy; I came here to do my time. So basically that's it.

A second approach to doing time emerged from a group of women whose interactions with staff and the prison environment appear to differ from those of whom we suggest choose an Adapted style of doing time. Most of the women in this second group report that they spend time with only one or two others, or alone and, like women in the Adapted group, these women have a high probability of enjoying their associations with other prisoners. However, unlike those in the Adapted class, these women are highly likely to report having difficulty dealing with the correctional officers. Not surprisingly, then, they also believe that earning the respect of prisoners is more important than earning the respect of staff and, relative to women in the Adapted class, they are much more likely to indicate that they feel they have little control over their prison environment. We refer to this as the "Convict" style of doing time, a term the women themselves use to describe certain types of prisoners (see also Owen 1998; Britton 2003: 109). Convicts are women who watch out for themselves and their friends. They don't associate widely with others, especially correctional officers. Bonnie described this distinction to us in the following ways:

> Convicts are the ones that are real tough, down to earth. Like if someone steals something, they're not going to let it go by. They're, you know, there's going to be a fight; they're both going to end up going to SHU [Secure Housing Unit]. You know a convict doesn't let things slide, you know. Like a convict stands up for their rights; doesn't let their rights go. An inmate will just . . . someone steals their stuff or something to violate their rights; they just let it slide, but a convict won't. Convicts are real, real hard, and usually those are the ones that usually do some time.

When we pressed Bonnie about whether length of time served is a critical determinant of this style of doing time, it was clear that attitude was more important, or as she put it, "it just depends on how you stand your ground." One of the most defining features of the Convict style is how women in this class stand their ground in encounters with staff. Pauleen, for example, explained that "inmates [by contrast to convicts] are up underneath the cop's ass telling them every little thing. Who's doing drugs, who fought or who's being homosexual." Those who have chosen a Convict style not only distain such behavior but also adopt a relatively uncompromising stance in their interactions with staff. As Tara, a short-term prisoner at CIW, told us when we inquired about relationships among staff and prisoners:

> Its just that we are on opposite sides of the fence and that's the way I want to maintain the relationship. I don't want any question of what it is I might be doing or that they might be doing. So I personally want the relationship, the line drawn and I'll stay here and you stay there.

Neva, who had put in twelve years on a life sentence at CIW, explained more precisely why she didn't want anything to do with the staff given the chances she felt prisoners had of winning any dispute with a correctional officer:

> They're gonna' take the staff's word over your word regardless of what happened, not unless you draw out a long investigation. And two out of three, most of the time, the staff is gonna' win anyway 'cuz they're gonna' have other staff to say this happened when it didn't actually happen. You know, and we go through a lot of that in here with the staff. You know disrespect toward inmates, you know, like you can go eat, and I'm sitting there and like if I'm talking, you'll have one staff over you, 'Ah no talking; you can't eat and talk at the same time; finish your dinner and get out.' You know ugly – just very ugly.

This description of how disputes and interactions among staff and prisoners are resolved also reflects the lack of control women who have chosen a Convict style feel they have over their lives in prison. This appears as well in their interactions with other prisoners who are typically described as limited to a trusted few. As Donna, a woman at VSPW recommended:

> Don't get involved in other people's relationships, affairs. Stay to yourself. Have a few friends. Don't trust anyone. Because you might go to Sally tomorrow and say oh I heard Jo say this or watch your back, and she's gonna' turn around and to, Jo, Kathy said, and then you're gonna' get beat up or get in a fight, you know. You don't hear nothing . . . I don't want to know; I don't care; it isn't my business, you know.

Finally, the third style of doing time that characterizes the prisoners is distinguished from both the Adapted style and the Convict style based on how women spend their free time and their attitudes toward other prisoners and staff. This third group of prisoners overwhelmingly indicated that they did not want to associate with other prisoners and would prefer to be alone when they are not locked in their cells. Further, while these women are about equally divided over whether they have difficulty with correctional officers, relatively few feel that it is more important to earn the respect of other prisoners than prison staff. These prisoners are also likely to feel they have no control over their prison environment. We refer to the style of doing time these prisoners have chosen as an "Isolate" style which is characterized by an approach to doing time that is very negative and singular. Descriptions of prisoners' relationships from women at each prison fit well with our sense of how alienated these women are from other prisoners. Marina, who was a novice to prison life, having been incarcerated for the first time at CIW as a white-collar offender, reflected on her preference for doing her own time and her distaste for her colleagues.

> I just tend to stay to myself . . . I just go pick up my lunch in the morning; I go get meds at night. In the morning I get up, go get my lunch, and then I go to work, and then I come back. I usually stay in my room most of the time, except if I have a visitor or something . . . I don't want to get involved with any of these women.

Yet, such a solitary stance on prison life didn't come only from women who were new to incarceration. Brenda, who had done considerable time in the county jail and was now incarcerated for a probation violation, expressed similar sentiments based on her knowledge of the problems that can come from establishing friendship networks in prison.

> I just don't like a lot of friends, you know, I don't. I don't see any sense in getting involved in all that emotional, you know, when somebody hurts somebody's feelings or something like that . . . They say "you're awful quiet";

I say "yeah." I said, I learned that silence is the only thing that can't be misquoted; that's so true. You can say something, and somebody will quote you and say it different, and there you got another problem.

Darlene who had served several years at CIW before being transferred to VSPW, expressed a similar sentiment. Soon to be released, she offered the following advice on what it is like doing time:

> It's hard to do time, you know. And then there's not many that offer friendship, and if they do they want something in return. That's why I stay to myself. Then people around me ... they start disliking you, you know, because you're different. They see you wanting to change and not come back to this place, so they don't even want to deal with you, talk behind your back and stuff.

When we asked Darlene how she related to staff, she described an approach that was different from both the Adapted and Convict styles. Unlike the women who had chosen the Adapted style, Darlene was not concerned with trying to interpret staff behavior or determine what type of person she was dealing with. But, unlike women who had chosen the Convict style, neither did she view staff as the enemy. Instead, for Darlene, consistent with our portrayal of the Isolate style of doing time, staff were there to do their jobs and sometimes they did it well and sometimes they didn't.

> There was this one time that one c.o. told me something and ah I looked at him and I didn't believe he was talkin' to me, you know. He called me out and I looked at him and I ... I just looked around ... and I looked at him and I said, I didn't even say anything. I was like, okay, and I went in my room. I came back out for the unlock and I looked at him and I shook my head and he told me you know what, I apologize. And I walked up to him and I said I accept your apology and I said you know I'm not one of the females, you know, that talks like that. I don't carry myself like that and I want my respect. And I respect you as authority and I want you to respect me as a person too. And he said okay ... I'll give him my respect. I could of sat and told him something you know out of line too, but I didn't.

Exploring Institutional Differences

The responses to prison life we uncovered resonate with some of the recent scholarship on women prisoners. Among those who chose the Convict style we see elements of active resistance to the most visible symbols of institutional control – correctional officers – as well as attempts to maintain a sense of personal identity by limiting their friendships with prisoners (Goffman 1963: 86). The prisoners who have chosen what we have termed the Adapted style have much in common with the prison-smart women discussed by Owen (1998: 168). These are women who maintain positive relationship with both correctional staff and other prisoners to facilitate some degree of freedom in, and control over, their prison world. Those choosing the Isolate style express the distrust and fear of other prisoners and self-imposed confinement characteristic of the "withdrawal patterns" others have documented (Mandaraka-Sheppard 1986; Girshick 1999). These similarities may suggest that regardless of the prison environment, there are a set of responses to prison life that are fairly typical among women prisoners. Yet, such an interpretation ignores the very real role of specific penal regimes in structuring how prisoners experience prison life (Sparks, Bottoms, and Hay 1996). As we have shown, CIW and VSPW vary considerably in their disciplinary and management practices – a variation that may bring into focus questions about the way in which women's responses to imprisonment have been traditionally portrayed.

To explore whether and how the prison context influences these styles of doing time, we tested the latent structure of doing time across prisons to see, for example, if the distribution of response items for those choosing an Isolate style differs between CIW and VSPW. The result of this test appears in Table 6-2.[2] The general pattern of response probabilities is very similar despite some subtle differences in the response probabilities for specific ways of doing time across the two prisons. For example, a larger proportion of women in all three groups reported feeling they had no control over their lives at VSPW than at CIW and a larger proportion of women at VSPW (except within the Adapted class) report having difficulty adjusting to the correctional staff. Despite these differences, a test to determine whether there are significant variations in how women do time at each prison revealed that there is substantive similarity in the structure of doing time across prisons.[3] Although there are the same three styles of doing time at each prison, the distribution of women among these styles of doing time differs by prison. As can be seen at the bottom of Table 6-2, while relatively similar proportions of women at CIW and VSPW are in the Isolate class (.20 and .23, respectively), those choosing the Adapted style are much more likely to be doing time at CIW than at VSPW (.47 vs. .29). By contrast, at VSPW it is the Convict style of doing time that predominates (.48 at VSPW vs. .33 at CIW).

There are several factors that may account for these different distributions. Based on the survey data on the demographics and criminal histories

[2] Specifically, we compared a homogeneous model, in which the latent structure of doing time was assumed to be the same across prisons (see BOLD probabilities in Table 6-2), with a heterogeneous model, in which the latent structure was allowed to vary across prisons (see probabilities in parentheses in Table 6-2). This was done by constraining the conditional probability of doing time within latent classes to be identical within each prison. We then compare goodness of fit statistics with those from the unconstrained model.

[3] The overall test of heterogeneity of doing time across the prisons was not significant [P = .1359].

of these women, it seems unlikely that the different distributions are the re-sult of compositional effects, or a concentration of certain types of offenders in one prison as opposed to the other. As we saw earlier, the backgrounds and criminal histories of the women at CIW and VSPW are very comparable. We cannot, however, rule out the possibility of unobserved heterogeneity in these two samples, or the possibility that different kinds of women, irrespec-tive of the similarities in their observed biographies, are sent to CIW and VSPW. Even though at the time of this research the California Department of Corrections (CDC) had not classified the women's facilities by security level, as we noted earlier, officials at CIW indicated that they were attempting to move their troublemakers to more secure prisons. Still another explanation for the different distributions of women across styles of doing time would focus on the differences in the organization and management of the two prisons we described earlier. From this structural perspective, it could be argued that the greater propensity for women to choose a Convict style at VSPW compared to CIW is because women at VSPW are responding to a harsher environment that has significant consequences for the types of rela-tionships they develop with both their fellow prisoners and the correctional staff. By contrast, the predominance of the Adapted style of doing time at CIW, relative to VSPW, may emerge from the physical and the philosophi-cal remnants of the rehabilitative era that have been sustained by long time staff and prisoners. We turn now to examine the relevance of some of these competing explanations to our understanding of how women do time.[4]

Understanding the Different Ways Women "Do Time"

In this section we focus on sorting out the relative contributions of women's life experiences and their carceral environments to how they do time. While this analysis draws upon the work done in the classic era of prison sociology – the juxtaposition of functional and importation paradigms – it also aims to build on recent feminist scholarship, which considers personal attributes and life experiences as critical "categories through which women define prison identity" (Bosworth 1999: 110). We examine associations between styles of doing time and various demographic (ethnicity, age) and personal

---

[4] At a second stage we assigned cases to latent classes. Specifically, we based assignment on the probability of each case falling into each class. We used a series of random numbers to assign cases to specific classes based on their latent class probabilities. This second stage analysis was conducted separately for each prison. We employ the results of this analysis for subsequent analyses. We also analyzed the missing cases in an attempt to determine whether the women who failed to answer one or more of these five questions could be assigned to a class based on the probability of their response to questions they did answer. The latent class analysis indicated that in both prisons, in most cases, the women with missing values formed a distinct fourth class. These women were eliminated from all subsequent analyses.

Table 6-3. *Unstandardized Coefficients: Multinomial Logistic Regression of Styles of Doing Time on Predictor Variables*[a]

	Latent Class I Adapted		Latent Class II Convicts		ANOVA
	B	S.E.	B	S.E.	X^2
Intercept	.24	.59	1.34	.57	7.79
Currently serving time at VSPW	−.65***	.17	.06	.17	30.61***
PERSONAL CHARACTERISTICS					
Ethnicity[b]					
African American	.30	.20	.35*	.20	3.26
Hispanic	.34	.25	.45*	.25	3.24
Other	.53*	.26	.46*	.25	4.56
Age	−.01	.01	−.04***	.01	14.78***
Education[c]					
High school	.07	.20	.13	.20	.46
More than high school	.02	.21	.20	.20	1.60
Married	−.21	.18	−.07	.18	1.55
Has Minor Children	.16	.19	−.03	.18	1.78
Substance Abuse					
Alcohol abuse	.17	.19	.49**	.18	8.89*
Drug abuse	.55**	.21	.11	.20	8.41*
OFFENSE CHARACTERISTICS					
Current Offense[d]					
Property	.06	.23	−.04	.23	.25
Drug	.22	.24	.37	.23	2.57
Other	−.59	.45	−1.20*	.49	6.09*
Parole/probation violation	.05	.18	−.05	.18	.41
INCARCERATION HISTORY					
Prior adult commitments[e]	.11	.09	.13	.09	2.18
Served time elsewhere?[f]					
Served time – CIW	.19	.23	.20	.23	.81
Served time – Madera	−.29	.22	−.21	.22	1.71
Served time – other	−.14	.23	−.12	.23	.40
SENTENCE CHARACTERISTICS					
Security Level[g]					
Custody Level 1	.05	.30	−.18	.29	1.07
Custody Level 2	−.09	.32	−.27	.31	.92
Custody Level 3	.16	.35	−.09	.34	.76
Other Custody Level	−.11	.38	−.63*	.38	3.85
Length of Time Spent					
Total time in prison – months	.003*	.002	.004*	.002	5.75*
Sentence length – months	−.001	.001	−.001	.001	.90

* $p < .10$
** $p < .01$
*** $p < .001$
[a] The contrast category is Latent Class III (Isolates).
[b] The reference category is "white."
[c] The reference category is "less than high school."
[d] The reference category is "violent" offenses.
[e] Prior adult commitments is an interval-level variable.
[f] The reference category is "served time – VSPW."
[g] The reference category is "level 4" – the highest level.

139

characteristics (e.g., education, marital status, drug and alcohol history), offense histories, and sentences.[5]

We pooled the data and estimated a model using multinomial logistic regression. Coefficients in this regression model estimate the independent effect of a given predictor on the odds of a respondent being in a particular category of the dependent variable, style of doing time, relative to an omitted category. The omitted category in all of our analyses, the group that provides the basis of comparison, is the Isolates. The results of this analysis appear in Table 6-3.

Controlling for personal attributes and background and sentence characteristics, the prison in which women are serving time has a significant and sizeable impact on how they do time. In fact, the effect of prison on how women do time, is more pronounced than any other predictor in the equations (as indicated by the ANOVA X^2 statistics); it is twice as large as the effect for age, four times as large as the effect of substance abuse problems, and six times greater than the effect of the length of time they have served at their respective institutions. Further, the effect that prison has on styles of doing time is consistent with the outcomes seen in Table 6-2. The probability that a woman will have developed an Adapted style of doing time, as opposed to Isolated style, is much lower at VSPW than it is at CIW. This effect cannot be attributed to the fact that there were more women with life sentences housed at CIW than at VSPW because the analysis partials out the effect of sentence length.[6] Rather it suggests that the physical, social, and political climate women encounter at CIW increases their probability of having less isolated responses to their carceral lives. Andrea, who had only been at CIW for a few months – having been transferred from the Central California Women's Facility, Madera – articulated a detailed and enthusiastic account of what she saw as the significant differences in penal regimes.

> Well, um, this, I love it here. The inmates call this CIWonderful and it's a
> lot more wonderful, trust me. It's like a college campus here, compared to
> the other prisons... There's trees, its easy going, the people are easy going

---

[5] The variables race, offense of conviction, time served, and custody level include other categories in their response codes. The responses coded in these other categories are as follows: (1) Other races includes Asians, Native Americans, and women of mixed racial heritage; (2) Other offenses include women who were convicted of prostitution, vehicular manslaughter, arson, and parole and probation violations; (3) Time served at prisons other than CIW, CCWF, or VSPW including forestry camps, the California Rehabilitation Center, the Northern California Women's Facility at Stockton, Avenal, Live Oaks, out of state prisons, and federal facilities; and (4) Women who were classified as having an other custody level were those who indicated that they had not yet been classified or they didn't know their custody level.

[6] Sentence length is the total number of months a woman has served at the present prison plus the time she has left to serve. For prisoners with no scheduled release date, sentence length was coded as 432 months (36 years) which was the maximum in the distribution of summing total months served with total time left to serve.

because if you get a 115 here, which is an order of disciplinary action, you can be shipped out of here somewhere else. That it's a privilege to be here, I believe. They have the camp people here, and industry. I work industry, which is really . . . I have a good job, great roommates, everything is happy-go-lucky, not happy-go-lucky, but it's just a lot better atmosphere. The atmosphere is just very pleasant, compared to Madera which there is eight women to a room. It gets about 115 degrees, there are no trees, and the attitudes there are very negative . . . The cops are really uninformed here. They don't know what's going on and they really don't care. This is Camp Snoopy. It's Camp Snoopy . . . this is Camp Snoopy, trust me compared to Madera this is Camp Snoopy. Cops have it easy here.

Sarah, a prisoner at VSPW who had also spent time at CIW, expressed a similar perspective. Characterizing the Adapted response pattern, she reflected on the differences each institution offered women in terms of their ability to control their environment. "You can run things better at CIW than here. You know they check up on you pretty much. Things can still be done here but not like CIW. You can really work it there."

Although the effect of the prison environment on how women manage their time is substantial, the data in Table 6-3 also show the effect of individual attributes and experiences when the prison environment is held constant. Here we find that age, a woman's history of substance abuse problems (drugs or alcohol), offense of conviction, and time served are all significant determinants of how women do time.[7] Older women are significantly less likely to adopt the Convict, relative to the Isolate, style of doing time regardless of their prison environment. This pattern is consistent with what long-termers told us about their perspective on prison time, which often was initiated by a period of rebellion and a denial of the restrictions imprisonment imposed upon them. As Marcy explained it:

> I've been here sixteen years, and the first ten years of my stay here at this institution was . . . chaos all the time. Ya' know, you come in here with an "I don't care" attitude and you still think you're out there on the streets . . . you wanna do things your way, and not adhere to the authorities. But the past six years have been . . . I don't think pleasant as such . . . but it hasn't been bad. It hasn't been at all bad.

Maxine, on the other hand, described her own development over time in terms of her relationship to staff. Note here how she enters the prison with a Convicts-style approach toward the staff but gradually develops a level of respect for staff that is more typical of the Isolate style.

[7] Race is also marginally significant. These findings suggest that by comparison to whites, Hispanic and African American prisoners are more likely to choose a Convict style than an Isolate style, but the effects are not substantially different from the effects of race on doing your time in an Adapted, as opposed to Isolated, manner.

First of all, initially, I had no sense of trust. Even when staff conducted them-selves appropriately, I did not trust. What was their motive? And so I was very hostile. It took more on their part...And so when I started testing the water, you might say...I started developing. They talked to me like a human being and that made a difference, and I would question it and look at them with why are you being good to me when Mr. or Miss so-and-so is so abusive and does these things to us? Why? And the difference is, some people care and some people don't. And I wanted to develop better relationships with them because I was gonna' be here, and when I wanted to have my door unlocked, I wanted to be able to go up there and be asked a question. I wanted to be able to have an answer; somehow be civil with one another. I'd go and get my door popped, or ask for a kotex, tampon, roll of toilet paper and they were responding positively and it was, okay, this will work."

Drug and alcohol abuse problems also significantly increase the odds that women will do their time in either an Adapted or a Convict style, rather than an Isolate style. These associations may reflect women's famil-iarity with a broad range of individuals in the criminal justice system since prisoners with substance abuse histories frequently have had multiple ar-rests before landing in prison. Such an interpretation is underscored by the significantly greater likelihood of adopting either of these two approaches to imprisonment (Convict or Adapted) as total time in prison accumulates. Finally, current offense also helps to distinguish the women who choose a Convict style from those who choose an Isolate style. Relative to the women incarcerated for the commission of a violent crime, those convicted of other offenses, are more likely to manage prison as with an Isolate style rather than a Convict style. These women represent a very heterogeneous group not just in terms of their commitment offenses (including, for example, arson, stalk-ing, and vehicular manslaughter) but also their life experiences. Roberta, a sixty-five-year-old alcoholic who was incarcerated for the first time in her life at VSPW for a hit and run "with bodily injuries," graphically depicts the Isolate approach to prison life. She begins by noting the problems she has in getting privacy in a room with seven other women, but rapidly digresses to the problems she has with prisoners generally.

They call me old lady and all this and that stuff and everything. I mean if something disappears, I've got it...I mean they're liars, cheats, and ah then [if you] don't believe in what they're doing, then you're way out in space some place. And they bawl me out; when they come out [of] the bathroom, why [do they] come out [with] no clothes on? I mean to me, that's gross. I mean, if they want to run around in the nude and play with each other and have sex, I mean, I go out of the room.

The evidence described thus far provides strong support for the classical paradigms of prison adaptation: functionalist, situational functionalist, and importation. While women have a common set of responses to prison life, the prison context itself, and to a lesser extent selected personal character- istics and preprison experiences, shapes their style of doing time. Women who choose as Adapted, as opposed to an Isolate style are much less likely to inhabit VSPW than CIW. Further, a woman's age, her substance abuse history, her offense, and the total length of time she has spent in prison also affect her style of doing time, irrespective of the prison in which she is serving her sentence.

A Different View of Women's Responses to Imprisonment

This analysis of styles of doing time relies on relatively broad-brush strokes to paint a picture of the different ways in which women respond to their prison time. Yet, we know that prison life creates and sustains much more complex sets of activities and emotional responses. What are these activities and responses and do the styles of doing time we identified, the different prisons women inhabit, and the markers of their identity and preprison lives, significantly affect them? It is to this subject we turn next as we explore a specific set of behavioral and emotional responses frequently labeled as indicators of prisoners' levels of coping and adaptation.

The behavioral responses we are interested in have typically been stud- ied as indicators of misbehavior and active resistance. We measure them with women's self reports of their disciplinary records, drug use, and sex- ual activity. We focus on disciplinary reports to capture the wide range of misbehaviors for which women can be sanctioned. In the California De- partment of Corrections, misbehavior or actions by prisoners for which a disciplinary report can be filed include: theft or acquisition or exchange of personal or state property, possession of contraband or controlled sub- stances or under the influence of such substances, misuse of food, misuse of telephone privileges, failure to meet work or program expectations, late for or absent without authorization from a work program assignment, use of vulgar or obscene language, failure to comply with departmental groom- ing standards, use of force or violence against another person, preparation to escape, tattooing, possession of five dollars or more without authoriza- tion, acts of disobedience or disrespect, inciting others to commit an act of force, gambling, and self-mutilation or attempted suicide (California Code of Regulations, Title 15). Here we are less concerned with the nature of the infractions on a women's disciplinary record than their total record of violations. Such a record reflects not only a woman's actual behaviors but also the way her behaviors are perceived by those who have the power to sanction her. Misconduct reports are a product of both the prisoner and the institution, and both should contribute to women's responses to prison life.

Because of the range of activities for which women can be sanctioned is extremely broad, and in some respects nebulous, we also include two specific misbehaviors that are prohibited under Title 15: sexual activity between prisoners and drug use. While female prisoners may not be aware of the number of actions that are prohibited by the California Department of Corrections, they are clearly aware that both of these acts are forbidden. As such, their choice of whether to participate in these activities also indicates something about their response to their carceral environments.

All of the information we have on these behaviors was self-reported by the women prisoners. There has been considerable criticism of official measures of prison misbehavior based on their susceptibility to organizational priorities and discretionary decision making (Van Voorhis 1994). Not only can the number and nature of such reports vary with institutional priorities but they also vary according to the subjective judgments of individual officers about particular prisoners and particular activities. As Britton (2003: 158) points out, regardless of prisoners' conduct, prisons are designed to reproduce bad behavior because, in the minds of their keepers, they hold "bad" people. This is especially problematic for female prisoners who are often described by male correctional officers as more emotional, manipulative, and generally more troublesome than their male counterparts (Pollock 1986; Carlen 1998: 86; Rasche 2001; Britton 2003). Official records are also less useful when the focus is on covert behaviors, especially sexual offenses that have a low probability of detection (Van Voorhis 1994). Of course, self-report data have their own set of validity issues revolving around questions of memory loss and deliberate over- or underrepresentation of infractions and illegal activities. Nevertheless, given our greater focus on covert behaviors, which may be less well-documented in official records, and the evidence that self-reports of misbehavior, such as insubordination, are just as valid as official records and are less likely to be affected by the prisoners' demographic profile (Van Voorhis 1994), we utilize prisoner self-reports of their disciplinary record, sexual relations with other prisoners, and drug use.

Roughly one-third of the women at each prison (35% at CIW and 33% at VSPW) indicated that they had received disciplinary reports since coming to the prison. Roughly similar proportions of women also indicated involvement in sexual relations with other prisoners during this term of imprisonment (38% at CIW and 36% at VSPW) but much lower proportions admitted to using illegal drugs (16% at CIW and 18% at VSPW; see Table 6-4). While it is difficult to gauge how accurate these self-reports are, we have some evidence of their validity based on both staff evaluations and information from other surveys of prisoners. In the case of disciplinary reports, various correctional administrators at both prisons noted they thought that our results were quite accurate. As one staff member put it, the bad apples

Table 6-4. *Behavioral and Emotional Responses to Imprisonment*

	Total % (N)	CIW % (N)	VSPW % (N)
MISCONDUCT			
Use illegal drugs in prison			
Yes	17 (293)	16 (133)	18 (160)
Involved in homosexual activity in prison			
Yes	37 (624)	38 (306)	36 (318)
Received disciplinary reports in prison			
Yes	34 (565)	35 (279)	33 (286)
MENTAL HEALTH ISSUES			
Worried about becoming a vegetable			
Never	80 (1308)	82 (644)	79 (664)
Rarely	11 (175)	10 (81)	11 (94)
Frequently	6 (96)	5 (37)	7 (59)
All the time	3 (50)	3 (21)	3 (29)
Worried about going mad			
Never	63 (1048)	69 (552)	57 (496)
Rarely	16 (266)	15 (117)	17 (149)
Frequently	10 (170)	8 (63)	13 (107)
All the time	11 (175)	8 (61)	13 (114)
Worried about feeling suicidal			
Never	77 (1268)	79 (625)	75 (643)
Rarely	14 (234)	13 (103)	15 (131)
Frequently	6 (103)	6 (48)	6 (55)
All the time	3 (44)	2 (18)	3 (26)

are a relatively concentrated group. Information on drug use during incarceration is more difficult to obtain. Surveys of prisoners in state and federal facilities in the United States assess drug and alcohol use *prior to incarceration*. In the case of drug use, these data indicate that 40% of women prisoners report using drugs at the time of their offense (Bureau of Justice Statistics 1997). While these estimates are higher than the current level of use our respondents report, the discrepancy is consistent both with the suggestion of some prior research that "the vast majority of women cease their drug use during their imprisonment" (Owen 1998: 47) and with the findings pertaining to drug usage prior to and during imprisonment among female prisoners in England and Wales.[8] Finally, despite the widespread attention

---

[8] Surveys of remanded and sentenced female prisoners in England and Wales indicate two-thirds (66%) of the remanded, and more than one-half (55%) of the sentenced, prisoners used drugs in the year before their incarceration but only one-quarter (25%) of the

given to same sex relations in the early research on female prisoners, today we have relatively little information about the prevalence of sexual relations among prisoners. Although virtually all recent studies of women's imprisonment note the presence of dyadic sexual relationships (see e.g., Owen 1998; Bosworth 1999; Girshick 1999; Greer 2000), there is some evidence that involvement in these relationships might not be as pervasive as previously thought. Greer (2000: 451), for example, found that while most of the female prisoners she interviewed believed that sexual relationships were extremely prevalent, only about of one-third of the women admitted being involved in a sexual relationship in prison. These findings are largely consistent with the results of our surveys where we found that across prisons the largest proportion of women estimated that anywhere from 50–70% of the prisoners were involved in sexual relations with other prisoners, yet only about one-third of the prisoners reported having been involved in such a relationship.

The emotional responses we examined are based on three items derived from a Situational Problems and Coping Difficulties scale (Richards 1978). These items have been used successfully in other studies of female prisoners (MacKenzie, Robinson, and Campbell 1989). Specifically, we asked the prisoners to indicate how often they worried about the following things since coming to prison: (1) becoming a vegetable, (2) being afraid of going mad, and (3) feeling suicidal. As the data in Table 6-4 indicate the prevalence of such distressed reactions to imprisonment is relatively low among these prisoners. Fewer than 10% of the women at either prison reported worrying about feeling suicidal either frequently or all the time and similarly small proportions reported being worried about becoming a vegetable either frequently or all the time. Nevertheless, the picture changes slightly when the prisoners were asked about going mad. At CIW 16% and at VSPW 26% reported this occurred either frequently or all the time. How does this compare with other estimates of prisoners' self-reported mental health? On the national level, there are some data on the prevalence of mental health problems that limits the kind or amount of work prisoners can do. Our data are fairly consistent with these national estimates that show that 16% of female prisoners report such a condition although the nature of the condition is not specified (Bureau of Justice Statistics 2001: table 2). Additionally, while the Bureau of Justice Statistics (2000) provides information on the number of suicides and other causes of death among prisoners in the United States, no comparable data are available on suicide ideation. However, a survey of sentenced female prisoners in England and Wales (Singleton et al. 1998) provides comparable estimates to ours: 8% of the

remanded, and one-third (34%) of the sentenced, female prisoners reported using drugs during their current prison terms (Singleton, Meltzer, and Gatward 1998).

surveyed women prisoners in England and Wales reported suicidal thoughts as did 8% of the women we surveyed at CIW and 9% of those we surveyed at VSPW.

We dichotomized the indicators of misbehavior by juxtaposing those women who reported they had engaged in a given misbehavior against those who did not. We also dichotomized the indicators of mental health problems by juxtaposing women who reported never or rarely experiencing problems against those who report experiencing problems frequently or all of the time. To estimate the relative effects of styles of doing time, the prison context, and the women's characteristics and criminal justice experiences on these activities and emotional responses, we used logistic regression.

We turn, first, to the results of our analyses of misbehavior. The styles of doing time we have identified are significantly related to all three of our indicators of misbehavior. Specifically, as can be seen in Table 6-5, women who choose the Convict style of doing time are more likely than women who choose the Isolate style to have disciplinary reports, use drugs, and engage in sexual activity. These relationships appear regardless of the prisoners' personal characteristics, offenses of conviction, prior prison experiences and current carceral environment. Recall that women who choose the Convict style felt that it was much more important to earn the respect of their fellow prisoners than the respect of the staff and that they clearly have the most trouble dealing with staff. Using drugs and maintaining an intimate relationship would certainly earn them the respect of some prisoners and the ire of staff. But such respect is also earned by standing up for yourself even when you know it will result in a disciplinary report. As Rosa, who was a relative newcomer to prison, told us: "I'm me. I'm who I am, regardless of what the staff thinks, or the administration thinks . . . So if I have a girlfriend out on the yard, oh well, you know."

The self-reported rates of disciplinary reports and drug use do not appear to be substantially different between the women choosing the Adapted and Isolate styles of doing time. In fact, only their greater likelihood of engaging in sexual relations with other prisoners distinguishes the former from the latter. What sets women who choose an Adapted style apart from other prisoners is their ability to traverse the social worlds of both the prisoners and the correctional officers with relative ease. This ability no doubt facilitates maintaining intimate sexual relations with other women while at the same time avoiding disciplinary reports. Alice, who had served well over twenty years at CIW, and who had clearly developed ways to manage her life in prison so as to reduce its pains, artfully frames the issue of sexual relations among prisoners by drawing attention to the bind staff are in given the changes that have occurred in social mores surrounding homosexuality. In making this comparison, it is obvious that she views sexual relations among

Table 6-5. *Binomial Logistic Regression of Misbehavior by Styles of Doing Time*

	Disciplinary Reports[a]		Use Drugs[a]		Homosexual Activity[a]	
	B	S.E.	B	S.E.	B	S.E.
Intercept	1.24	.50	−.72	.60	1.81	.49
STYLES OF DOING TIME[b]						
Adapted	.01	.19	.27	.24	.37*	.19
Convict	.34*	.19	.50*	.23	.61***	.18
PERSONAL CHARACTERISTICS						
Ethnicity[c]						
African American	.45**	.17	−.76***	.22	.53**	.16
Hispanic	.37*	.20	−.05	.23	.30	.20
Other	.52*	.20	−.09	.23	.63**	.20
Age	−.06***	.01	−.06***	.01	−.08***	.01
Education[d]						
High school	−.18	.17	.26	.20	−.15	.16
More than high school	.24	.17	.34	.21	.17	.17
Married	.03	.16	−.02	.18	−.18	.15
Has Minor Children	.14	.16	−.10	.19	−.13	.15
Substance Abuse						
Alcohol abuse	.26*	.15	.003	.18	.06	.15
Drug abuse	.22	.18	1.16***	.25	.13	.18
OFFENSE CHARACTERISTICS						
Current Offense[e]						
Property	−.22	.19	−.20	.23	−.32*	.19
Drug	−.45***	.19	−.27	.23	−.25	.19
Other	.17	.45	−1.58	1.05	−.76	.51
Parole/probation Violation	−.56***	.16	−.47*	.19	−.43**	.15
INCARCERATION HISTORY						
Prior Adult Commitments[f]	.05	.06	.06	.07	.09	.06
Served Time Elsewhere?[g]						
Served time – CIW	.13	.19	−.12	.24	.40*	.18
Served time – Madera	.13	.18	.50*	.22	.18	.17
Served time – other	.04	.18	−.21	.22	−.17	.17
SENTENCE CHARACTERISTICS						
Currently Serving Time at VSPW	−.10	.15	.18	.17	−.02	.14
Security Level[h]						
Custody Level 1	−1.18***	.23	−.86***	.25	−.69**	.23
Custody Level 2	−.90***	.25	−.60	.27	−.70**	.25
Custody Level 3	−.42	.26	−.28	.28	−.56*	.27
Other Custody Level	−1.05***	.31	−1.22**	.40	−.92**	.31

	Disciplinary Reports[a]		Use Drugs[a]		Homosexual Activity[a]	
	B	S.E.	B	S.E.	B	S.E.
Length of Time Spent						
Total time in prison – months	.01***	.001	.01***	.001	.01***	.001
Sentence length – months	.001*	.001	.002***	.001	.001*	.001

* p < .10
** p < .01
*** p < .001
[a] The categories "never" and "rarely" are combined and contrasted with the categories "frequently" and "all the time."
[b] The contrast category is Latent Class III (Isolates).
[c] The reference category is "white."
[d] The reference category is "less than high school."
[e] The reference category is "violent" offenses.
[f] Prior adult commitments is an interval-level variable.
[g] The reference category is "served time – VSPW."
[h] The reference category is "level 4" – the highest level.

prisoners as just part of life in prison; they are not problematic as long as they are handled discretely.

> As the administration and the line staff don't condemn it, they don't condone it either, but they don't condemn it. As it is socially more accepted in the world out there, it is socially more accepted in here. Sex is still a violation of Title 15 in the prison, and if you're caught in a compromising position, you're going to get written a "115" [a disciplinary report]. But it's not quite as looked down upon.

A number of factors related to the prison environment (custody level, total time in prison, and sentence length) are also significantly associated with our different measures of misbehavior in ways consistent with prior research. Female prisoners with longer sentences, more accumulated time in prison, and lower custody levels report significantly more misbehavior than prisoners with shorter sentences, less time served, and the highest custody level.[9] By contrast, those prisoners who have been returned to prison for a probation or parole violation report significantly fewer disciplinary reports, and are less likely to report drug use or sexual activity relative to

---

[9] These time served effects might be interpreted as merely a function of opportunity since women who have accumulated more time in prison have had more time to acquire disciplinary reports. However, we are hesitant to conclude these are just opportunity effects since we found no relationship between number of disciplinary reports and having a life sentence. At both CIW and VSPW, 60% of the women with life sentences reported no infraction.

their counterparts who are serving time on their original offense. Further, many of the personal characteristics of these women predict misbehavior in ways that are similar to those we observed in our analysis of styles of doing time. For example, younger women, women of color, and women with substance abuse histories are more likely to report misbehavior than older women, white women, and women who do not report drug or alcohol problems. However, unlike our previous analysis, here we find that the prison context itself (CIW and VSPW) has no relationship to self-reported rates of misbehavior.[10] Based both on our experiences and on the female prisoners' responses to these two institutions, this finding is contrary to what we would have anticipated. CIW maintains a relaxed atmosphere that at least by all outward appearances would seem to be more tolerant of prisoners' misbehavior than VSPW. However, as we have seen, the growth in imprisonment in California over the past two decades produced a concerted effort by the California Department of Corrections to closely regulate prisoners' behavior across institutions. Nancy, who has been incarcerated at CIW for at least eighteen years, explained the changes she has witnessed in the way the staff and administration handle disciplinary problems, making it clear that the increasing punitiveness of the modern prison era is not just evident in the newer institutions for women.

> I see people getting locked up more than I used to. I live in the unit where . . . they bring people when they go to lock them up, and write them up and so on. And I see more people in there than I used to. You know I hear more incidents . . . well I know there are more incidents, because I record that. They tried to say that there was less, that there was decrease. They have made more stringent rules and changes . . . they did something just recently. They used to have . . . it was part of the Work Incentive Program, the "115." When you had a 115 . . . you served a sixty or I mean a three month and you got your time back, that kind of thing . . . you know, you were able to earn things back, and do different things and it was lighter. Well actually, I think in a lot of ways it was a mistake 'cuz nothing ever really happened. Because they would end up getting their time back anyway, so what did they care? So they cracked down on that and they made up a whole bunch of new rules as far as 115's. You know that's all through the CDC, it's not just here.

The overall effect then may be that misbehavior is fairly well scrutinized in this atmosphere, irrespective of where you are incarcerated, and as we have seen, relative distinctions between the two prisons – at least with respect to monitoring misbehavior – are difficult to distinguish.

In Table 6-6, we examine the effect of the same variables on our indicators of mental health. Styles of doing time are strongly related to mental

---

[10] Because the prison has a significant effect on styles of doing time, and these styles of doing time also are significantly related to misbehavior, we expected that the prison context might have an indirect relationship on misbehavior through styles of doing time. Subsequent analyses, however, revealed no main effect of prison on misbehavior.

Table 6-6. *Binomial Logistic Regression of Mental Health Issues by Styles of Doing Time*

	Vegetable[a]		Go Mad[a]		Suicidal[a]	
	B	S.E.	B	S.E.	B	S.E.
Intercept	−3.59	.83	−.004	.53	−.56	.74
STYLES OF DOING TIME[b]						
Adapted	−.69*	.32	−.88***	.20	−.78**	.30
Convict	.06	.28	−.30	.18	−.14	.26
PERSONAL CHARACTERISTICS						
Mental Health History	.38	.25	.60***	.15	.73**	.22
Ethnicity[c]						
African-American	−.16	.30	.19	.19	−.65*	.31
Hispanic	.11	.37	.37*	.22	−.01	.33
Other	.29	.32	.41*	.22	.42	.28
Age	.03*	.01	−.04***	.01	−.03*	.02
Education[d]						
High school	−.46	.32	−.20	.18	.10	.28
More than high school	.39	.28	.21	.19	.50*	.28
Married	.24	.25	.24	.16	.50*	.23
Has Minor Children	−.06	.26	.11	.17	−.18	.24
Substance Abuse						
Alcohol Abuse	−.33	.26	.20	.16	.04	.24
Drug Abuse	.05	.28	−.24	.19	−.14	.27
OFFENSE CHARACTERISTICS						
Current Offense[e]						
Property	−.85*	.36	−.18	.21	−.27	.30
Drug	−.54	.33	−.14	.21	−.64*	.32
Other	.25	.63	.27	.44	−.02	.66
Parole/probation Violation	−.60*	.30	−.26	.17	.01	.26
INCARCERATION HISTORY						
Prior Adult Commitments[f]	.13	.11	.06	.06	−.02	.11
Served Time Elsewhere?[g]						
Served time – CIW	−.93*	.38	.02	.22	.04	.33
Served time – Madera	.66[+]	.35	−.07	.20	.04	.32
Served time – other	−.02	.34	−.04	.20	.27	.31
SENTENCE CHARACTERISTICS						
Currently Serving Time at VSPW	.66*	.27	.38*	.16	−.25	.23
Security Level[h]						
Custody Level 1	−.14	.36	−.38	.24	−.75*	.32
Custody Level 2	−.15	.41	−.12	.26	−.40	.35
Custody Level 3	.59	.37	−.06	.28	−.13	.36
Other Custody Level	.39	.51	−.10	.33	−.68	.49

(*continued*)

Table 6-6 (*continued*)

	Vegetable[a]		Go Mad[a]		Suicidal[a]	
	B	S.E.	B	S.E.	B	S.E.
Length of Time Spent						
Total time in prison – months	−.002	.002	.002	.001	−.002	.002
Sentence length – months	.003***	.001	.0005	.001	.002*	.001

* p < .10
** p < .01
*** p < .001

[a] The categories "never" and "rarely" are combined and contrasted with the categories "frequently" and "all the time."
[b] The contrast category is Latent Class III (Isolates).
[c] The reference category is "white."
[d] The reference category is "less than high school."
[e] The reference category is "violent" offenses.
[f] Prior adult commitments is an interval-level variable.
[g] The reference category is "served time – VSPW."
[h] The reference category is "level 4" – the highest level.

health experiences, with women choosing an Adapted style reporting that they are significantly less likely to worry about becoming a vegetable, going mad, or feeling suicidal than women in the Isolated class. Relative to style of doing time, personal characteristics and criminal justice experiences generally seem to have less of an impact on these women's mental health responses. An important exception, however, is mental health history. We find, consistent with prior research on prisoner mental health, that prisoners who have experienced emotional difficulties in the past are more likely to report emotional problems during periods of incarceration (Adams 1992: 306). Age and sentence length also have significant effects, indicating that younger women and women with longer sentences are more likely than older women and women with more abbreviated prison terms to self-report these signs of mental deterioration.

Our interviews with the women suggest, as the quantitative results do, that the mental health of prisoners is a complex problem. Frida, who has had relatively little prison experience, told us about a particularly traumatic experience she witnessed and reflected on the possible causes of depression and self-harm among women who have been institutionalized at a very early age:

> I have a friend, she's on medication, she's been in the institution, in the CDC [California Department of Corrections] since she was thirteen years old. She has problems with cutting herself, and hurting herself. About six months ago

she told the police [correctional officers] and they let her go in her room, and when they came back to her room she was sitting in the bathroom with her arm cut. She had said that she needed to talk to the doctor, like she's going to ... she was feeling like she was getting to that point. And they thought well whatever, and put her in her room. And then they had to come back to a pool of blood and a big gash, you know because she didn't only just slice her arm, but she cut it to where there was a big hole.

Marina, also a relative new comer to prison, referred to the depersonalization of the prison experience as depressing:

And then you don't have your clothes; you don't have your make-up; you don't have anything; so you ... you know, you're just, you don't care about yourself, you know? I mean, I take a bath; well over there in SCU [the receiving center] all you have is showers, but I really didn't care how I looked. Why? My family wasn't here; why should I care?

While these feelings may be common among many prisoners, as we have seen, they seem to be particularly acute for women who choose to isolate themselves from the other prisoners. As Stacey, who is doing a life sentence at VSPW, characterized prison life:

In my opinion, prison just does something to you. It's emotionally abusive. It's hard to describe. You know, it like when you have a problem or just need to talk to someone for advice, there's nobody you can go to. You can't talk to a c.o. [correctional officer] because a c.o.'s going to talk to another c.o. You can't talk to a psychologist, unless of course you can put that kind of trust in them, you know, because you never know where they're taking it. You can't talk to another inmate, because then everybody's going to know about it. I mean one thing somebody told me one time that before they ever say anything to anybody, they decide if they want everybody to know or not. And if they don't want everybody to know, they don't tell anyone ... you have to be your own best friend because there's really nobody you can trust. The isolation is hard. That's um, something that just nags at you, you know? And you have all these thoughts going through your mind. You have no inside advice; you have no second opinion; you have no one to help you to look at it in a different light. So you're really only seeing things from your perspective, and you're not getting any insight on it. So it's ... it's harder to make decisions. It's harder to come to terms with it because there's nobody who can understand you, but you. And you're not even understanding yourself at the time, you know? It's not until later that you might be able to look back and reflect on it. But that's only if you're lucky, you know? And to me, I think it's amazing that more people haven't gone crazy.

The data in Table 6-6 also suggest that, irrespective of personal attributes and previous life experiences, mental health problems may be more likely to occur at VSPW than at CIW. Considering not only the differences we have described in these two facilities but also women's subjective comparisons of the two prisons, we should not be surprised women at VSPW report being more worried about their emotional state than women at CIW. Toni, who has three prior prison commitments, describes doing time at VSPW in the following way: "It sucks; it's hard. It's mentally draining to the person. A lot of the staff is really degrading to the inmates. They have no conception of treating a person like a human being, regardless of individuality." Wilma, who had previously done time at CIW but was now housed at VSPW, provides an equally negative picture of prison life:

> Doing time here is like runnin' a concentration camp because the way they treat you, and the way they talk to you is... they act... treat you like you're children. And if you have a problem – like your mother dies, or your husband dies, those are close-knit family members. You aren't allowed to go to their funeral, even if you have never been a high security risk. And at CIW, they've always allowed you to go to the funeral, you know.

Contrary to Wilma's remarks, decisions regarding whether a prisoner can leave for a family member's funeral are based on security risk, number of prior leaves, and sentence. Nevertheless, what is interesting about her comments are her perceptions that VSPW has a more restrictive environment than CIW.

In summary, extending our view of how women respond to prison life, we find that their styles of doing time are associated with specific behaviors and emotional reactions independent of their carceral settings. Women who choose a Convict style of doing time and, to a lesser extent, those who choose an Adapted style report engaging in more misbehavior than those in the Isolate class; women in the Adapted class report significantly fewer emotional problems than those in the Isolate class. Further, our ability to predict emotional problems with personal attributes and prison terms is generally more limited than is the case of misbehavior. Women's emotional reactions to prison are shaped primarily by their prior mental health history, their age and prison sentence and to a lesser extent the prison in which they are serving time.

Evaluating Women's Responses to Prison

Roughly forty years ago, the introduction of gender into studies of how prisoners do time produced not just a different reading of the functional model of prison adaptation but also a relatively universal picture of the female prison experience. Today, contemporary work on women's imprisonment has somewhat altered this picture with new interpretations of women's prison lives that highlight the relevance of their subjective experiences and active resistance but leave open the question of how different penal regimes shape these experiences. In an era when these regimes are being transformed and repackaged, some containing elements that are more consistent with older rehabilitative philosophies and others containing hallmarks of the new punitiveness, we sought to determine whether these transformations are both reflected in and a determining facet of how women experience prison life. By so doing, we found that women respond to prison life in very predictable ways: by accommodation as in the Adapted style, by refusing to accommodate to prison authority as in the Convict style, and by seclusion as in the Isolate style. And, while these three responses transcend specific prison environments, the particulars of these environments determine how women will be arrayed among them. It is at CIW, an institution that retains much of the rehabilitative temperament of past, that we find a greater proportion of the women effectively managing the contradictions and tensions of the prison world and relatively fewer women openly rejecting the conditions and symbols of their confinement.

Our analyses also drew attention to sets of behaviors and emotional responses that in more recent prison research are considered important indicators of coping and adjustment. Targeting and classifying prisoners who are perceived to be troublemakers or emotionally vulnerable facilitates more effective prison administration. However, we think these behaviors and emotional responses tell a different story about the effects of specific carceral settings on women's lives and perhaps beyond. As Goffman (1961: 123) suggested in his classic essay on total institutions, one of the most interesting differences among these institutions is "the fate of their graduates." While we have no way of directly addressing this issue, our findings certainly have implications for these women's postprison lives.

There are two perspectives on the effects of prisoner misbehavior for postrelease adjustment (Adams 1992: 338–339). Some have argued that active resistance to prison authority makes for better adjustment upon release because such behavior demonstrates the independence and autonomy needed for life outside of the prison (Kassebaum, Ward, and Wilner 1971; Miller and Dinitz 1973; Goodstein 1979). Others, however, have argued that such rebellious behavior predicts recidivism (Gottfredson and Adams 1982). While we will not know the fates of these women prisoners, we do know that the women who choose what we call an Adapted approach to incarceration and the active resisters of the Convict style, engage in more misbehavior than those who choose an Isolate style. And, at least in the case of those choosing an Adapted style there were significantly fewer mental health problems than among those choosing an Isolate style. There is ample evidence of continuity in mental health problems from prison to community settings (Feder 1989) and, as our quantitative data showed, from community settings to prison. But, perhaps what is of more central concern is our finding that, independent of a woman's mental health history, the prison itself can have an impact on the emotional well-being of its charges. While depersonalization and loss of liberty are characteristic of virtually all prisons, the new wave of prisons that has emerged in what some refer to as the era of hyperincarceration may be exacerbating these problems.

Of course, all of this suggests the importance of taking account of multiple perspectives on women's responses to incarceration. To focus only on acts of resistance – a constant feature of prison life that seems to be unrelated to specific prison contexts – can obscure the importance of how changes over time and across institutions alter prisoners' general responses, and emotional reactions, to their environments (cf., e.g., Bosworth 1999). In the next, and final, chapter, we examine this issue in the context of current scholarly research and discourse on the "get tough" or "penal harm" movement.

Conclusion: The Spectrum of Women Prisoners' Experiences

IN THE FALL OF 1998, shortly after we completed our field research, Amnesty International singled Valley State Prison for Women (VSPW) out for a visit during its investigation of human rights violations in women's prisons. A year later, thousands of television viewers were introduced to VSPW through American Broadcasting Company's (ABC) six-part *Nightline* series on women in prison. As part of that series, Ted Koppel interviewed the prison's chief medical officer, Dr. Anthony DiDomenico, who commented that prisoners at VSPW liked having pelvic exams because "it's the only male contact they have." When DiDomenico was relieved of his duties shortly after the interview, VSPW's fame spread even further as newspapers across the United States and Canada picked up the story.[1] The image conveyed by this publicity was of a massive, overcrowded and underresourced institution where sexual abuse and medical maltreatment of prisoners were commonplace. But while that image might grab public attention and describe some aspects of prison life at VSPW, it simplifies a much more complex picture. The experience of imprisonment at VSPW, the epitome of the neoliberal era prison, also incorporates elements of other penal regimes and political eras. The "intertwining of established and emergent structures" (Garland 2001: 168) of imprisonment can be seen in the continuing abuse and neglect of women prisoners and in the recent and dramatic increase in the numbers of women subject to long periods of carceral control. VSPW is, then, an ongoing and unfinished project just as the California Institution for Women (CIW) is.

---

[1] For excerpts from Dr. Anthony DiDomenico's interview with Ted Koppel, see Jon Barlow, "Crime and Punishment: Women in Prison," ABCNEWS.com: *Nightline*: Women in Prison, October 29, 1999. A news item on DiDomenico's dismissal appeared in dozens of U.S. newspapers and in at least one Canadian newspaper. See "Doctor reassigned after TV interview," *The Globe and Mail*, October 16, 1999, p. A18.

Ours is a story that speaks to the gap in prison sociology between analyses of macrolevel trends in the contexts of state punishment and microlevel studies of those who live out that punishment on a day-to-day basis (Sparks et al. 1996). To address this omission, we have tried to depict women's carceral experiences across two different penal eras and two different prison contexts in California. We found that the changes in penal ideologies, rationales, and practices described in recent prison scholarship translated into changes in the experiences of female prisoners, how they are treated, and the explicit and implicit messages about who they were. As prison administrators and staff increasingly shifted their focus to managing ever larger female prison populations with shrinking resources, the expectations they held for these prisoners diminished. Staff foresaw recidivism not rehabilitation upon prisoners' release, as the women repeatedly noted to us. Unlike the past, then, these carceral warehouses hold out little hope for their charges but instead function primarily as long-term shelters. The temporal changes in the administration and staff's view of female prisoners were matched by changes in the ways in which the women themselves related to their colleagues and staff. Although female prisoners have always been distrustful of one another, in the punitive era of the 1990s, this attitude seemed to have crystallized. More than ever, women limited their associations and friendships with other prisoners and distanced themselves from correctional staff, especially at VSPW, an institution largely viewed by its inhabitants as only a place to punish women.

We also found that the prison context had a substantial bearing on how women chose to do their time. It was in the most punitive environment, an environment that captured some of the essential features of the new penology, where women prisoners were least likely to approach their confinement in what we have called an adapted, as opposed to an isolated, manner and where they were more likely to report emotional distress. Overcrowding, the lack of meaningful programs, and the oppressive regimentation of life at VSPW may all contribute to these outcomes but so also did the staff's treatment of the prisoners. Women at both CIW and VSPW complained about their interactions with staff but, as we have noted, the women at VSPW were far more outspoken about what they saw as arbitrary restrictions, inhumane treatment, and abuse from staff. While most women enter prison with a long history of disadvantages, often including histories of both abuse and mental illness (Kruttschnitt and Gartner 2003), particularly punitive penal environments may turn such disadvantages into more acute problems and ones that serve to increase the risk of both self-harm and, ultimately, reoffending.

Despite the ways in which VSPW's regime departed from traditionally gendered modes of female imprisonment, the fundamental experiences of women housed there would be familiar to women at CIW in both the 1960s and the 1990s. Assumptions about criminal women changed little over time and place, even as occasional attempts were made by the media and politicians to reinvent their images as more violent or drug-crazed. But the women, and increasingly men, who worked with these prisoners generally did not see them as particularly dangerous but instead as emotionally needy, inadequate, and criminally immature. Administrators and staff depicted women's crimes not as a product of their own doing but as a reflection of bad choices they have made about partners and, often, their susceptibility to drug addiction. Volition, a key element in the rationale of the new "culture of crime control" (Garland 2001), is missing, as it always has been, for female offenders.

Although this new culture of crime control formulated a different set of standards for evaluating and controlling prisoners' behaviors, the prisoners themselves faced many of the same types of contradictions and challenges. During the rehabilitative period, which emphasized the malleable nature of human thought and behavior, women prisoners were told to open up, disclose problems, and embrace the potential of treatment and getting well. Yet, as these women acknowledged, failing to partake in the rhetoric of disclosure would earn them the ire of staff while fully accepting it could undermine their chances for release. This paradox of imprisonment did not disappear with the demise of rehabilitation. It reappeared in the form of responsibilization in the punitive era. Administrators, staff, and prisoners all readily acknowledged that if a prisoner wanted to be rehabilitated it was up to her. But as the women were quick to point out to us, while readily acknowledging their problems with drugs and alcohol, education and employment, there were few if any resources available to help them with such an endeavor.[2]

Other very visible signs of continuity in female prisoners' experiences across time and place can be found in the overall lack of violence and racial animosity women exhibited toward their fellow prisoners, and the prevalence of drug use and sexual relationships among prisoners. Sexual relationships have been a long-standing focus of scholarly work on female prisoners and today these relationships are being recast by some scholars as a sign of women's agency, signaling resistance, or one way in which women manage prison time. Our assessment of women's styles of doing time was more broadly conceived and designed to capture both their attitudes and actions toward other prisoners, the correctional staff, and the prison regime itself. Taking this approach, we found some important similarities in how women respond to prison that transcended the two prison contexts where we carried out our research and that characterize women's carceral experiences

---

[2] If the success of rehabilitative endeavors depend upon individual receptivity to change (see e.g., Baskin and Sommers 1998; Maruna 2001), it would appear that the demise of these endeavors have surely been ill-timed.

in other times and places. Ward and Kassebaum (1965), although primarily focusing on women's sexual relationships in prison, also noted that they employed several modes of adaptation that varied with the stage of their institutional career. Withdrawal, colonization (or cooperation), and rebellion were three responses identified as central types of adaptation in the early sociology of imprisonment – the deprivation/importation research (Matthews 1999: 55) – and they have reappeared to various degrees in contemporary studies of women prisoners (e.g., Eaton 1993; Owen 1998; Bosworth 1999), including this one.

Our ability to identify elements of both change and continuity in the prison experience was a consequence of our effort to bridge the gap between macrotheoretical prison scholarship and microstudies of the prison environment. We see the former as indispensable to the latter as it illuminates how political shifts in punishment become a lived reality. But the rays cast by research on prison life will be sufficiently enlightening only to the extent that women's prison experiences are considered. As others have noted, the general longstanding neglect of gender in studies of macrochanges in penality has meant that our understanding of contemporary penal life has been incomplete (Howe 1994).

Although female prisoners are still a relatively small proportion of the U.S. prison population, they may have been disproportionately affected by the political changes that have culminated in this new era of punitiveness. The passage of the Uniform Determinate Sentencing Act in California increased women's likelihood of going to prison; once there, it increased their likelihood of staying. Unlike the indeterminate sentencing system that was "offender-based," determinate sentencing is explicitly "offense-based" (Zimring et al. 2001: 114). The character of the individual and her situation are seen as irrelevant to the sentencing process, and the only factor deemed important in the sentencing decision is what the offender has done. If judges were inclined to take family responsibilities or an offender's role in a given offense into account when deciding sentence length under the indeterminate system, the move to determinate sentencing has surely diminished such discretion. For female offenders, who are more likely than male offenders to have dependent children living with them, the effect of eliminating childcare responsibilities as a mitigating circumstance in sentencing decisions reduces the odds that judges will consider alternatives to incarceration for them (Daly 1995; Raeder 1995; Hagan and Dinovitzer 1999). Determinate sentencing has also affected sentenced offenders' ability to secure earlier release dates. Good time credits can be removed for misconduct, a particular vulnerability for female prisoners who are often viewed as more troublesome than male prisoners (McClellan 1994; Britton 2003). The subsequent introduction of mandatory prison sentences for certain drug crimes in the 1980s contributed further to the growth in the numbers of women being sent to prison, as women's arrests for drug law violations increased dramatically over most of the 1980s. Finally, other mandatory minimum sentencing legislation passed in California since the 1980s also increased the odds that women would be spending time behind bars, as the legislation targeted less serious offenses, the crimes in which women are disproportionately likely to be involved.

These changes in criminal justice policy over the last forty years have resulted in enormous growth in the female prison population, but not a total transformation of the prison experience for women as much as a reconfiguration of it. This finding no doubt reflects the ways in which women's imprisonment has generated its own discourses and, at least until recently, its own techniques of punishment. But it also reflects the fact that prisons, while fundamentally all about punishment and deprivation, about manipulating the interrelationships of time, place, and self in highly controlled environments, do so to different degrees in different contexts. As Sparks and his colleagues (1996: 301) so aptly put it:

> Even within one system at one time there are variable as well as constant features in the ways that order in prisons is conceived of and achieved. Thus, the continual tendency in prison studies to seek to show that there exists some essential irreducible ideal type of The Prison is almost certainly misleading . . . It is more productive and more sociologically sensitive to think of a spectrum of possible ordering relations of which "actually existing prisons" in any given society accentuate certain features.

Our consideration of the relations existing in two women's prisons was based on what we perceived to be the contingent relationship between macrochanges in penal policy, practice, and discourse and the lived experience of imprisonment. For the women we studied that experience reflected the interplay of historical context, the gendered character of punishment, and more. The moments of the rehabilitative and neoliberal eras of punishment we have captured suggest that while timeworn practices of punishment have changed, the prevailing relations of power and contradictions of discourse and practice that shape the meaning of women prisoners' lives have not.

Characteristics of Interviewees

To protect the anonymity of the interviewees, we have assigned a pseudonym to each woman and provided only limited information about each of them. For some of the women interviewed by Ward and Kassebaum, very little personal information was available.

Women Interviewed by Ward and Kassebaum at CIW in the early 1960s

April had been at CIW for three weeks after spending two months in jail. She was serving a twenty-year sentence for manslaughter; she stabbed a man, probably her boyfriend or husband, to death. Before this commitment, she had served jail time on drunk and disorderly charges. The interviewer notes she had lived "under authority" in a state mental hospital.

Barbara was an eighteen-year-old who had been transferred to CIW from a youth facility because she was "unmanageable" and had escaped once. Although she admits to having committed a number of felonies, she did not have a felony conviction. The interviewer notes that Barbara had been in and out of jail and girls' schools for seven years. She was interviewed after only one week at CIW.

Corinne had served one year at CIW on a conviction for grand theft and forgery. A representative on the inmate council, she had been a truck driver before coming to prison. Corinne, white, was twenty-seven years old, and had children. She had dropped out of high school before finishing tenth grade.

Doris was a regular user of marijuana and pills on the outside, which got her into trouble with the law. She had been in prison before, and her criminal

163

record included three prior felony convictions. She told the interviewer that she had attempted suicide twice before when she was not in prison, the most recent attempt five years ago. Raped at age sixteen by her mother's boyfriend, she had been married once, but only for a week. She referred to herself as bisexual. She was interviewed a second time after she returned to prison on parole violation.

Edith was serving time on either a drug or prostitution charge. She described herself as a "lush" and "hype," but denied any involvement in prostitution.

Faye had worked as a secretary, "figure model," and prostitute on the outside to support her heroin habit. She had previously done time at CIW and in several jails and reform schools. A white woman, Faye was divorced with one child, who had been adopted by her cousin when she went to prison.

Ginger worked in the sex trade. We have very little other information on her except that she is white.

Helen worked in the sex trade. We have very little other information on her except that she is black.

Irene was serving her third commitment at CIW. As a teenager, she had been sent to a reform school and subsequently served time at CIW when it was located at Tehachapi. She was divorced and referred to herself as a "true homosexual."

Joanne was serving two years for the sale of marijuana. She had previously served a few months in federal prison. A white woman in her early twenties, she was married to a man who was also in prison.

Kay was serving five years for drug sales. She had separated from her husband after coming to prison.

Lana had worked in burlesque as a "muscular control dancer" and as a stripper. She had been married twice, the second time to a gay man for what she called "business purposes"; she lived with a female partner during her second marriage. Lana, a white woman, was in her late twenties or early thirties.

Madeleine had served three years at CIW for a drug offense. She had previously served time in federal prison. A white woman in her thirties, she was described by the interviewer as "a hard-looking girl."

Nora was serving a six month to fourteen year sentence on a forgery conviction, which she said resulted from her drug problem. This was her first time in prison. A vocational nurse, she was forty-seven years old and had children.

Olive was in prison for the first time on a robbery conviction. She committed the robbery with her husband, to whom she was "happily married." She explained her role in the robbery this way: "I just stood there."

Patty a white woman, was probably serving time for a drug offense.

Queenie was at CIW for violating her parole. She was thiry-five, had three children, and was divorced. The interviewer described her as "extremely masculine in appearance."

Rhonda, a white woman, had worked as a cocktail waitress, model, and prostitute before prison. She was due to be released in a few weeks. She had given birth to eight children in eight years (four of whom had died at birth) by six different men. Two of the children were in foster care and two had been adopted by her parents.

Sandy was a member of the inmate council.

Teresa was at CIW for violating parole. She had previously served fourteen months for possession of narcotics. She also had been in jail several times before coming to CIW.

Ursula was serving time for check fraud. At age eight, her father had tried to molest her; at age fourteen, she was sent to a convent/reformatory. She was divorced.

Vicky had served at least ten months for either a drug offense or prostitution. This was her first time in prison. She reported having been raped by her father when she was a child and described herself as a heroin addict.

Wanda was divorced with one child. She had served several months on an indeterminate sentence of up to fifteen years.

Xena has a release date coming up soon. She revealed little about herself during the interview.

Yvonne, a white women, had served four months of a five year to life sentence for armed robbery. As a teenager, she had spent time in a youth facility.

Zoe had served over a year at CIW. On the outside, she'd worked as a prostitute. She was once married for ten years, but was currently divorced.

Women Interviewed by Kruttschnitt and Gartner at CIW

Nancy, a white woman, was in her fifties and had served eighteen years of a life sentence. This was her first time in prison. She described herself as an incest survivor, an alcoholic, and, pill user.

Tara had served two years at CIW for check fraud and was due to be released in three months. This was her first time in prison. Tara, a thirty-eight-year-old white woman, had worked as an accountant before coming to prison. She had one child and was in the process of divorcing her husband.

Heidi had served four months for possession of methamphetamines and had another five months left to serve. It was her second time in prison. Heidi, a white woman, and the single mother of two children was in her late twenties or early thirties.

Debbie had served about four months for sale of methamphetamines and had about six months left to serve. It was her first felony commitment. Debbie, a white woman, was thirty, unmarried, and pregnant with her fourth child. She reported having been physically abused by some of her male partners.

Katherine was in prison for the third time and had served two years of a three to four year sentence. Her first prison term was for robbery, but the last two terms were for drug offenses. She was forty-five and had lived on the streets before coming to prison.

Carol had served thirteen years on a life sentence for killing her husband, whom she said had abused her. It was her first time in prison. Carol, a black woman, was in her early fifties and had three children.

Georgia had served twelve years at CIW for second degree murder of a woman. Part Native American and part Hispanic, she was in her thirties, and described herself as having an alcohol problem.

Tina had served eight years on a sentence of life without parole. It was her first time in prison. She, a Hispanic, was forty years old and had two children and two step-children. She said she had been abused by her former husband.

Neva had served twelve years of a life sentence for the second degree murder of a female friend in a drug dispute. This was her first time in prison. Neva, an African American, was in her late thirties or early forties. She was not married and had no children.

Maureen had served six months at CIW and had six months left to serve on a conviction for theft. She had served two years at CIW many years ago for shoplifting and had done federal time for counterfeiting. A sixty-two year-old African American, she had two living children and was married.

Marcy had served sixteen years at CIW on a twenty-five to life sentence for a crime she had committed with her husband, whom she had since divorced. Marcy, Puerto Rican and in her early forties, revealed that she had been molested by an uncle when she was a child.

Deedee had served about four months of a two-year sentence for armed robbery. She had done time at CIW years ago for drug sales and had served considerable jail time. Deedee, a white woman in her late thirties, had three children and was a self-described drug addict.

Maxine had served ten years on a fifteen to life sentence for murder. A white woman in her late forties, she was a self-described drug addict. She divorced her husband when she went to prison and arranged to have her children move out of the state.

Elizabeth had done four months on a two-year sentence for burglary. She described herself as having a cocaine habit and as having sold sex for drugs. Elizabeth, African American and in her early twenties, was married with two children. This was her first time in prison.

Belinda had served nine months for a residential burglary conviction, the last six of these at CIW. She expected to be released in five months. This was her first time in prison. She admits to having a cocaine habit. Belinda, a Hispanic woman in her late twenties, had one child.

Stella had served three months for selling marijuana out of her home. This was her first time in prison. Stella, Hispanic, was in her late forties or early fifties and had thirteen children.

Ellen had served about two years of a three-year sentence for armed robbery. This was her first time in prison. White, in her late twenties or early thirties, Ellen was separated from her husband and had two children. She had worked in construction before coming to prison.

Hilary had served nine years on a twenty-five to life sentence. This was her first time in prison. Mixed race (white and Hispanic), she was in her mid-forties and had not married or had children.

Bonnie had served three months for a drug-related crime and expected to be released in six more months. This was her first time in prison. She told us that she has a serious drug problem. Bonnie, white, in her late twenties, had one child.

Carla had served seven months on a three-year sentence for selling drugs to an undercover cop. This was her first time in prison. She is Hispanic and/or white and in her late twenties.

Margaret had eight previous commitments to prison and had served sixteen years in total at CIW and CCWF. On this commitment, she had served about six months on a two-year sentence. A self-described thief and heroin addict, she had been married for over thirty years and had many grandchildren.

Anne had served about six months for drug and weapons possession. This was her first time in prison, but her second drug conviction. She had given birth right after she got to CIW. White and in her late twenties, Anne was divorced and had four children.

Beverly had served fifteen years of a twenty-five to life sentence for armed robbery and murder. This was her first time in prison although she said she had worked as a prostitute to supply her drug habit for a few years. Beverly, Puerto Rican and in her late thirties, was married and had two children.

Brenda was about to be released after serving six months for violating probation. While she had often been in jail, this was her first time in prison. A white woman in her early sixties, Brenda had been living in her car before coming to prison. She was divorced and had five children and some grandchildren.

Alice had served over twenty years on a life sentence. This was her first time in prison. Alice, white, was in her mid-forties and married.

Julia had served over three years on a twenty-five to life sentence for murder. This was her first time in prison. White and in her fifties, Julia was college educated, had been married three times, and had two children.

Andrea had served about five months for violating probation, three of those at CIW, and had about five more months to serve. She was in prison for the first time on a drug conviction. Prior to coming to prison she had worked as a prostitute to support a drug habit. White, thirty-two, and with two children, Andrea had some college education.

Marina had served about six months of a two year sentence for embezzlement. This was her first time in prison. Married with four children and one grandchild, Marina, a Hispanic woman, was in her late forties or early fifties.

Pauleen had served six years of a seventeen-year sentence for residential burglary. She had served two previous prison terms, which she attributes to her drug habit. Hispanic, she was in her late thirties and was neither married nor had any children.

Charlotte had served seven years of a fifteen to life sentence for murder. She had never been in trouble with the law before this. White and in her late fifties or early sixties, she had three children and four grandchildren.

Margo had served over twenty years on a life sentence for murder. She had never been in prison or jail before. White and in her late forties, she was not married nor did she have any children.

Nina was serving time for petty theft with priors and had been at CIW for about seven months. She had previously spent four years at the California

Rehabilitation Center because of a drug habit. Native American, she was in her late thirties and divorced.

Eva had served over fifteen years at CIW on a fifteen to life sentence for robbery/murder. She had served time before this and claimed drug abuse was behind her criminal behavior. Eva, Native American, was forty-two years old.

Helenora had served ten years at CIW on a life sentence for murder. Hispanic, she was in her late forties and had two children.

Penny had served about two years at CIW for petty theft and had been given a third strike. She had done two other prison terms, one on a robbery conviction. Penny attributed her crimes to her history of drug abuse. Penny, Hispanic, was in her mid-forties.

Women Interviewed by Kruttschnitt and Gartner at VSPW

Darlene had been transferred to VSPW after serving five years at CIW on a property crime conviction. A Hispanic woman in her early thirties, she had been at VSPW for seven months when we interviewed her.

Christine had served over twenty years at CIW on a life sentence for murder before being transferred to VSPW. She was in her mid-forties and had been at VSPW for sixteen months. This was her first time in prison.

Sally had served two years at VSPW on a life sentence. In prison for the first time, she was about nineteen years old and white.

Toni had served three months at VSPW for a property crime conviction. Her third time in prison, she had also been at CIW and CCWF. Toni, white and in her late twenties, was divorced with two children.

Mandy was transferred to VSPW after serving ten months on a drug charge at CCWF. She had been at VSPW for two months. This was her third time in prison. She had lived on the streets and worked as a prostitute since age fourteen. Mandy, white, was thirty-two and divorced.

Colleen had served three years on a drug charge at CIW before being transferred to VSPW three months earlier. She had a year left to serve. Colleen, a thirty-eight-year-old African American, related a history of child sexual abuse.

Clair had served fifteen months at VSPW on a four-year sentence for a violent crime. This was the first time she had been in prison. Clair, Hispanic, was thirty-three years old.

Angela was sent to VSPW for violating the conditions of her probation and had been there for five months. She had been convicted of a property crime and this was her first time in prison. Angela, a white woman, was thirty-one years old.

Evelyn had been at VSPW for ten months after spending two months at CIW and CCWF. She would not discuss her crime. In her mid-thirties, white, and college educated, this was the first time she had been in prison.

Jackie spent five months at CIW for violating her probation on a property crime conviction before being transferred to VSPW, where she had spent the last four months. This was the first time in prison for Jackie, an African American, who was in her late-twenties and married with children.

Dina had served about a year at VSPW for violating probation on a property crime conviction. A white woman, she was in her late-twenties and in prison for the first time.

Janeen had served six months at VSPW for violating probation on a drug conviction and expected to be released in two months. This was her first time in prison. Janeen, African American, was thirty-two years old, had one child and was pregnant with her second.

Dana had been convicted of a property crime and had served five months at VSPW. A white woman, she was twenty-five years old and in prison for the first time.

Jill had served over twelve years on a life sentence at CIW, CCWF, and, finally, VSPW, where she had been for a few months. She had never been in prison before this. She was in her mid-forties and white.

Nicole was convicted of manslaughter and given a fourteen-year sentence. She had served almost two years at CIW before being transferred to VSPW. This was the first time in prison for Nicole, a Hispanic woman in her late thirties with five children.

Ivy had served five months of a two year sentence (for manufacturing amphetamines) at CIW before being transferred to VSPW, where she had been for about six months. Ivy, a white woman in her late thirties, had children.

Dawn was in prison for the fourth time and had served two months at CCWF before being transferred to VSPW fourteen months previously. A thirty-seven-year-old African American, she had convictions for robbery and petty theft.

Marva had served three months at VSPW on a four-year sentence for "manufacturing" and for an undisclosed crime. Marva, an African American, was thirty-five years old and had three children.

Wilma had served seven months at VSPW for a conviction on a drug offense. She had previously done time at CIW on a lengthy sentence in the 1970s and 1980s. Wilma, an African American, was forty-seven and had three children.

Miriam had served about twenty years on a seven to life sentence for murder at CCWF and CIW before being transferred to VSPW. The thirty-eight year old had not been in prison before this term.

Renee had served almost three years of an eighteen-to-life sentence for murder. A white woman in her mid-thirties, Renee had no children and had never been in prison before.

Rosa was in prison for the first time and had served four months at VSPW on a drug charge. The thirty-one-year-old mother of two, who is Hispanic, said she had never used drugs.

Mona had served eight months at VSPW on a five-year sentence for attempted murder. This was the first time the nineteen-year-old Hispanic woman had been in prison.

Jocelyn was a thirty-nine-year-old African American woman in prison for the first time. She had served five months at VSPW for possession and sale of drugs. Jocelyn was married and had children and grandchildren.

Kelly, thirty-six, had been at CIW and CCWF before being transferred to VSPW nine months earlier. She was given a two-year sentence for a property crime conviction.

Sarah had served about a year at VSPW and expected to be released in a few weeks. This was her second time in prison: In the 1980s she had done time at CIW. Sarah, white, was in her mid-thirties.

Natasha had been transferred from a youth facility, where she'd been for seven years, to VSPW about a year before the interview. The twenty-five-year-old African American was serving a ten-year sentence for a violent crime.

Stacey, a nineteen-year-old white woman, was in prison for the first time on a life sentence for murder. She had lived on her own since she was fifteen and had never had a problem with drugs.

Tamara had been in and out of prison since the early 1980s and had served nine months of a life sentence at VSPW. Hispanic and a self-described drug addict, she was in her mid-forties.

Frida had served one year of a fifteen-year sentence at VSPW for an undisclosed offense. This was her first time in prison. She was divorced and had one child.

Hanah had served seven months for possession of cocaine and expected to serve another ten months before her release. Although she was a self-described "gang banger" and had two strikes, she had never been in prison before. Hanah, Hispanic, was thirty-one years old.

Tanya, twenty-seven, was convicted for robbery and had served about two years at VSPW. This was the third time she had been in prison. She described herself as having a drug problem.

Roberta had served six months at VSPW on a two-year sentence for driving while intoxicated with bodily injury. This was the first time in prison for this sixty-five-year-old white woman who was divorced with two children.

Lindsey had spent ten years in prison on three different convictions. She had been at VSPW for eighteen months on a drug conviction when we interviewed her. Lindsey, African American, was forty-four years old.

Diana had been at VSPW for four months for violating parole and gave birth just after her arrival. She had been convicted of a property crime and was in prison for the first time. A thirty-eight-year-old African American, she was married and had children.

Donna was serving a life sentence for manslaughter. She had been at CIW for fourteen years before being transferred to VSPW a few months earlier. She was a self-described "career criminal" having had several criminal convictions beginning when she was a teenager. Donna, a forty-seven-year-old white woman, was divorced and had one child.

Delia was doing her fifth term in prison, this time for three parole violations. She had received a four-year sentence for petty theft and her second strike. Delia was in her late thirties, described herself as mixed race, had four children, and had a drug problem.

Stephanie, a thirty-something African American woman, had served almost two years at VSPW on her second commitment to prison. She had previously done time at CCWF and CIW.

References

Abramsky, Sasha. 2002. *Hard Time Blues*. New York: St. Martin's Press.

Adler, Michael and Brian Longhurst. 1994. *Discourse, Power, and Justice: Toward a New Sociology of Imprisonment*. London: Routledge.

Adams, Kenneth. 1992. Adjusting to Prison Life. In *Crime and Justice: An Annual Review of Research*, vol. 16, edited by Norval Morris and Michael Tonry. Chicago: University of Chicago Press.

Adams, R., D. Onek and A. Riker. 1998. *Double Jeopardy: An Assessment of the Felony Drug Provision of the Welfare Reform Act*. Washington D.C.: Justice Policy Institute.

Alarid, Leanne Fital. 1997. Female Inmate Subcultures. In *Contemporary and Classical Readings*, edited by James W. Marquart and J.R. Sorensen. Los Angeles: Roxbury.

Alpert, Geoffrey P., George Noblit, and John J. Wiorkowski. 1977. A Comparative Look at Prisonization: Sex and Prison Culture. *Quarterly Journal of Corrections* 1: 29–34.

Austin, James and John Irwin. 2001. *It's About Time: America's Imprisonment Binge*. Belmont, Calif.: Wadsworth.

Austin, James, John Irwin, and Charis E. Kubrin. 2003. It's About Time: America's Imprisonment Binge. In *Punishment and Social Control*, 2nd ed., edited by Thomas Blomberg and Stanley Cohen. New York: Aldine de Gruyter.

Baldassare, Mark. 2000. *California in the New Millennium: The Changing Social and Political Landscape*. Berkeley: University of California Press.

Baskin, Deborah R. and Ira B. Sommers. 1998. *Casualties of Community Disorder: Women's Careers in Violent Crime*. Boulder, Colo.: Westview.

Beckett, Katherine. 1997. *Making Crime Pay: Law and Order in Contemporary American Politics*. New York: Oxford University Press.

Bedrick, Brooke G. 1993. "The Retreat from Justice in the Women's Campaign for California's First Women's Prison, 1912 to 1936." Master's thesis, Columbia University.

Berk, Bernard. 1966. Organizational Goals and Inmate Organization. *American Journal of Sociology* 71: 522–34.

Berk, Richard, Harold Brackman, and Selma Lesser. 1977. *A Measure of Justice: An Empirical Study of the Changes in the California Penal Code, 1955–1971.* New York: Academic Press.

Biles, David. 1981. *Criminal Justice Research in California.* Canberra: Australian Institute of Criminology.

Blomberg, Thomas G. and Stanley Cohen. 2003. Introduction to Part I. In *Punishment and Social Control,* edited by Thomas G. Blomberg and Stanley Cohen. New York: Aldine de Gruyter.

Bloom, Barbara, Meda Chesney-Lind, and Barbara Owen. 1994. *Women in California Prisons: Hidden Victims of the War on Drugs.* San Francisco: Center on Juvenile and Criminal Justice.

Bondeson, Ulla V. 1989. *Prisoners in Prison Societies.* New Brunswick, N.J.: Transaction.

Bookspan, Shelley. 1991. *A Germ of Goodness: The California Prison System, 1851–1944.* Lincoln, Nebr.: University of Nebraska Press.

Boothby, Jennifer L. and Thomas W. Durham. 1999. Screening for Depression in Prisoners Using the Beck Depression Inventory. *Criminal Justice and Behavior* 26: 107–24.

Bosworth, Mary. 1996. Resistance and Compliance in Women's Prisons: Towards a Critique of Legitimacy. *Critical Criminology* 7: 5–19.

Bosworth, Mary. 1999. *Engendering Resistance: Agency and Power in Women's Prisons.* Brookfield, Vt.: Ashgate Dartmouth.

Bosworth, Mary. 2000. Confining Femininity: A History of Gender, Power, and Imprisonment. *Theoretical Criminology* 4: 265–84.

Bottoms, Anthony E. 1977. Reflections on the Renaissance of Dangerousness. *Howard Journal* 16: 70–6.

Bottoms, Anthony E. 1983. Neglected Features of Contemporary Penal Systems. In *The Power to Punish,* edited by David Garland and P. Young. London: Heinemann.

Bottoms, Anthony E. 1995. The Philosophy and Politics of Imprisonment and Sentencing. In *The Politics of Sentencing Reform,* edited by C. Clarkson and R. Morgan. Oxford: Clarendon.

Bottoms, Anthony E. 1999. Interpersonal Violence and Social Order in Prisons. In *Prisons,* edited by Michael Tonry and Joan Petersilia. Vol. 26 of *Crime and Justice: A Review of Research,* edited by Michael Tonry and Norval Morris. Chicago: University of Chicago Press.

Britton, Dana M. 2003. *At Work in the Iron Cage: The Prison as Gendered Organization.* New York: New York University Press.

Bukstel, L. and P. Kilmann. 1980. Psychological Effects of Imprisonment on Confined Individuals. *Psychological Bulletin* 88: 469–93.

Bureau of Justice Statistics. 1997. *Prisoners in 1996.* NCJ-164619. Washington, D.C.: U.S. Department of Justice, Bureau of Justice Statistics.

Bureau of Justice Statistics. 2000. *Correctional Populations in the United States, 1997.* NCJ-177613. Washington D.C.: U.S. Department of Justice, Bureau of Justice Statistics.

Bureau of Justice Statistics. 2001. *Medical Problems of Inmates, 1997.* NCJ-181644. Washington, D.C.: U.S. Department of Justice, Bureau of Justice Statistics.

Bush-Baskette, Stephanie. 1999. The "War on Drugs": A War on Women? In *Harsh Punishment: International Experiences of Women's Imprisonment*, edited by Sandy Cook and Susanne Davis. Boston: Northeastern University Press.

Bush-Baskette, Stephanie. 2000. The War on Drugs and the Incarceration of Mothers. *Journal of Drug Issues* 30: 919–28.

Bushman, Betty. 1964. Meet Mrs. Dianne Feinstein – Housewife with a Cause. *Riverside Press-Enterprise*, Aug. 16, C-10.

Buwalda, May. 1963. California Institution for Women. *Correctional Review* (Sept./Oct.): 14.

California Advisory Commission on the Status of Women. 1971. *California Women*. Sacramento: California Advisory Commission on the Status of Women.

California Assembly Select Committee on Corrections. 1977. *The California Institution for Women: One Year Later – A Follow-up Report*. Frontera: Assembly Select Committee on Corrections, July 21, 1977.

California Bureau of Criminal Statistics. Various years. *Crime and Delinquency in California*. Sacramento: Department of Justice.

California Council on Criminal Justice. 1972. *Synopsis of the 1972 California Comprehensive Plan for Criminal Justice*. Sacramento: California Council on Criminal Justice.

California Council on Criminal Justice. 1973. *1973 Comprehensive Plan for Criminal Justice*. Sacramento: California Council on Criminal Justice.

California Department of Corrections. 1957. *Orientation to Employment in State Correctional Service*. Sacramento: California Department of Corrections.

California Department of Corrections. 1960. *Rules of the Director of Corrections and of the Superintendent of the California Institution for Women*. Sacramento: California Department of Corrections.

California Department of Corrections. 1962. *Biennial Report*. Sacramento: California Department of Corrections.

California Department of Corrections. 1994. *Inside Corrections: Public Safety, Public Service*. Sacramento: California Department of Corrections.

California Department of Corrections. Various years. *Characteristics of Population in California State Prisons by Institution*. Sacramento: California Department of Corrections.

California Department of Finance. 1999. *California Statistical Abstract*. Sacramento: California Department of Finance.

California Department of Housing and Community Development. 2000. *Raising the Roof*. Sacramento: California Department of Housing and Community Development.

California Employment Development Department. 2000. *Occupations with Projected Declines: California, 1998–2008*. Sacramento: California Employment Development Department.

California Judicial Council Advisory Committee. 1997. *Final Report on Racial and Ethnic Bias in the Courts*. Sacramento: California Judicial Council Advisory Committee.

California Senate. 1991. Concurrent Resolution 33; Resolution Chapter 129. Filed with the California Secretary of State, September 26.

California Senate Concurrent Resolution 33 Commission Report. 1994. *Female Inmate and Parolee Issues.* Sacramento: California Department of Corrections.

Campbell, Nancy D. 2000. *Using Women: Gender, Drug Policy, and Social Justice.* New York: Routledge.

Caplow, Theodore and Jonathan Simon. 1999. Understanding Prison Policy and Population Trends. In *Prisons,* edited by Michael Tonry and Joan Petersilia. Vol. 26 of *Crime and Justice: A Review of Research,* edited by Michael Tonry and Norval Morris. Chicago: University of Chicago Press.

Carlen, Pat. 1994. Why Study Women's Imprisonment or Anyone Else's? *British Journal of Criminology* 34: 131–40.

Carlen, Pat. 1998. *Sledgehammer: Women's Imprisonment at the Millennium.* Houndsmills, Basingstoke: Macmillan.

Carlen, Pat. 2002. New Discourses of Justification and Reform for Women's Imprisonment in England. In *Women and Punishment. The Struggle for Justice,* edited by Pat Carlen. Devon, U.K.: Willan.

Carter, Iverne. 1963. The Challenge at C.I.W. *Correctional Review* (Sept./Oct.): 12.

Casper, Jonathan D., David Brereton, and David Neal. 1982. *The Implementation of the California Determinate Sentencing Law.* Washington D.C.: U.S. Department of Justice.

Cassel, Raymond and Robert B. Van Vorst. 1961. Psychological Needs of Women in a Correctional Institution. *American Journal of Corrections* 23: 22–24.

Christiansen, Kim, James V. Grimaldi, and Donna Wares. 1990. Prison. *Orange County Register,* July 29 1990.

Clear, Todd. 1994. *Harm in American Penology: Offenders, Victims and Their Communities.* Albany: State University of New York Press.

Clemmer, Donald. 1940 (2nd ed., 1958). *The Prison Community.* New York: Holt, Rinehart and Winston.

Cline, Hugh and Stanton Wheeler. 1968. The Determinants of Normative Patterns in Correctional Institutions. *Scandinavian Studies in Criminology* 2: 173–84.

Clogg, Clifford. 1995. Latent Class Models. In *Handbook of Statistical Modeling for the Social and Behavioral Sciences,* edited by Gerhard Arminger, Clifford Clogg, and Michael Sobel. New York: Plenum Press.

Cohen, Stanley. 1985. *Visions of Social Control.* Cambridge: Polity.

Colvin, Mark. 1992. *The Penitentiary in Crisis: From Accommodation to Riot in New Mexico.* Albany N.Y.: State University of New York Press.

Craddock, Amy. 1996. A Comparative Study of Male and Female Prison Misconduct Careers. *Prison Journal* 76: 60–80.

Cross, Jennifer. 1968. American's Laboratory for Social Change. In *The California Revolution,* edited by C. McWilliams. New York: Grossman.

Cummins, Eric. 1994. *The Rise and Fall of California's Radical Prison Movement.* Stanford: Stanford University Press.

Daly, Kathleen. 1995. Gender and Sentencing: What We Know and Don't Know from Empirical Research. *Federal Sentencing Reporter* 8: 163–68.

Dallek, Matthew. 2000. *The Right Moment: Ronald Reagan's First Victory and the Decisive Turning Point in American Politics.* New York: Free Press.

Danner, Mona. 1998. Three Strikes and It's Women Who Are Out. In *Crime Control and Women,* edited by Susan Miller. Thousand Oaks: Sage.

Davies, Malcolm. 1996. *Penological Esperanto and Sentencing Parochialism: A Comparative Study of the Search for Non-Prison Punishments.* Aldershot U.K.: Dartmouth.

Davis, Lynn. 1973. Life in Frontera Prison. *Ms. Magazine* 8 (1): 54–63.

Diaz-Cotto, Juanita. 1996. *Gender, Ethnicity and the State: Latina and Latino Prison Politics.* Albany, N.Y.: State University of New York Press.

Dietrich, Lisa C. 1998. *Chicana Adolescents: Bitches, 'Hos', and Schoolgirls.* Westport, Conn.: Praeger.

DiIulio, John J. 1987. *Governing Prisons: A Comparative Study of Correctional Management.* New York: Free Press.

Dirsuweit, Teresa. 1999. Carceral Spaces in South Africa: A Case Study of Institutional Power, Sexuality, and Transgression in Women's Prison. *Geoforum* 30: 71–83.

East, Patricia L. and Marianne E. Felice. 1996. *Adolescent Pregnancy and Parenting: Findings from a Racially Diverse Sample.* Mahwah N.J.: Lawrence Erlbaum.

Eaton, Mary. 1993. *Women After Prison.* Philadelphia: Open University Press.

Eisenstein, Zillah. 1988. *The Female Body and the Law.* Berkeley: University of California Press.

Elliott, Mabel A. 1966. Book Department, *Women's Prison: Sex and Social Structure* by David A. Ward and Gene G. Kassebaum. *The Annals of the American Academy of Political and Social Science* 368: 232–33.

Faith, Karlene. 1993. *Unruly Women: The Politics of Confinement and Resistance.* Vancouver: Press Gang.

Feder, L. 1989. "The Community Adjustment of Mentally Disordered Offenders." Ph.D. dissertation, State University of New York at Albany, School of Criminal Justice.

Feeley, Malcolm M. and Jonathan Simon. 1992. The New Penology: Notes on the Emerging Strategy of Corrections and Its Implications. *Criminology* 30: 449–74.

Feeley, Malcolm M. and Jonathan Simon. 1994. Actuarial Justice: The Emerging New Criminal Law. In *The Futures of Criminology,* edited by David Nelken. London: Sage.

Foucault, Michel. 1979. *Discipline and Punish: The Birth of the Prison.* London: Penguin.

Fox, James. 1982. Women in Prison: A Study in the Social Reality of Stress. In *The Pains of Imprisonment,* edited by Robert Johnson and Hans Toch. Beverly Hills, Calif.: Sage.

Fox, James. 1984. Women's Prison Policy, Prisoner Activism, and the Impact of the Contemporary Feminist Movement: A Case Study. *The Prison Journal* 1: 15–36.

Freedman, Estelle B. 1981. *Their Sisters' Keepers: Women's Prison Reform in America, 1830–1930.* Ann Arbor: University of Michigan Press.

Garbedian, Peter. 1963. Social Roles and Process of Socialization in the Prison Community. *Social Problems* 11: 139–52.

Garbedian, Peter. 1964. Social Roles in a Correctional Community. *Journal of Criminal Law, Criminology and Police Science* 55: 235–47.

Garland, David. 1990. *Punishment and Modern Society: A Study in Social Theory.* Chicago: University of Chicago Press.

Garland, David. 1995. Penal Modernism and Post-modernism. In *Punishment and Social Control: Essays in Honor of Sheldon L. Messinger,* edited by Thomas G. Blomberg and Stanley Cohen. New York: Aldine de Gruyter.

Garland, David. 1996. The Limits of the Sovereign State: Strategies of Crime Control in Contemporary Society. *British Journal of Criminology* 36: 445–71.

Garland, David. 1997. 'Governmentality' and the Problem of Crime: Foucault, Criminology, and Sociology. *Theoretical Criminology* 1: 173–214.

Garland, David. 2001. *The Culture of Control: Crime and Social Order in Contemporary Society.* Chicago: University of Chicago Press.

Garland, David. 2003. Penal Modernism and Postmodernism. In *Punishment and Social Control,* 2nd ed., edited by Thomas G. Blomberg and Stanley Cohen. New York: Aldine De Gruyter.

Gartner, Rosemary and Candace Kruttschnitt. 2004. A Brief History of Doing Time: The California Institution for Women in the 1960s and the 1990s. *Law and Society Review* 38: 267–304.

Gaubatz, Kathlyn Taylor. 1995. *Crime in the Public Mind.* Ann Arbor: University of Michigan Press.

Genders, Elaine and Elaine Player. 1990. Women Lifers: Assessing the Experience. *Prison Journal* 80: 46–57.

Giallombardo, Rose. 1966. *Society of Women: A Study of a Women's Prison.* New York: Wiley.

Gibbs, Jewelle Taylor and Teiahsha Bankhead. 2001. *Preserving Privilege: California Politics, Propositions, and People of Color.* Westport Conn.: Praeger.

Girshick, Lori B. 1999. *No Safe Haven: Stories of Women in Prison.* Boston: Northeastern University Press.

Goetting, Ann and Roy Michael Howsen. 1986. Correlates of Prisoner Misconduct. *Journal of Quantitative Criminology* 2: 49–67.

Goffman, Erving. 1961. *Asylums.* Garden City, N.Y.: Anchor Books.

Goffman, Erving. 1963. *Stigma: Notes on the Management of Spoiled Identity.* Englewood Cliffs, N.J.: Prentice Hall.

Gomez, Laura E. 1997. *Misconceiving Mothers: Legislators, Prosecutors, and the Politics of Prenatal Drug Exposure.* Philadelphia: Temple University Press.

Goodstein, Lynn. 1979. Inmate Adjustment to Prison and the Transition to Community Life. *Journal of Research in Crime and Delinquency* 16: 246–72.

Goodstein, Lynn and K. Wright. 1989. Inmate Adjustment to Prison. In *The American Prison,* edited by Lynn Goodstein and Doris MacKenzie. New York: Plenum.

Gordon, Walter. 1981. *Crime and Criminal Law: The California Experience, 1960–1975.* Gaithersburg Md.: Associated Faculty Press.

Gottfredson, Michael and Kenneth Adams. 1982. Prison Behavior and Post Release Performance: Empirical Reality and Public Policy. *Law and Policy Quarterly* 4: 373–91.

Greer, Kimberly. 2000. The Changing Nature of Women's Interpersonal Relationships in a Woman's Prison. *The Prison Journal* 80: 442–68.

Grusky, Oscar. 1959. Organizational Goals and the Behavior of Informal Leaders. *American Journal of Sociology* 65: 59–67.

Hagan, John and Ronit Dinovitzer. 1999. Collateral Consequences of Imprisonment for Children, Communities, and Prisoners. In *Prisons*, edited by Michael Tonry and Joan Petersilia. Vol. 26 of *Crime and Justice: A Review of Research*, edited by Michael Tonry and Norval Morris. Chicago: University of Chicago Press.

Hallinan, Joseph T. 2001. *Going Up the River: Travels in a Prison Nation*. New York: Random House.

Haney, Lynn. 1996. Homeboys, Babies, and Men in Suits: The State and the Reproduction of Male Dominance. *American Sociological Review* 61: 759–78.

Hannah-Moffat, Kelly. 1995. Feminine Fortresses: Women-Centered Prisons? *Prison Journal* 75: 135–64.

Hannah-Moffat, Kelly. 1999. Moral Agent or Actuarial Subject: Risk and Women's Imprisonment. *Theoretical Criminology* 3: 71–94.

Hannah-Moffat, Kelly. 2001. *Punishment in Disguise: Federal Imprisonment of Women in Canada*. Toronto: University of Toronto Press.

Harris, John C. and Paul Jesilow. 2000. It's Not the Old Ball Game: Three Strikes and the Courtroom Workgroup. *Justice Quarterly* 17: 185–203.

Hart, Dianne Walta. 1997. *Undocumented in L.A.: An Immigrant's Story*. Wilmington Del.: SR Books.

Hartnagel, Timothy F. and Mary Ellen Gillan. 1980. Female Prisoners and the Inmate Code. *Pacific Sociological Review* 23: 85–104.

Heffernan, Esther. 1972. *Making It in Prisons: The Square, the Cool and the Life*. New York: Wiley-Interscience.

Housing California. 2000. *The Long Wait: The Critical Shortage of Housing in California*. Sacramento: Housing California.

Howe, Adrian. 1994. *Punish and Critique: Towards a Feminist Analysis of Penality*. New York: Routledge.

Hudson, Barbara. 2002. Gender Issues in Penal Policy and Penal Theory. In *Women and Punishment: The Struggle for Justice*, edited by Pat Carlen. Cullompton, Devon: Willan.

Irwin, John. 1970. *The Felon*. Englewood Cliffs, N.J.: Prentice-Hall.

Irwin, John. 1980. *Prisons in Turmoil*. Chicago: Little, Brown.

Irwin, John and James Austin. 1994. *It's About Time: America's Imprisonment Binge*. Belmont: Wadsworth.

Irwin, John and Donald Cressey. 1962. Thieves, Convicts and the Inmate Culture. *Social Problems* 10: 145–47.

Jacobs, David and Ronald E. Helms. 1996. Toward a Political Model of Incarceration: A Time-Series Examination of Multiple Explanations for Prison Admission Rates. *American Journal of Sociology* 102: 323–57.

Jacobs, James. 1974. Street Gangs Behind Bars. *Social Problems* 21: 395–409.

Jacobs, James. 1977. *Stateville: The Penitentiary in Mass Society*. Chicago: University of Chicago Press.

Jacobs, James. 1983. *New Perspectives on Prison and Imprisonment*. Ithaca: Cornell University Press.

Jensen, Gary F. and Dorothy Jones. 1976. Perspectives on Inmate Culture: A Study of Women in Prison. *Social Forces* 54: 590–603.

Jewkes, Yvonne. 2002. *Captive Audience: Media, Masculinity and Power in Prisons.* Portland, Ore.: Willan Publishing.

Johnson, James A.R., Elisa Jayne Bienenstock, Walter C. Farrell, Jr., and Jennifer L. Glanville. 2000. Bridging Social Networks and Female Labor Force Participation in a Multiethnic Metropolis. In *Prismatic Metropolis: Inequality in Los Angeles,* edited by Lawrence D. Bobo, Melvin Oliver, James A. Johnson, and Abel Valenzuela. New York: Russell Sage.

Joint Committee on Prison Construction and Operations. 1983. *California Institution for Women: Present Problems – Future Needs.* Hearing held at Frontera, Calif., November 29, 1983.

Jones, Richard S. 1993. Coping with Separation: Adaptive Responses of Women Prisoners. *Women and Criminal Justice* 5: 71–97.

Justice Now and Prisoners Action Coalition. 2000. *Legislative Hearing on the Conditions of Confinement for California's Women Prisoners.* San Francisco: Justice Now and Prisoners Action Coalition.

Kassebaum, Gene, David Ward, and Daniel Wilner. 1971. *Prison Treatment and Parole Survival.* New York: Wiley.

Kohpahl, Gabriele. 1998. *Voices of Guatemalan Women in Los Angeles: Understanding Their Immigration.* New York: Garland.

Kotkin, Joel and Paul Grabowicz. 1982. *California Inc.* New York: Rawson Wade.

Kruttschnitt, Candace. 1981. Prison Codes, Inmate Solidarity, and Women: A Re-examination. In *Comparing Female and Male Offenders,* edited by Marguerite Q. Warren. Beverly Hills, Calif.: Sage.

Kruttschnitt, Candace and Rosemary Gartner. 2003. Women's Imprisonment. In vol. 30 of *Crime and Justice: A Review of Research,* edited by Michael Tonry. Chicago: University of Chicago Press.

Kruttschnitt, Candace, Rosemary Gartner, and Amy Miller. 2000. Doing Her Own Time? Women's Responses to Prison in the Context of the Old and the New Penology. *Criminology* 38: 681–718.

Larson, J.H. and Joey Nelson. 1984. Women's Friendships and Adaptation to Prison. *Journal of Criminal Justice* 12: 601–15.

Leger, Robert G. 1987. Lesbianism Among Women Prisoners: Participants and Nonparticipants. *Criminal Justice and Behavior* 14: 448–67.

Leps, Marie-Christine. 1992. *Apprehending the Criminal: The Production of Deviance in Nineteenth-Century Discourse.* Durham, N.C.: Duke University Press.

Liebling, Alison. 1992. *Suicides in Prison.* London: Routledge.

Liebling, Alison. 1999. Prisoner Suicide and Prisoner Coping. In *Prisons,* edited by Michael Tonry and Joan Petersilia. Vol. 26 of *Crime and Justice: A Review of Research,* edited by Michael Tonry and Norval Morris. Chicago: University of Chicago Press.

Lilliston, 1971. Women's Prison Goal: A Campus Image. *Los Angeles Times,* March 7, 1971, E1 and E6.

Little Hoover Commission. 1994a. *Putting Violence Behind Bars: Redefining the Role of California's Prisons.* Sacramento: Little Hoover Commission.

Little Hoover Commission. 1994b. *The Juvenile Crime Challenge: Making Prevention a Priority.* Sacramento: Little Hoover Commission.

Little Hoover Commission. 1995. *Boot Camps: An Evolving Alternative to Traditional Prisons.* Sacramento: Little Hoover Commission.

Little Hoover Commission. 1998. *Beyond Bars: Correctional Reforms to Lower Prison Costs and Reduce Crime.* Sacramento: Little Hoover Commission.

Loader, Ian and Richard Sparks. 2002. Contemporary Landscapes of Crime, Order, and Control: Governance, Risk, and Globalization. In *The Oxford Handbook of Criminology,* edited by Mike Maguire, Rod Morgan, and Robert Reiner. Oxford: Oxford University Press.

Loucks, Alexander D. and Edward Zamble. 2000. Predictors of Criminal Behavior and Prison Misconduct in Serious Female Offenders. *Correctional Service Canada, Empirical and Applied Criminal Justice Review,* vol. 1, no. 1. (online journal of the Research on Criminal Justice Network): *http://qsilver. queensu.ca/rcjnet/journal.* (Accessed October 15, 2001).

Lynch, Mona. 1998. Waste Managers? The New Penology, Crime Fighting, and Parole Agent Identity. *Law and Society Review* 32: 839–70.

Lynch, Mona. 2000. Rehabilitation as Rhetoric: The Idea of Reformation in Contemporary Parole Discourse and Practices. *Punishment and Society* 2: 40–65.

MacKenzie, Doris Layton, James W. Robinson, and Carol S. Campbell. 1989. Long-term Incarceration of Female Offenders: Prison Adjustment and Coping. *Criminal Justice and Behavior* 16: 223–38.

Mahan, Sue. 1984. Impositon of Despair: An Ethnography of Women in Prison. *Justice Quarterly* 1: 357–84.

Maher, Lisa. 1997. *Sexed Work: Gender, Race, and Resistance in a Brooklyn Drug Market.* New York: Oxford University Press.

Mandaraka-Sheppard, Alexandra. 1986. *The Dynamics of Aggression in Women's Prisons in England.* Aldershot: Gower.

Maruna, Shadd. 2001. *Making Good: How Ex-convicts Reform and Rebuild Their Lives.* Washington, D.C.: American Psychological Association.

Mathews, Glenna. 2003. *Silicon Valley, Women, and the California Dream: Gender, Class, and Opportunity in the 20th Century.* Stanford: Stanford University Press.

Matthews, Roger. 1999. *Doing Time: An Introduction to the Sociology of Imprisonment.* Houndsmills, Basingstoke, Hampshire: Palgrave.

Mauer, Marc, Cathy Potler, and Richard Wolf. 1999. *Gender and Justice: Women, Drugs, and Sentencing Policy.* Washington D.C.: Sentencing Project.

Mawby, R. I. 1982. Women in Prison: A British Study. *Crime and Delinquency* 28: 24–39.

May, Christine. 1995. *50 Years: Public Safety, Public Service.* Sacramento: California Department of Corrections.

McClellan, Dorothy Spektorov. 1994. Disciplinarity in the Discipline of Male and Female, Inmates in Texas Prisons. *Women and Criminal Justice* 5: 71–9.

McClellan, Dorothy Spektorov, David Farabee, and Ben M. Crouch. 1997. Early Victimization, Drug Use, and Criminality: A Comparison of Male and Female Prisoners. *Criminal Justice and Behavior* 24: 455–76.

McCorkle, Jill A. 1998. Going to the Crackhouse: Critical Space as a Form of Resistance in Total Institutions and Everyday Life. *Symbolic Interaction* 21: 227–52.

McGuire, James. 1995. *What Works: Reducing Re-offending*. New York: John Wiley.

Medlicott, Diana. 2001. *Surviving the Prison Place: Narratives of Suicidal Prisoners*. Aldershot, England: Ashgate.

Messinger, Sheldon. 1967. Book Reviews of *Society of Women: A Study of a Women's Prison* by Rose Giallombardo and *Women's Prison: Sex and Social Structure* by David A. Ward and Gene G. Kassebaum. *American Sociological Review* 32: 143–46.

Miller, S. and S. Dinitz. 1973. Measuring Institutional Impact: A Follow-up. *Criminology* 11: 417–26.

Minton, Robert J. 1971. *Inside: Prison American Style*. New York: Random House.

Morales, Richard. 1980. "History of the California Institution of Women, 1927–1960: A Woman's Regime." Ph.D. dissertation, University of California, Riverside, Department of Sociology.

Morgan, Rod. 2002. Imprisonment: A Brief History, The Contemporary Scence, and Likely Prospects. In *The Oxford Handbook of Criminology*, edited by Mike Maguire, Rod Morgan and Robert Reiner. Oxford: Oxford University Press.

Office of Economic Research. 2000. *California: An Economic Profile*. Sacramento: Office of Economic Research.

Ohlin, Lloyd. 1959. "The Theory of Individualization in Treatment and Institutional Practice." Paper presented at the Ninth Annual Institute of the Illinois Academy of Criminology, Chicago, Illinois, April.

O'Malley, Pat. 1992. Risk, Power, and Crime Prevention. *Economy and Society*, 21: 252–75.

O'Malley, Pat. 1996. Risk and Responsibility. In *Foucault and Political Reason: Liberalism, Neo-Liberalism, and Rationalities of Government*, edited by A. Barry, T. Osbourne, and N. Rose. Chicago: University of Chicago Press.

O'Malley, Pat. 1999. Volatile and Contradictory Punishment. *Theoretical Criminology* 3: 175–96.

Owen, Barbara. 1998. *In the Mix: Struggle and Survival in a Women's Prison*. Albany: State University of New York Press.

Owen, Barbara. 1999. Women and Imprisonment in the United States: The Gendered Consequences of the U.S. Imprisonment Binge. In *Harsh Punishment: International Experiences of Women's Imprisonment*, edited by Sandy Cook and Susanne Davies. Boston: Northeastern University Press.

Owen, Barbara and Barbara Bloom. 1995. *Profiling the Needs of California's Female Prisoners: A Needs Assessment*. Final Report to the National Institute of Corrections, U.S. Department of Justice, February.

Parsons, Talcott. 1951. *The Social System*. Glencoe, Ill.: Free Press.

Petersilia, Joan. 1999. Parole and Prisoner Reentry in the United States. In *Prisons*, edited by Michael Tonry and Joan Petersilia. Vol. 26 of *Crime and Justice: A Review of Research*, edited by Michael Tonry and Norval Morris. Chicago: University of Chicago Press.

Pollock, Joycelyn M. 1986. *Sex and Supervision: Guarding Male and Female Inmates*. New York: Greenwood.

Pollock-Byrne, Joycelyn M. 1990. *Women, Prison and Crime.* Pacific Grove, Calif.: Brooks/Cole.

Pratt, John. 2000. The Return of the Wheelbarrow Men; Or the Arrival of Postmodern Penality? *British Journal of Criminology* 40: 127–45.

Pratt, John. 2002. *Punishment and Civilization: Penal Tolerance and Intolerance in Modern Society.* London: Sage.

Putnam, Jackson K. 1994. The Progressive Legacy in California. In *California Progressivism Revisited,* edited by William Deverall and Tom Sittons. Berkeley: University of California Press.

Quigley, John, Steven Raphael, and Eugene Smolensky. 2001. *Homelessness in California.* San Francisco: Public Policy Institute.

Raeder, Myrna S. 1995. The Forgotten Offender: The Effect of Sentencing Guidelines and Mandatory Minimums on Women and Their Children. *Federal Sentencing Reporter* 8: 157–62.

Rafter, Nichole Hahn. 1990. *Partial Justice: Women, Prisons and Social Control,* 2nd ed. New Brunswick, N.J.: Transaction.

Rasche, Christine. 2001. "Cross-Sex Supervision of Female Inmates: An Unintended Consequence of Employment Law Cases Brought by Women Working in Corrections." Paper presented at the annual meeting of the American Society of Criminology, Atlanta, Ga., Nov. 6–10.

Reiner, R. 1992. Policing a Postmodern Society. *Modern Law Review* 55: 761–81.

Reingold, Beth. 2000. *Sex, Gender and Legislative Behavior in Arizona and California.* Chapel Hill: University of North Carolina Press.

Richards, B. 1978. The Experience of Long-term Imprisonment. *British Journal of Criminology* 18: 162–69.

Rierden, Andi. 1997. *The Farm: Life Inside a Women's Prison.* Amherst: University of Massachusetts Press.

Riveland, Chase. 1999. Prison Management Trends, 1975–2025. In *Prisons,* edited by Michael Tonry and Joan Petersilia. Vol. 26 of *Crime and Justice: A Review of Research,* edited by Michael Tonry and Norval Morris. Chicago: University of Chicago Press.

Roberts, Jerry. 1994. *Dianne Feinstein: Never Let Them See You Cry.* New York: Harper Collins.

Rock, Paul. 1996. *Reconstructing a Women's Prison: The Holloway Redevelopment Project, 1968–1988.* Oxford: Clarendon.

Rose, Nikolas. 2000. Government and Control. In *Criminology and Social Theory,* edited by David Garland and Richard Sparks. Oxford: Oxford University Press.

Roundtree, George A., Brij Mohan, and Lisa W. Mahaffey. 1980. Determinants of Female Aggression: A Study of a Prison Population. *International Journal of Offender Therapy and Comparative Criminology* 24: 260–69.

Ruback, R. Barry and Timothy B. Carr. 1984. Crowding in a Women's Prison: Attitudes and Behavioral Effects. *Journal of Applied Social Psychology* 14: 57–68.

Scheingold, Stuart A. 1984. *The Politics of Law and Order: Street Crime and Social Policy.* New York: Longman.

Schiraldi, Vincent. 1994. *The Undue Influence of California's Prison Guards' Union: California's Correctional-industrial Complex.* San Francisco: Center on Juvenile and Criminal Justice.

Schrag, Clarence. 1944. "Social Types in a Prison Community." Master's thesis, University of Washington, Department of Sociology.

Shaw, Margaret. 1992a. Issues of Power and Control: Women in Prison and Their Defenders. *British Journal of Criminology* 32: 438–52.

Shaw, Margaret. 1992b. *Paying the Price: Federally Sentenced Women in Context.* Ottawa: Ministry of Solicitor General of Canada.

Silberman, Matthew. 1995. Review of *The Rise and Fall of California's Radical Prison Movement. Contemporary Sociology* 24: 94–5.

Simon, Jonathan. 1991. Exchange with B. Traugher. In *Growth and Its Influence on Correctional Policy: Perspectives on the Report of the Blue Ribbon Commission.* Proceedings of a Conference at the University of California, Berkeley, May 10–11, 1990. Berkeley: Guggenheim Criminal Justice Program.

Simon, Jonathan. 1993. *Poor Discipline: Parole and the Social Control of the Underclass, 1890–1990.* Chicago: University of Chicago Press.

Simon, Jonathan. 1994. In the Place of the Parent: Risk Management and the Government of Campus Life. *Social and Legal Studies* 3: 15–45.

Simon, Jonathan. 1997. Governing Through Crime. In *The Crime Conundrum: Essays on Criminal Justice,* edited by George Fisher and Lawrence Friedman. Boulder, Colo.: Westview.

Simon, Jonathan. 2000. The 'Society of Captives' in the Era of Hyper-incarceration. *Theoretical Criminology* 4: 285–306.

Simon, Jonathan. 2001. 'Entitlement to Cruelty': The End of Welfare and Punitive Mentality in the United States. In *Crime, Risk, and Justice: The Politics of Crime Control in Liberal Democracies,* edited by K. Stenson and R. Sullivan. Devon U.K.: Willan.

Simon, Jonathan and Malcolm M. Feeley. 1995. True Crime: The New Penology and Public Discourse on Crime. In *Punishment and Social Control: Essays in Honor of Sheldon L. Messinger,* edited by Thomas G. Blomberg and Stanley Cohen. New York: Aldine de Gruyter.

Simon, Jonathan and Malcolm M. Feeley. 2003. The Form and Limits of the New Penology. In *Punishment and Social Control,* 2nd ed., edited by Thomas G. Blomberg and Stanley Cohen. New York: Aldine De Gruyter.

Singleton, Nicola, Howard Meltzer, and Rebecca Gatward. 1998. Psychiatric Morbidity among Prisoners in England and Wales. ISBN 011-6210-45. London: National Statistics Office.

Smart, Carol. 1990. Feminist Approaches to Criminology or Postmodern Woman Meets Atavistic Man. In *Feminist Perspectives in Criminology,* edited by L. Gelsthorpe and A. Morris. Milton Keynes: Open University Press.

Sparks, Richard, Anthony E. Bottoms, and Will Hay. 1996. *Prisons and the Problem of Order.* Oxford: Clarendon Press.

State of California. 1998. *California Code of Regulations. Title 15: Crime Prevention and Corrections. Division 3, Department of Corrections, Chapter 1: Rules and regulations of the Director of Corrections.* Sacramento: State of California.

Stoll, Michael A. 2000. Search, Discrimination, and the Travel to Work. In *Prismatic Metropolis: Inequality in Los Angeles,* edited by Lawrence D. Bobo, Melvin Oliver, James A. Johnson, Jr., and Abel Valenzuela. New York: Russell Sage.

Stoller, Nancy. 2000. *Improving Access to Health Care for California's Women Prisoners: Executive Summary*. Santa Cruz, Calif.: California Policy Research Center.

Street, David, Robert D. Vinter, and Charles Perrow. 1966. *Organization for Treatment*. London: Collier-Macmillan.

Sykes, Gresham. 1958. *The Society of Captives: A Study of a Maximum Security Prison*. Princeton: Princeton University Press.

Sykes, Gresham. 1995. The Structural-Functional Perspective on Imprisonment. In *Punishment and Social Control: Essays in Honor of Sheldon L. Messinger*, edited by Thomas G. Blomberg and Stanley Cohen. New York: Aldine De Gruyter.

Taylor, J. Edward, Philip L. Martin, and Michael Fix. 1997. *Poverty Amid Prosperity: Immigration and the Changing Face of Rural California*. Washington D.C.: Urban Institute Press.

Thomas, Charles W. 1977. Theortical Perspectives on Prisonization: A Comparison of the Importation and Deprivation Models. *Journal of Criminal Law and Criminology* 68: 135–45.

Tillman, Robert. 1990. The Prevalence and Incidence of Adult Arrests: An Update. *Crime and Delinquency in California, 1980–1989*. Sacramento: Department of Justice.

Tittle, Charles R. 1969. Inmate Organizations: Sex Differentiation and the Influence of Criminal Subcultures. *American Sociological Review* 34: 492–505.

Tonry, Michael. 1999. Why Are U.S. Incarceration Rates So High? *Crime and Delinquency* 45: 419–37.

Traugher, Brian. 1991. Commentary. In *Growth and Its Influence on Correctional Policy: Perspectives on the Report of the Blue Ribbon Commission*. Proceedings of a Conference at the University of California, Berkeley, May 10–11, 1990. Berkeley: Guggenheim Criminal Justice Program.

Tyler, Tom R. and Robert J. Boeckmann. 1997. Three Strikes and You Are Out, but Why? The Psychology of Public Support for Punishing Rule Breakers. *Law and Society Review* 31: 237–65.

United States Bureau of the Census. 1963. *1960 Census of the Population*. Volume 1: *Population Characteristics*. Washington, D.C.: U.S. Government Printing Office.

United States Bureau of the Census. 1993. *Census of Population and Housing*. Volume 1: *Population Characteristics*. Washington, D.C.: U.S. Department of Commerce, Economic and Statistics Administration.

United States Bureau of the Census. 1999. *Poverty in the United States, 1998*. Washington, D.C.: U.S. Government Printing Office.

Valverde, Mariana. 1998. *Diseases of the Will: Alcohol and the Dilemmas of Freedom*. Cambridge: Cambridge University Press.

Van Voorhis, Patricia. 1994. Measuring Prison Disciplinary Problems: A Multiple Indicators Approach to Understanding Prison Adjustment. *Justice Quarterly* 11: 679–709.

Vigil, James. 2002. *A Rainbow of Gangs: Street Cultures in the Mega-City*. Austin: University of Texas Press.

Waller, Maureen R. 2001. *Unmarried Parents, Fragile Families: New Evidence from Oakland*. San Francisco: Public Policy Institute of California.

Ward, David A., Maurice Jackson, and Renee E. Ward. 1969. Crime of Violence by Women. In *Crimes of Violence*, vol. 13. A Staff Report Submitted to the National Commission on the Causes and Prevention of Violence. Co-Directors, Donald J. Mulvihill and Melvin M. Tumin. Washington D.C.: U.S. Government Printing Office.

Ward, David and Gene Kassebaum. 1963. Patterns of Homosexual Behavior Among Female Prison Inmates. Los Angeles, Calif.: School of Public Health, University of California.

Ward, David and Gene Kassebaum. 1965. *Women's Prison: Sex and Social Structure.* New York: Aldine Publishing.

Ward, Joyce. 1982. Telling Tales in Prison. In *Custom and Conflict in British Society*, edited by Ronald Frankenberg. Manchester: Manchester University Press.

Warren, Carol A. B. 1987. *Madwives: Schizophrenic Women in the 1950s.* New Brunswick, N.J.: Rutgers University Press.

Weitzman, Lenore. 1985. *The Divorce Revolution: The Unexpected Social and Economic Consequences for Women and Children in America.* New York: Free Press.

Wellford, Charles. 1967. Factors Associated with Adoption of the Inmate Code: A Study of Normative Socialization. *Journal of Criminal Law, Criminology and Police Science* 58: 197–203.

Wilkins, John and Jeremy Coid. 1991. Self-mutilation in Female Remanded Prisoners. I. An Indicator of Severe Pathology. *Criminal Behavior and Mental Health* 1: 247–67.

Wilson, Thomas P. 1968. Patterns of Management and Adaptations to Organizational Roles: A Study of Prison Inmates. *American Journal of Sociology* 74: 146–57.

Worrall, Anne. 1990. *Offending Women: Female Lawbreakers and the Criminal Justice System.* London: Routledge.

Worrall, Anne. 2002. Rendering Women Punishable: The Making of a Penal Crisis. In *Women and Punishment: The Struggle for Justice*, edited by Pat Carlen. Cullompton U.K.: Willan.

Zahn, Margaret A. and Patricia L. McCall 1999. Homicides in the 20th Century United States. In *Studying and Preventing Homicide*, edited by M. Dwayne Smith and Margaret A. Zahn. Thousand Oaks, Calif.: Sage.

Zalba, Serapio R. 1964. Women Prisoners and Their Families. Department of Social Welfare and Department of Corrections. Sacramento: State of California.

Zavella. 1997. *Immigrants Out! The New Nativism and Anti-immigrant Impulse in the United States.* New York: New York University Press.

Zedner, Lucia. 1995. Wayward Sisters: The Prison for Women. In *The Oxford History of the Prison: The Practice of Punishment in Western Societies*, edited by N. Morris and D.J. Rothman. New York: Oxford University Press.

Zimring, Franklin. 1991. Correctional Growth in Context. In *Growth and Its Influence on Correctional Policy: Perspectives on the Report of the Blue Ribbon Commission.* Proceedings of a Conference at the University of California, Berkeley, May 10–11, 1990. Berkeley, Calif.: Guggenheim Criminal Justice Program.

Zimring, Franklin and Gordon Hawkins. 1992. *Prison Population and Criminal Justice Policy in California.* Berkeley, Calif.: Institute of Governmental Studies Press.

Zimring, Franklin and Gordon Hawkins. 1994. The Growth of Imprisonment in California. *British Journal of Criminology* 34: 83–95.

Zimring, Franklin and Gordon Hawkins. 1995. *Incapacitation, Penal Confinement and the Restraint of Crime.* Oxford: University Press.

Zimring, Franklin E., Gordon Hawkins, and Sam Kamin. 2001. *Punishment and Democracy. Three Strikes and You're Out in California.* New York: Oxford University Press.

Zingraff, Matthew T. and Rhonda Zingraff. 1980. Adaptation Patterns of Incarcerated Female Delinquents. *Juvenile and Family Court Journal* (May): 35–47.

Author Index

Subject Index